*A Pocket Guide to Superstitions
of the British Isles*

STEVE ROUD

A Pocket Guide to Superstitions of the British Isles

PENGUIN BOOKS

PENGUIN BOOKS

Published by the Penguin Group
Penguin Books Ltd, 80 Strand, London WC2R 0RL, England
Penguin Group (USA) Inc., 375 Hudson Street, New York, New York 10014, USA
Penguin Books Australia Ltd, 250 Camberwell Road, Camberwell, Victoria 3124, Australia
Penguin Books Canada Ltd, 10 Alcorn Avenue, Toronto, Ontario, Canada M4V 3B2
Penguin Books India (P) Ltd, 11 Community Centre, Panchsheel Park, New Delhi – 110 017, India
Penguin Group (NZ), cnr Airborne and Rosedale Roads, Albany, Auckland 1310, New Zealand
Penguin Books (South Africa) (Pty) Ltd, 24 Sturdee Avenue, Rosebank 2196, South Africa

Penguin Books Ltd, Registered Offices: 80 Strand, London WC2R 0RL, England

www.penguin.com

First published 2004
1

Set in 10/12 pt PostScript Adobe Caslon
Typeset by Rowland Phototypesetting Ltd, Bury St Edmunds, Suffolk
Printed in Great Britain by Clays Ltd, St Ives plc

ISBN 0140–51549–6

Contents

Introduction   vii

Superstitions Around the Year
FESTIVALS   3
LUCKY AND UNLUCKY DAYS   20

The Cycle of Life
BIRTH   31
MARRIAGE   47
DEATH   57

The Human Body
PARTS OF THE BODY   75
ACTIONS   88

Domestic Superstitions
IN AND AROUND THE HOUSE   97
FURTHER AFIELD   122
CLOTHES AND ACCESSORIES   131
FOOD AND DRINK   139

The Occult
PREDICTING THE FUTURE   151
CHARMS AND CURSES   163
LUCKY AND UNLUCKY NUMBERS   182

The Natural World
ANIMALS   195
BIRDS   219
INSECTS   236
PLANTS   244

TREES   257
NATURAL PHENOMENA AND WEATHER   263

Bibliography   274
Index   276

Introduction

Superstition is a pretty slippery concept, and first we need to examine what we mean by it. The simple statement that a superstition is an irrational belief is quite adequate for most purposes, as long as we don't enquire too closely into the meaning of the word 'irrational'. But not every irrational belief gets labelled as superstition, so we need to look a bit closer. One of the key characteristics of superstition is a belief in the existence of *luck*, as a real force in life, and that luck can be *predicted* by signs, and can be *controlled* or *influenced* by particular actions or words. Other key elements include a belief in *fate*, which again can be predicted and manipulated, and a belief in what can only be described as *magic* – the idea that people can be harmed or protected by spells, charms, amulets, curses, witchcraft, and so on.

Superstitions are also *unofficial* knowledge, in that they run counter to the official teachings of religion, school, science, and government, and this is precisely why – even in the twenty-first century – many of us like to hold on to a few, to show that we are not totally ruled by science and hard fact.

This book doesn't follow the general pattern of popular books on superstition, in that it does not simply repeat the many recent theories of origin that pass as knowledge in the subject. What is offered instead is historical research – the result of years of searching for examples of superstitions, not just by me, but by many other researchers before me (most notably Iona Opie and Moira Tatem) in every source we can think of – novels, plays, poetry, children's books, newspapers, magazines, diaries – going back as far as we can. As folklorists, we also listen to people on buses, on the radio, in the playground, in the supermarket, and so on, to learn what is being said and done now.

We examine statements, and ask questions. It is frequently said, for example, that the fear of spilling salt goes back to the Last Supper, and that to prove it Leonardo Da Vinci's painting of that event shows Judas spilling the salt. But it doesn't. One piece of 'evidence' put forward to support the completely groundless idea that 'Ring a ring a roses' goes back to the plague is that sneezing was a main symptom of that disease. It wasn't. It turns out that Friday 13th is a Victorian invention. 'Touch wood', it is claimed, is based on a belief in tree spirits, but is there evidence we ever believed in tree spirits?

What we end up with is a huge mass of material on the subject, which can be organized and analysed to provide data for informed judgements instead of guesses. The first principle of the historical approach is that if a superstition cannot be found before, say, 1850, the idea that it has survived from an ancient fertility ritual or pre-Christian sacrifice 1,200 years before seems a bit far-fetched to say the least. If it existed in that time, how come nobody noticed it? And if there is no evidence for its existence, how can we base our theory of origin on it? If it had existed underground all that time it would probably have changed beyond all recognition anyway (imagine a game of Chinese whispers lasting for 1,200 years), so an examination of the modern version is unlikely to tell us anything about the original. What our historical approach enables us to do is to make estimates of age, development, and relative popularity of particular beliefs, and we can start to make general statements about how superstitions function. Occasionally, historical research also throws light on how the superstitions arose in the first place.

One thing which becomes obvious when comparing a whole mass of reported superstitions is that most are based on a small number of principles which are repeated time and again in different guises, and these formulae can tell us a great deal. The two most widespread, for example, are that you must not *tempt fate* (don't count your chickens before they're hatched, don't boast about your good fortune) and that *beginnings* dictate the future course of events. The concern for good beginnings is reflected in first-footing customs at New Year, giving a baby a coin to ensure future good fortune, getting out of bed on the correct side to start the day well, and so on. On the negative side, don't stumble as you leave the house, don't see an unlucky person on the way to your fishing boat, and so on. A third principle, which is in fact far more complex if fully analysed, is that the natural world 'knows' what is to happen in human life – a robin tapping at the window means a death in the house very soon, a dog howling at your door means the same.

The world of superstition is essentially a symbolic one, although in most cases only on a very simple level. Money in the pocket at a key moment (for example, when hearing the first cuckoo in spring) stands for prosperity in the coming year, whereas an empty purse symbolizes want. A piece of coal carried by a first footer represents warmth and comfort; an upturned bowl in a seafaring family stands for an upturned ship. This feeling for the symbolic is often little more than a weak pun – washing on certain days 'washes one of the family away', 'turn your chair to turn your luck'.

Another conclusion that is clearly supported by a historical review is that we, as a society, are much less superstitious than we were a hundred, or even fifty, years ago. Although we like to pretend that we have our little irrationalities, and few people (myself included) can claim to be completely free of superstition, many of us only *play* at it nowadays. This claim can be demonstrated in several ways, most notably by asking anyone to name ten superstitions; many will not be able to get beyond five without really thinking hard about it, whereas a century ago the average person would have known dozens.

Even those we still know are relatively colourless, being nearly always simply a matter of 'bad luck', whereas in the past they would have had more individual meanings – a death, you won't get married, a stranger is coming, and so on. Regional differences have been largely ironed out, and the same beliefs are found all over the country. But the real acid test is that however superstitious a person may think they are, few act on them in the way that previous generations did. Who would accept being turned down for a job because they had red hair or had the wrong sun sign? Who would phone work and say, 'I can't be in today because I saw a magpie as I left home'? We might try a traditional cure like a key down the back for a nosebleed, but who would accept a verbal charm rather than hospital treatment to stop real bleeding? Who would tell a young mother that her baby will die if she weighs it, or lets it see its reflection in a mirror? And so on, through hundreds of different superstitions which were believed and acted upon only a century ago.

But why were people so superstitious? It is usually assumed that superstition is the result of fear and uncertainty – an attempt to control the parts of life that are in fact beyond our understanding or control. This is largely true, and there is some evidence that superstition is more prevalent in people involved in dangerous occupations, and increases in times of particular uncertainty, such as during a war. But there are other forces involved. Superstitions are passed on from person to person, often within a family, and take on the authority of tradition. It must also be said that, in the past, various people made a living out of their neighbour's willingness to believe in magical cures, love potions, and the need for protection against ill-wishing.

The main reason for the decline of superstition in modern times is that many of these uncertainties have declined – whole areas of life, from the trivial to the life-threatening, have had the mystery and danger removed from them to a large extent. Childhood diseases still exist, and parents still have worries, but this is nothing compared to how it was a century ago. Changes in everyday technology have brought almost instant death to many beliefs. The light-bulb and the radiator provide little scope for superstition, or romance, whereas the candle and the open fire had plenty. Baking bread, turning the bed, churning butter, washing by hand, sweeping the house, laying out a corpse in the front room, killing a pig – all these activities were highly charged with beliefs, but have changed beyond recognition, or disappeared from our lives completely. How many of us know the phases of the moon?

It could be argued that superstitious impulses in society are not dead, but are simply resurfacing in the guise of alternative medicines, un-official pick-and-mix religions, astrology, X-File conspiracy theories, and new age cults and gurus of various kinds, but that is beyond the scope of this small book. But one major area where most of us can claim to be less prone to irrational thinking is in the matter of *witchcraft*. However badly things are going, however ill we may feel, few would think that the cause was our neighbour's spite or the spells of a witch. In this area at least, people nowadays have more sense.

The present book is a much-abridged and edited version of my *Penguin Guide to the Superstitions of Britain and Ireland*, published in 2003. Anyone who is interested in finding out more about the superstitions included here, and dozens more, is referred to that work. In particular, the full Guide gives details of the sources of the verbatim quotations included here. Readers with a serious interest in the subject should also consult Iona Opie and Moira Tatem, *Dictionary of Super-stitions* (Oxford University Press, 1989), and the other works listed in the bibliography. Finally, I would like to thank Kate Faulkner for help with the text and for preparing the index.

Steve Roud
Maresfield, E. Sussex

Superstitions Around the Year

FESTIVALS

Lucky Being first-footed by a man • Gathering cream of the well on New Year's Day • Keeping bread baked on Good Friday • Eating twelve mince pies in twelve different houses

Unlucky Letting fire out of the house on New Year's Day • Leaving Christmas decorations up after Twelfth Night • Starting any project on Holy Innocents' Day

LUCKY AND UNLUCKY DAYS

Lucky Saying 'rabbits' on the first day of the month • Gathering dew on May Day

Unlucky Starting anything on a Friday • Doing anything on Friday 13th • Being born in May

FESTIVALS

New Year

The importance of beginnings is one of the fundamental principles of superstition in Britain and Ireland. Beliefs cluster round the beginning of the day, of a journey, of spring, of a marriage, of a life, and so on. The New Year is an obvious addition to this list, and is still regarded as a key turning-point, even by those who claim to be non-superstitious. The feeling of a new beginning pervades our cultural and personal responses to the season. As Pliny asked, nearly 2,000 years ago, 'Why on the first day of the year do we wish one another cheerfully a happy and prosperous new year?' (*Natural History*, AD 77).

> The character of the coming twelve months, for good or bad fortune, is foretold by the appearance of things on the morning of the new year. A trivial mishap, or the slightest instance of good luck, has now more than its usual significance, inasmuch as it predicts, in a general way, the course of events through the coming year.   Cornwall (1871)

It is not easy to reach an accurate synthesis of New Year beliefs and customs in the past. While underlying principles are remarkably constant, details vary considerably across Britain and Ireland, and even in a single county there could be sharp disagreement over essential details such as the preferred hair colour of the 'first footer'. Confusion also reigns over nomenclature. The generic term 'letting' or 'bringing' in the New Year can cover a variety of activities designed to mark the turn of the year, and 'first footing' in Scotland could mean the New

Year custom of the first person to enter the house, or the first person met – at any time of year – in the morning or at the start of a journey.

first footing at New Year

First footing is regarded as the archetypal Scottish custom but in fact it was previously common in England and parts of Wales as well. Nevertheless, it was certainly taken more seriously in Scotland than elsewhere, and it has continued to operate there while virtually dying out in other areas. The basic tenet of the custom is that the first person who enters the house in the New Year brings either good or bad luck for the next twelve months, depending on whether or not s/he conforms to the local idea of being 'lucky', and whether s/he performs the expected tasks. Each community formerly had its own rules for the custom, and these varied widely, within a basic broad format. Indeed, it seems to be the case that many households had their own individual ways of proceeding, but the tendency over time has definitely been towards uniformity.

Elements of the first-footing custom can be assigned to one of four main categories: (1) positive personal characteristics of the first footer, which were sought after; (2) negative personal attributes, which should be avoided; (3) symbolic gifts which were carried into the house; and (4) symbolic actions carried out by him/her, or the occupants of the house.

Most accounts stress some physical aspect of the first footer, and the modern positive stereotype is a 'tall, dark-haired man', but this was not always the case. Dark hair is definitely the most often quoted attribute, but it was certainly not universal, even in Scotland, and a small minority of descriptions even say a fair- or red-haired man was preferred. Despite the wide variety of acceptable or desirable physical attributes, almost all agree that a woman would be bad luck. Some sources indicate ambivalence, or at least differing views on this question:

> In most places throughout West Wales, even at the present day, people are very particular as to whether they see a man or a woman the first thing on New Year's morning. Mr. Williams in his 'Llen-Gwerin Sir Gaerfyrddin' says that in parts of Carmarthenshire in order to secure future luck or success during the coming year, a man must see a woman and a woman a man. And the Rev.

N. Thomas, Vicar of Llanbadarn Fawr, informed me that he has met people in his parish who consider it lucky to see a woman first. As a rule, however, the majority of people both men and women deem it lucky to see a man, but unlucky to see a woman.

Wales (1911)

The seriousness with which some householders took this matter is demonstrated in many accounts of specific instances, such as the following extract reporting a case at Mansfield Police Court. A man was charged with assaulting a young woman on New Year's Day, and the following explanation for her being out of doors at the time was given:

The young woman attended the midnight service at the parish church, and returned home a few minutes past twelve o'clock; but the mother, believing in the superstition that it is unlucky for a female to enter the house on New Year's morning before a man, told the daughter that neither her father nor brother had yet come home, and she was to wait until they came to enter the house first. The girl, in consequence, went for a stroll, the morning being moonlight, and returned to the house five times, but, as her father and brother had not returned, the mother kept the door locked. For the sixth time she went for a walk along the streets, this being about a quarter to one o'clock, when the prisoner met and assaulted her.   Nottinghamshire (1890)

Apart from colour of hair, and sex, there have been many other negative characteristics of the first footer. A representative list given by Mrs Macleod Banks (*British Calendar Customs: Scotland*, Vol. 2, 1939), taken from a variety of late nineteenth-century Scottish sources, includes people who are pious and sanctimonious, flat-footed, barefooted, stingy, lame, who have a blind eye, who are midwives, ministers, doctors, gravediggers, thieves, who have met with an accident on the way, and who are carrying a knife or a pointed tool. Despite the apparently bewildering variety of attributes to avoid, the underlying principles are clear. The first footer must be whole, socially acceptable, and lucky, to guarantee those desirable qualities for the house for the forthcoming year.

The next key point of first footing is that the person must not arrive empty-handed. The overwhelming importance of bringing something into the house before anything is taken out at this season is treated below and, as the first person to enter, the first footer must be careful not to break this rule. A wide variety of items have been reported, but most of them carried symbolic weight by being staples of life such as food, drink, heat, or light. The first footer's symbolic actions are not always recorded, but in many cases there were set things that he should do. He nearly always has to wish everyone a happy New Year, sometimes has to cut a special cake, stir the fire, or visit every room in the house. Some households stipulate that the first footer should enter by the front door and leave by the back, which is directly opposed to how it would be at other times of the year.

Records show that few people left the matter to chance, and most householders who believed in the custom arranged beforehand with someone who fitted the ideal to come along soon after midnight. Some accounts show that people as well as houses could be 'first footed':

> The old folk go off to bed but many of the young ones will not be there for hours yet. Each girl is expecting the first-foot from her sweetheart, and anxious to be the first to open the door to him, and many a quiet stratagem is sometimes spent in the endeavour to outwit her, and get the old grandmother, or some dooce serving-lass, to be the first to meet the kiss-expecting lover. Quieter folks will put off their first footing until morning, but in nearly all Scottish families the first-foot is looked upon as a matter of no little importance, and notes will be compared among the neighbours in country villages as to who was their first-foot-luck or ill-luck, according to the character of the visitor.
>
> Scotland, *All the Year Round* (31 December 1870)

The biggest mystery about New Year first footing is that it cannot be traced before the mid nineteenth century, and even if we allow some earlier references which refer to similar first-foot customs on Christmas Day, the documentary record still reaches back to only about 1804/5. It is not at all unusual for calendar customs to have a much shorter history than has been assumed, but given the popularity and wide geographical distribution of first footing, it is surprising that earlier descriptions have not been found. The central motif of good/bad luck being predicted by a person met in the morning or the start of a journey certainly goes back much further, and a tentative suggestion is that the New Year custom was simply a specialized version of the former belief, which was later incorporated into a calendar custom.

The geographical distribution is interesting, but the evidence is not conclusive. It is clear that first footing was strongest in Scotland and northern England – particularly Yorkshire and Lancashire – but Ireland hardly appears in the documentary record at all. Nevertheless, of the five references so far found from before 1850, two are from Scotland, two from Herefordshire, and one from the Isle of Man.

letting in the New Year

In many homes, the central symbolic focus of the turning of the year took the form of physical steps to 'let the New Year in'. In most cases it was simply a question of opening doors or windows:

> As the clock struck twelve, it was customary to open the back door
> first, to let the old year out; then, the front door was opened, to let
> the new year in.   Herefordshire (1912)

There was also a deep-felt need to set a good precedent, something which underlies many of the superstitions of New Year's Day, and this was manifest in a concern about the inward and outward flow of items which symbolize luck and prosperity. Thus there was a wide-spread feeling that nothing should be taken out of the house before something was brought in. This is one of the main points of many versions of first footing; however, where that custom did not take place, or where householders felt in need of even more assurance, further steps had to be taken to ensure the balance of incomings and outgoings remained firmly in favour of the former. For some, this idea was confined to certain symbolic staples such as money, but many people took the principle to its logical conclusion and forbade all outgoings, however mundane:

> I remember accompanying the mistress of the house to her kitchen
> on New Year's Eve, when she called together all her servants, and
> warned them, under pain of dismissal, not to allow anything to be
> carried out of the house on the following day, though they might
> bring in as much as they pleased. Acting on this order, all ashes,
> dish-washings, or potato-parings, and so forth, were retained in
> the house till the next day, while coals, potatoes, firewood, and bread

were brought in as usual, the mistress keeping a sharp look-out on
the fulfilment of her orders.   N. England (1866)

Particular concern focused on fire:

If any householder's fire does not burn through the night of New
Year's Eve, it betokens bad luck during the ensuing year; and if any
party allow another a live coal, or even a lighted candle, on such an
occasion, the bad luck is extended to the other party for commiserat-
ing with the former in his misfortunes.   Lancashire (1851)

It was further believed that your situation or main occupation on the
day would affect your life for the next twelve months. So, for example,
people tried to be active and happy, to wear new clothes, and so on.

New Year's Day was also one of several days in the year when
washing was prohibited in many households, for fear it would cause a
death in the family:

On New Year's day one of our maids (not a Devonshire one)
was going to do the family washing, when our West-country girl
exclaimed in horror

Pray don't 'ee wash on New Year's day
Or you'll wash one of the family away
Devon (1896)

Reported examples of this superstition are overwhelmingly from
southern England, with a particular concentration in the West
Country, but it was also believed in fishing families elsewhere in the
country. In common with the other major New Year superstitions,
there is no indication that this fear of washing is older than the mid
nineteenth century, and indeed it seems to have been most widespread
in the twentieth.

collecting water on New Year's Day

A firm conviction that the special character of New Year's Day is
reflected in the natural world led to a range of customs based on the
first water collected on that day. The most widespread of these,
variously known as the cream, flower, crop, or ream of the well, held
that whoever succeeded in getting the first water from any well would
be lucky in some way – usually in love:

The maiden who, on New Year's morning, first draws a pailful of water from the village well is accounted singularly fortunate. She has, in truth, secured the 'flower o' the well', and will be happy for the succeeding year. The lassies often sing this couplet:

> The flower o' the well to our howse gaes
> And the bonniest lad'll be mine.
>
> Caithness (1895)

The custom was almost exclusively confined to females, and in some versions the water had similar cosmetic qualities to May dew. The earliest clear reference to it appears in one of the Revd James Nicol's Scottish poems in 1804, with lines very similar to the Caithness example quoted above, but long before that, the West Country poet Robert Herrick may have referred to the idea in 1648 when he wrote that 'Perilla' should 'bring Part of the creame from that Religious Spring' to wash his body after death.

Easter

The vast majority of superstitions which have gathered around Easter are concerned specifically with Good Friday, but one widespread Easter Sunday belief was that when the sun rose on that day, it danced:

On Easter Sunday, people at Castleton, Derbyshire, used to climb the hill on which the castle is built, at six o'clock in the morning, to see the sun rise. On this day the sun is said to dance for joy at his rising. On the Wednesday before Easter Sunday a Derbyshire man said, 'I think the sun will hardly be able to contain himself till Sunday'. In Derbyshire they say that the sun spins round when he sets on Easter Sunday, and people go out to see this spinning.

Derbyshire (1895)

In answer to those who said they could not see the performance, believers had two replies – either the watcher lacked faith, which is the standard reply to all doubters of supernatural phenomena the world over, or the Devil had obscured the wondrous sight.

The notion was clearly already well known in the mid seventeenth century, when Sir John Suckling (*Ballade Upon a Wedding*, 1646) used the image in his description of a girl dancing at a wedding, and it was still very widely known and believed in the early twentieth century.

Good Friday

Popular traditions and beliefs about Good Friday reveal a long-standing ambivalence about the meaning of the day in the minds of the people. In the eyes of the official religion, the commemoration of the death of the founder would clearly be a day set aside from all others as one of mourning, fasting, prayer, and penitence, but for very many individuals, the day has long been far from gloomy. The confusion is certainly not helped by the term *Good* Friday, in common use since the thirteenth century, and originally meaning *Holy* or *God's* Friday. The notion that the day was 'good' because Christ's sacrifice opened to us the gates of everlasting life was a distinction which was lost on many English-speaking folk. In the early nineteenth century, before the introduction of bank holidays, Good Friday and Christmas Day were the only two days of leisure which were almost universally granted to working people, and rural workers, in particular, regarded Good Friday as the ideal time to plant their potatoes and to get forward on their gardens and allotments. They also indulged in many traditional games, from skipping to marble-playing, on the day. In popular superstition, therefore, we find the day treated as good or bad, almost at random. Thus, bread baked on Good Friday is lucky and cures all ills, but 'He who bakes or brews on Good Friday will have his house burnt down before the end of the year' (Northamptonshire, 1851). Similarly, 'Potatoes must always be planted on Good Friday' (Devon, 1972), but 'Potatoes must not be dibbled on Good Friday or bad crop will follow' (*c.*1932), and so on.

The picture is further complicated by the widespread fear of Friday as the unluckiest day of the week. It is likely that this reputation itself came about in pre-Reformation Britain by extension from Good Friday, but as it became widespread in its own right, it in turn strengthened the original negative reputation of Good Friday. The most widespread beliefs about Good Friday are detailed below, but there were many others.

One notable characteristic of Good Friday prohibitions is the frequency with which they are explained and supported by stories based on apocryphal events which took place when Christ was on his way to Calvary. But one continuing puzzle over Good Friday traditions and beliefs is the apparently late date at which they start to be recorded.

As far as the written record goes, most of them seem to be no older than the nineteenth century.

Good Friday bread

Undoubtedly the most widespread of Good Friday beliefs concern the special food associated with the day – bread, buns, and eggs. The basic tradition is that bread and buns baked on the day never grow mouldy but remain edible for ever, and similarly, eggs laid on Good Friday never go bad. They were also believed to have considerable power in the medicinal sphere, and were routinely kept in many a home for use during the coming year:

> Calling at a cottage one day, I saw a small loaf hanging up oddly in a corner of the house. I asked why it was placed there, and was told that it was Good Friday bread; that it would never grow mouldy (and on inspecting it I certainly found it very dry) and that it was very serviceable against some diseases, the bloody flux being mentioned as an example.   Suffolk (1867)

Good Friday bread was also held to have protective properties, most commonly against fire, but also in some coastal areas against shipwreck, and its presence in the kitchen also assured good luck in baking throughout the coming year. A short legend explains why baked products should have so much power on this day, but it is difficult to assess how widely known it was:

> As our Blessed Lord was carrying His cross on his way to His crucifixion, a woman who had been washing came out of the house and threw her dirty water over the Saviour; another woman who was standing near with some freshly baked bread said to her, 'Why do you treat that poor man like that, One who never did you any harm?' and she gave our Blessed Lord a loaf, which He ate, and said 'from henceforth blessed be to the baker, and cursed be the washer.'   Herefordshire (1912)

The history of the belief in the potency of Good Friday bread is unclear. Certainly it was extremely well known and widely reported throughout the nineteenth century, and was already in circulation in the mid eighteenth century, but before that the record is blank, apart from a very early reference identified by Iona Opie and Moira Tatem:

in a letter to Bishop Wulfsige, written around the year 1001, the English abbot Aelfric refers to priests keeping 'the sacrament conse-crated on Easter Day the whole year long for sick men'. If this tradition remained active from medieval times to the eighteenth century, it is a mystery why it does not seem to be mentioned by anyone. Similarly, if the belief was re-introduced after a long lapse, it is difficult to see why, or how.

no work on Good Friday

Other Good Friday superstitions are couched in terms of prohibitions on certain activities, and one of the most widespread was the ban on washing. Various calamities could be the result of such a sinful act: clothes washed or hung out to dry would be found spattered with blood, soap suds would turn red, the family would be dreadfully un-lucky, or someone would die because you 'washed them away'. This belief is found in a surprisingly restricted area – all the known refer-ences are from English locations – and the earliest is from only 1836.

Given the nature of Good Friday as the key day for Christian mourning, it is not surprising that there was a general feeling that, like a sort of super-Sunday, no work should be done on the day. The ambivalent nature of Good Friday beliefs is shown most clearly in the realm of work on the land and the planting of crops, where completely opposite advice was given:

> I learn from a clergyman familiar with the North Riding of York-shire, that great care is there taken not to disturb the earth in any way; it were impious to use spade, plough, or harrow. He remem-bers, when a boy, hearing of a villager, Charlie Marston by name, who shocked his neighbours by planting potatoes on Good Friday, but they never came up.   Yorkshire (1866)

> Many people then begin to toll their gardens, as they believe, to use their own words, that all things put in the earth on Good Friday will grow 'goody', and return to them with great increase.
>
>   Devon (1838)

Unfortunately, it is not simply a geographical north-south divide, as positive attitudes to the day have been found in each region, although the strongest prohibitions have been found in Scotland and Northern England. Potatoes and parsley were particularly singled out as suited

for Good Friday planting, but all growing things were thought suscep-
tible to the influence of the day, and were often expected to 'come up
double'.

One worker reported as unwilling to work on Good Friday was the
blacksmith. Many would not allow a fire in their forge, or would have
anything to do with nails:

> A friend who passed his boyhood in the north of Durham informs
> me that no blacksmith throughout that district would then drive a
> nail on that day; a remembrance of the awful purpose for which
> hammer and nails were used on the first Good Friday doubtless
> held them back.   Co. Durham (1866)

Other versions of this prohibition include the blacksmith's wife. The
story goes that when the bellows refused to work on the first Good
Friday, she used her apron to fan the flames to make the nails, or she
carried them to the executioners in her apron. Some nineteenth-century
blacksmiths' wives thus refused to wear an apron on Good Friday.

Hallowe'en (31 October)

Hallowe'en is probably the most misrepresented and misunderstood
festival in the British traditional calendar. The widespread notion that
the day (or rather the night) is a pre-Christian pagan celebration of
the dead is not historically correct, but is now so well entrenched as
to be immovable. Certainly, the festival on 1 November, called *Samhain*, was by far the most important of the four quarter days in the
medieval Irish calendar, with gatherings and feasts, and a sense that
this was the time of year when the physical and supernatural worlds
were closest and magical things could happen. But however strong
the early evidence is in Ireland, in Wales it was 1 May and New Year
which took precedence; in Scotland there is hardly any mention of
31 October/1 November until much later, and in Anglo-Saxon England
even less. Samhain's importance has thus been extrapolated from the
Irish evidence and overemphasized for the rest of the British Isles. As
the historian Ronald Hutton (1996) comments:

> It must be concluded, therefore, that the medieval records furnish
> no evidence that 1 November was a major pan-Celtic festival, and
> none of religious ceremonies, even where it was observed.

On the other hand, it was a very important time of year in the Catholic Church. Hallowe'en is the Eve of All Hallows or All Saints (1 November), which, along with All Souls (2 November), constitute Hallowtide. These festivals were confirmed at these dates from about AD 800 to 1000, but later gradually coalesced around the night of 31 October/1 November, and All Souls took the highest profile. The key element was that this was the time for commemoration of the departed faithful, and in particular the day when prayers could be said and bells could be rung, to get souls out of purgatory and into heaven. The connection between the dead and this time of year was thus a Christian invention. The reforming Protestant churches abolished these notions, but they continued in Catholic areas and in the popular mind and tradition.

When folklore records began to be made in the eighteenth and nineteenth centuries, the overwhelming features of Hallowe'en were divination (usually love divination) and games. Few of these were reported as happening solely at this season, but those concerned with seasonal plants – apples, nuts, cabbages – were more in evidence than at other times.

Beyond the modern obsession with witches' hats and brooms, our view of the traditional Hallowe'en has been heavily influenced by the catalogue of divinations so entertainingly provided by Robert Burns in his poem 'Hallowe'en' (1786), and his basic accuracy is confirmed by other sources. Similar activities were still popular in Ireland over 150 years later:

> Fortune-telling has a place in all Hallowe'en parties, and the for-
> tunes are usually concerned with love and marriage. Girls used to
> veil mirrors and hope to see the face of a future husband when the
> veil was removed at midnight. Young men pulled cabbage-stalks,
> kale-runts. And from their size and the amount of earth which
> adhered to them they foretold whether their future wives would be
> tall or short, rich or poor. I saw this done at a Hallowe'en party a
> few years ago. The burning of nuts is still practised. Couples place
> nuts in pairs on the hearth and from their behaviour they draw
> conclusions about their own future love-life.   N. Ireland (1951)

In England, the festival remained far less prominent in the traditional calendar, although the closer one gets to Scotland the higher its profile appears to have been.

Christmas

All seasonal festivals attract superstitions, which usually focus on whatever elements are considered particularly special to the season. So, for example, the singing of carols being fundamental to the Christmas season, many people once believed that it was unlucky to sing them at any other time. Christmas has been one of the most popular festivals in the calendar for a long time, so it is no surprise that it has had more than its fair share of beliefs, and those which are still widely known concentrate on decorations and seasonal food.

Christmas decorations

The main areas in which belief comes to the fore in respect of Christmas decorations are: (1) which plants can be used and which, if any, forbidden; (2) when the decorations are put up; (3) when they are taken down; (4) what happens to them then, and the key question in the past was whether they should be burnt or not. The term 'Christmas decorations' here refers solely to evergreens and other plants. Artificial decorations were not introduced until late Victorian times, and do not seem to have gathered any beliefs of their own.

Holly and ivy have been the mainstay of Christmas decoration for church use since at least the fifteenth and sixteenth centuries, when they are mentioned regularly in churchwardens' accounts, but many of the specific traditions about them are found only in much later sources:

> It depends upon the kind of holly that comes into a house at Christmas which shall be master during the coming year, the wife or the husband. If the holly is smooth, the wife will be master, if the holly is prickly, the husband will be the master. It is considered very unlucky for a house unless some mistletoe is brought in at Christmas.   Derbyshire (1871)

> In decorating the house with evergreens at Christmas, care must be taken not to let ivy be used alone, or even predominate, as it is a plant of bad omen, and will prove injurious. Northamptonshire (1851)

Throughout the historical record, other plants are also mentioned, including laurel, box, bay, rosemary, and mistletoe. There is no indication that any particular plant was deliberately avoided, until the

constant reiteration in recent times of dubious notions of sacredness
and Druid connections led to people questioning mistletoe's inclusion.
Some even claim that it was historically banned from sacred buildings
(see pp. 251–2 for further discussion).

The only genuine belief about mistletoe is that anyone who stands
under it cannot refuse to be kissed. This was already widespread in
the early nineteenth century, as John Brand (1813), Washington Irving
(1820), and John Clare all describe it in their works:

> The shepherd now no more afraid,
> Since custom doth the chance bestow,
> Starts up to kiss the giggling maid
> Beneath the branch of mistletoe
> That 'neath each cottage beam is seen,
>
> John Clare, *Shepherd's Calendar* (1827)

and it has continued to the present day. It has been suggested that
this is a survival of a classical belief recorded by Pliny (AD 77) that
mistletoe promotes conception in women if they carry a piece with
them, but it is difficult to see how this belief survived the intervening
1,800 years without being noticed elsewhere, unless it was re-
introduced to British tradition directly by translation of Pliny's works.

As regards the correct time for putting up and taking down decorations, there is little similarity between the present day and previous
era. A little over a century ago, decorations were put up just before
Christmas (usually Christmas Eve); nowadays, most people put them
up a fortnight to a week before Christmas Day, and public displays
are usually in place around 1 December. Few people would now wait
until Christmas Eve, but in the past many believed that it was
extremely unlucky to bring evergreens into the house before that date.

> Early in December, 1905, I was carrying some fine holly through
> Chelford, and a group of women in the street commented on
> the ill-luck that would follow my taking it into the house before
> Christmas day.   Gloucestershire (1912)

Although fairly generally reported, we have no evidence that this
concern over timing existed before the 1870s.

Similarly, the norm for modern Christmas decorations is that they
have to be removed on or before Twelfth Night, but for previous
generations by far the most common time was Candlemas Day

(2 February). This had been so at least since the mid seventeenth
century. Robert Herrick alluded to Candlemas several times in his
poems, including the famous lines:

> Down with the rosemary, and so
> Down with the baies, and misletoe;
> Down with the holly, ivie, all,
> Wherewith ye drest the Christmas hall.
>
> Robert Herrick,
> 'Ceremony upon Candlemas Eve' (1648)

Candlemas was being named as the proper time by some informants
right up to the turn of the twentieth century. It demonstrates the
power of contemporary custom that most people nowadays would
recoil in horror from any suggestion that their Christmas decorations
should stay up until February.

> If every scrap of Christmas decoration is not removed from the
> church before Candlemas-Day, there will be a death within a year
> in the family occupying the pew where a leaf or berry is left.
>
> Suffolk (1864)

There was also a sharp disagreement between those who believed
that the plants should then be burnt and those who insisted they
should not. Both sides maintained it would lead to dreadful bad luck
not to follow their rule, but there is no discernible geographical pattern
to explain the different views on burning. The chronological spread is
perhaps more telling. The earliest anti-burning piece dates from only
1866, but there are references which support burning right back to the
eleventh century. On this evidence, it would seem that burning the
Christmas evergreens was the norm until quite late in the nineteenth
century.

Christmas food

There is a distinct tendency for food which is customary at particular
festivals to develop connotations of luck, and this is particularly true
of Christmas puddings and mince pies:

> Mince pies, too, have their own magic; if you eat twelve of them,
> from twelve separate friends, during the twelve days of Christmas,
> you are promised a lucky twelve months to follow.   Wiltshire (1975)

The 'twelve separate friends' is more usually given as 'twelve different houses' – presumably it would be too easy to eat twelve in one house. This notion was widespread across England in the late nineteenth and twentieth centuries, but it has not been found before the 1850s. This was the period when Christmas was being drastically remodelled, and it is quite possible that it was a new fancy of the time. There is still a vague feeling in many people's minds that one should not refuse a mince pie at Christmas, and the saying is still quoted regularly as an excuse for mild festive overeating.

The custom of getting everyone in the household to stir the Christmas cake or pudding mix, at least in token terms, is still well known and widely practised.

> When I was a child in the 1940s, we all had to help to make the Christmas cake. Mother used a large yellow mixing bowl and a big wooden spoon. We were called into the kitchen and had to stand on a chair to reach the bowl. You had to close your eyes and stir the mixture round three times, then you made a wish for what you wanted Santa to bring.   Lincolnshire (1992)

As with other Christmas food beliefs, this one is not recorded before the mid Victorian era.

Holy Innocents' Day (28 December)

In the Christian churches, Holy Innocents, or Childermas, is dedicated to the first-born children massacred by Herod (Matthew 2: 1–18). To commemorate that awful event, the day was a 'dismal' (*dies mala* means 'bad day' in Latin) day, with muffled peals of bells and, despite falling within the twelve days of Christmas, with a subdued and penitential air. This official religious background was reflected in superstitions surrounding the day, which was generally considered very unlucky. If anything was started on the day, it would never be finished or would go disastrously wrong, fishermen refused to leave harbour, and, in the home, no major housework was attempted, and in particular no washing done. The latter would be certain to result in a death in the family.

Not only was the day itself unlucky, but the day of the week on which it fell would also be unlucky for the coming year, and in some communities that day would be referred to as a 'Cross day' all year.

The earliest references are from the early seventeenth century, with Richard Carew's description of Cornwall in 1602, and John Melton's attack on superstitions in his *Astrologaster* (1620):

> That it is not good to put on a new sute, pare ones nailes, or begin any thing on a Childermass day.

And even in the late twentieth century a few people still remembered not to wash on the day.

LUCKY AND UNLUCKY DAYS

unlucky days

The notion that particular days are lucky or unlucky is, presumably, universal. In antiquity, the Egyptians, Jews, Greeks, and Romans all had complex systems which either identified specific unlucky days or assigned each day in the year as either lucky or unlucky. These notions were certainly known in England in Saxon times, and medieval calendars also identified days as good or bad. In Britain, since at least the turn of the fifteenth century, unlucky days were called 'Egyptian days', either because it was thought that the system used for calculating them went back to Egyptian times, or because they were believed to be connected with events such as the ten plagues of Moses, so that the adjective 'Egyptian' came to signify gloom and misery. From about the same time, they were also termed 'dismal days' – the word dismal being derived from the Latin *dies mala* (bad day), with which the days were marked on medieval calendars. Unlucky days were also called 'Cross days'.

As an example of the list of unlucky days, the following is from a manuscript *Kalendar* of the time of Henry VI (1422–61):

> These underwritten be the perilous days, for to take any sickness
> in, or to be hurt in, or to be wedded in, or to take any journey upon,
> or to begin any work on, that he would well speed. The number of
> these days be in the year 32; they be these: – January 1, 2, 4, 5, 7,
> 10, 15; February 6, 7, 18; March 1, 6, 8; April 6, 11; May 5, 6, 7;
> June 7, 15; July 5, 19; August 15, 19; September 6, 7; October 6; November 15, 16; December 15, 16, 17.   Robert Chambers, *Book of Days* (1864)

Such lists, when compared, seem to bear little relationship to each
other, although, to be fair, if they were calculated on forthcoming
astronomical features they could indeed be different each year. However, there is no reason to think that they were any more scientific
than the daily horoscope predictions in a modern tabloid newspaper.
Ordinary people will have known little of the 'science' of astrology
anyway, but a simplified and popular form was filtered down to them
via the almanacs which sold in their hundreds of thousands each year.
These cheap publications also provided data on the phases of the
moon, which were taken into account when planning many aspects of
daily life, especially on the farm.

Apart from those unlucky days set by almanac and calendar makers,
there seems to have been little structure to the days individuals
regarded as unlucky or lucky. Fridays have generally been regarded as
unlucky since at least the medieval period, and Good Friday was
singled out for gloom in some contexts. Nowadays, of course, Friday
13th is widely feared, but this can be traced back only to Victorian
times. The only other day which was widely regarded as unlucky was
Holy Innocents' Day or Childermas (28 December), and those who
took this seriously also regarded the day of the week on which it fell
as suspect for the rest of the year.

The antiquarian John Aubrey was interested in the topic of unlucky
days, and he devoted a chapter to 'day fatality' in his *Miscellanies*
(1696), in which he discussed the way particular dates seem to be
significant to individuals and to nations, but his thoughts on the
matter are anything but convincing. His method is to list events which
had happened on a certain date, and then stand back in amazement
at the coincidence of it all. He was particularly fascinated by people
who had been born and had died on the same date in the year, and as
he thought their deaths were a 'good thing' (they were going to meet
their maker) he could declare this their lucky date. Most other attempts

to prove the reality of individual lucky and unlucky days, even down
to present times, are similarly unconvincing.

Fridays

Across the whole British Isles, Friday has long had the reputation of
being the unluckiest day of the week, and there were numerous
traditional restrictions and prohibitions about what should or should
not be done on the day. In accordance with the general superstitious
fear of bad beginnings particular concern was felt about starting
anything on a Friday – a new journey, business project, job, marriage –

> My wife recently wanted a fresh servant, and advertised for one in
> a local newspaper. A girl, a native of Devonshire, applied for the
> situation, and appearing to be in every way suitable, she was
> engaged, and asked to come on a given date. That date happened
> to be on a Friday, but the girl positively refused to enter on a new
> situation on a Friday. She said she would 'rather give up the place'.
> We had to submit, and she came to our house on a Saturday.
>
> Devon (1900)

As late as the 1950s, this superstition still had strong influence in many
quarters:

> The Amusement Caterers' Association in reply to a query arising
> from a report in *The Times* (2 May 1951) of a meeting of showmen
> 'to hear what could be done to overcome the fact that a Friday
> would be the first day on which visitors would be admitted to the
> fun fair' stated . . . it is quite true to say that, especially among the
> older showmen and amusement caterers, there is a superstition
> that it is unlucky to open on a Friday, but, so far as we know, it is
> dying out as the newer generations come into the business. The
> feeling, however, has been strong enough to encourage showmen
> of Battersea Park to stage the reported unofficial opening (or 'dress
> rehearsal') on Thursday next when, as you have read, several thou-
> sand children will be invited to the amusement park as guests of
> the concessionaires.
>
> London (1951)

People would not move house ('Friday flit, short sit'), and fishermen
would not set sail. In the domestic sphere, it was thought unlucky to
cut fingernails and hair.

Numerous minor beliefs also clustered around the day: 'Adam and Eve ate the forbidden fruit on a Friday' (Sussex, 1878); 'A Crow would not carry a straw to its nest on a Friday' (Orkney, 1909); 'Criminals are very superstitious – there are fewer burglaries on Fridays' (c.1932); 'If people marry on Friday they will "lead a cat-and-dog life", that is, they will quarrel' (England, 1895); and many others.

There is little doubt that this belief has simple Christian roots. The medieval Catholic church promoted Friday across Europe as a day of penance and abstinence in commemoration of Christ's death on the day. The unluckiness of Fridays is well documented since the late fourteenth century, when Chaucer wrote 'And on a Friday fell all this mischance' in the *Nun's Priest's Tale* (c.1390). In the last century or so, the rise of Friday 13th as unlucky has all but eclipsed the idea that all Fridays are suspect.

Friday 13th

The belief that Friday 13th is an especially unlucky day is one of the widest-known superstitions in Britain today, and is erroneously assumed to be of great antiquity. The notion that thirteen is a generally unlucky number has not been found earlier than 1852, and although Fridays have been regarded as unlucky since medieval times, it is quite certain that the fear of Friday 13th is a Victorian invention. Indeed, the first definite reference to Friday 13th we have is from 1913:

> I have met a 'coach' of fine mental capacities, which had been carefully cultivated, who dreaded the evil luck of Friday the 13th.

But what may be a point in the development of Friday 13th is provided by a piece from *Notes & Queries* in 1873:

> Thirteen at Dinner: I apprehend that there is no doubt that this notion has reference to the Last Supper, at which thirteen were present. Some, I believe, have carried it to the extent of disliking that number at all times; but the commoner form limits it to Friday. Not that there is any ground of fact for this, for the Last Supper was on the fifth, not the sixth, day of the week. Sailors are held somewhat superstitious and I know an eminent naval officer who, though I do not know that he acted on it earlier in his life, actually would walk out of the room when the conjunction happened on a

Friday, after the death of his wife and daughter, both of which
events were preceded by the said conjunction.

It is not quite clear which particular 'conjunction' this writer means,
but it seems to be thirteen at table and Friday rather than the date. It
does show, however, that Fridays and thirteens were beginning to be
connected in the 1870s.

The idea that Friday 13th is an ancient superstition is so ingrained
that the assertion that it is no older than Victorian is frequently
met with disbelief, even anger, but the evidence is overwhelming.
Historical research into folklore topics is routinely bedevilled by the
problem of negative evidence. To put it simply, we cannot be sure
that a belief or custom did not exist at a particular time simply because
a written reference to it has not been found. Nevertheless, with a belief
such as Friday 13th, we are on much safer ground than usual, for the
obvious reason that it concerns a particular calendar date, and there is
no shortage of date-based material. From the seventeenth century
onwards, the printing presses poured forth almanacs – publications
whose whole *raison d'être* was to provide information about dates,
including lucky and unlucky ones. None of them single out Friday
13th. Since before Samuel Pepys's time, people have kept detailed
diaries and journals, scores of which have been published and are
generally available – those before the twentieth century do not mention
Friday 13th being unlucky. Our sixteenth- and seventeenth-century
dramatists, great and small, wrote tragedies full of omens – dogs howl,
owls shriek, ravens, comets and thunderstorms predict disaster – but
no tragedy happens on Friday 13th. And so on.

Even in the later nineteenth and early twentieth centuries, the belief
does not seem to be nearly as widely known as today. The Victorian
folklore collectors do not mention it, and even popular turn-of-the-
century books on superstitions often omit it. T. Sharper Knowlson,
for example, devotes a section of his *Origins of Popular Superstitions
and Customs* (1910) to the unlucky nature of Fridays, and another to
thirteen at the table, but does not connect the two. The same situation applies in the USA, where the Friday 13th superstition is today
as strong as it is in Britain. For example, the article 'The Thirteen
Superstition among the Fair Sex' (*Belford's Magazine*, 1891) printed
letters from well-known American women who were asked if they
believed in 'the thirteen superstition'. Every one of them interpreted

the title as referring to thirteen at table; none of them mentioned
Friday 13th.

the month of May

May is the only month which appears in its own right in a range of
beliefs, and although May Day itself has nearly always been viewed in
a positive light, the rest of the month was curiously regarded with
suspicion in a number of contexts. The best-known positive feature
of the month is that May dew is excellent for the complexion – in
particular for the removal of freckles – and some said the effect of one
bathing lasted all year:

> Washing the face with dew gathered on the morning of the first
> day of May kept it from being tanned by the sun and becoming
> freckled.   N.E. Scotland (1881)

It was still being recommended in the late twentieth century. The
earliest clear reference is as late as the seventeenth century, and occurs
in Pepys's *Diary*. On 28 May 1667 he describes how his wife, Elizabeth,
got up early to gather the dew:

> After dinner, my wife away down with Jane and W. Hewer to
> Woolwich in order to a little ayre, and to lie there tonight and so
> to gather May dew tomorrow morning, which Mrs. Turner hath
> taught her as the only thing in the world to wash her face with, and
> I am contented with it.

She went out again on 10 May 1669, and it is worth noting that
Elizabeth Pepys clearly believed in the efficacy of the dew throughout
May rather than being restricted to the first of the month as was later
the case. The wording of Pepys's entry indicates that the idea of May
dew for the complexion was new to him, and as we have no earlier
description in Britain it is quite possible that it was a new fashion,
probably introduced from the Continent.

The early history of the custom is unfortunately confused by impre-
cise reading of primary sources. There are numerous references, going
back at least as far as Chaucer's time, to the custom of 'going a-Maying',
in which parties would go out to the woods to fetch green boughs to
decorate their homes and public buildings. It is often assumed that
these trips included bathing in the dew, but this is unwarranted.

May dew was also recommended for a range of children's ailments, and a relatively minor belief was that while gathering it for cosmetic purposes, there was an opportunity to make a wish:

> On the first day of May girls went to wash their faces in the dew and wish before sunrise – while doing this they name some lad and wish in their own mind that he may become their sweetheart, and they get their wish.   Ross & Cromarty (1939)

It was commonly believed that kittens born in May were unlucky, no use as mousers, and brought snakes into the house. It was thus not at all uncommon for all kittens born in the month to be unceremoniously drowned. A similar, but less widespread, belief spilled over into the human sphere, and held that babies born in May were sickly and unlucky, as reported in the journal *Folk-Lore* in 1957:

> May-born babies, like May kittens, are said to be weakly and un- likely to thrive. Whenever any misfortune befell my grandmother, who died in 1925, she never failed to remind us that she had been born in May.

saying 'rabbits' on the first day of the month

A strange but widespread custom which exists mainly in the domestic setting of a family. It involves marking the first day of the month, and sometimes the night before, by saying out loud 'rabbits' or 'hares'. Those who do so ensure a wish comes true, or good luck through the coming month. Details vary considerably, but the broad outline is always recognizable:

> On the first of each month as soon as you realise it is the first, say 'White rabbits, white rabbits, white rabbits'. This will ensure luck for the rest of the month.   Co. Tyrone (1972)

The almost universal rule is that whatever words are prescribed for the last night must be the last thing said, and those for the morning must be the first. In some families it is the first to say it who gets the wish, while others more diplomatically promise a lucky month for everyone who keeps within the rules.

The earliest concrete dating for the custom is found in a correspon- dence which appeared in the *Saturday Westminister Gazette* in March and April 1919. The first writer simply asks for details, and others reply from various parts of England stating that their families already carry out the custom every month. One writer claims to have known it for about twenty-five years, but it is clear that the custom was not by any means universally known at that time, and many regarded it as relatively new.

The Cycle of Life

❧

BIRTH

Lucky Being born with a caul • Carrying the baby upstairs before down •
Letting a baby's hands stay unwashed • Letting a good-tempered person be
first to kiss the baby • Wrapping the baby in old clothes • Giving the baby
money on a first visit • Making sure the baby cries at christening •
Helping the baby's teething with a coral necklace

Unlucky Boasting about your baby • Sitting on a chair just vacated by a
pregnant woman • Letting a pregnant woman see anything ugly or
frightening • New mothers leaving the house before being 'churched' •
Bringing a new cradle or pram into the house before the baby is born •
Cutting the baby's fingernails before he or she is a year old • Baby teething
too early • Weighing the baby before he or she is a year old

❧

MARRIAGE

Lucky Getting married while the sun is shining • Throwing the bride's
stocking or bouquet • Getting married in white or blue • Putting wedding
cake under your pillow

Unlucky Losing a wedding ring • Wearing black or green at a wedding •
Reciting Psalm 109 to curse a marriage • Wedding party meeting a funeral

❧

DEATH

Lucky A piece of hangman's rope • Touching a corpse to avoid dreaming
of it • Opening all the doors when death occurs • Stopping clocks and
covering mirrors • Holding a funeral in the rain • Walking a few steps
with a funeral if you meet one

Unlucky Three unexplained loud knocks • A corpse staying limp • A
grave being open on a Sunday • Treading on graves • Being buried on the
north side of a church • Being the first or last person buried on a given day

BIRTH

Numerous beliefs concerning pregnancy, childbirth, and babies existed in the nineteenth century which have almost completely disappeared, as much of the danger and uncertainty involved has diminished. The basic superstitious principles involved are mostly clear enough – babies are vulnerable to ill-wishing by witches and fairies as well as to physical disease; they are at the beginning of their lives, and things that happen to them could influence their future fortune; and whatever traits they exhibit will predict their future character. Most importantly, however, parents must not tempt fate by being too pleased with themselves, or by boasting, or over-praising the baby. Even before birth the baby's future is at risk, and expectant mothers need to be careful what they do, and even what they see. For each of these areas of concern there was a range of traditional beliefs and customs on which those involved could rely for guidance, or at least for explanation.

pregnancy: chair and bed

For at least the last forty years, it has been said that a female should not sit down on a chair just vacated by a pregnant woman, or she herself will fall pregnant in the near future. This notion does not seem to have been noted by folklorists, and it is perhaps a relatively modern belief, but it has undoubtedly been widespread in Britain since at least the 1960s, and the symbolism involved is not hard to find. A similar belief in the 1930s warned women not to sit on a bed in which a baby had recently been born.

pregnancy: pendulum divination

A traditional way of determining the sex of an unborn baby is to
suspend a wedding ring or a needle, by a hair or thread, over the
mother-to-be's abdomen, and watch for oscillations. The item will
move either in a circular manner, or in a straight line from side to
side, and this indicates a boy or a girl. Unfortunately, there is no
agreement about which movement means which sex. Pendulum divination has been practised in Britain in many other contexts since at
least the sixteenth century, but for determining sex its first recorded
version dates from only around the First World War. In March 2002,
an expectant mother posted a message to a baby discussion list on the
Internet asking for details:

> Does anybody know when you dangle your wedding ring on a piece
> of cotton over your bump, and it either goes left–right, or round in
> a circle, which means a boy and which means a girl. Thanks, Bev.

A few responses were posted, which showed continued confusion over
whether the circles meant a girl or a boy, but the correspondence
demonstrated that this method of prediction was still being regularly
tried, even if only in fun. Interestingly, one detailed response from the
daughter of a pet-shop manager claimed that the procedure was still
used routinely by breeders to sex young birds.

birthmarks and pre-natal impressions

Birthmarks and other unusual physical characteristics of a new baby
were explained by reference to the belief that strong influences on a
pregnant woman could have a lasting effect. This influence could be
any strong emotion, usually fear, or it could simply be the sight of
something unusual or repellent. Birthmarks would usually take on the
shape of whatever caused the emotion, but sometimes the influence
could be much more extensive:

> Just before she was born, her father had some ferrets. He was nearly
> caught with them one day, and he ran home thinking he was
> followed, and threw the ferret into his wife's lap, telling her to hide
> it under her apron; but she was frightened, and fell right down on
> the floor, and the ferret ran away. Soon after, she had this little girl
> born, with red eyes, as red as flames, and white hair, as white as

snow. She is married now and gets a lot of money by going about
to fairs.   Essex (*c.*1830)

It was thus everybody's duty to ensure that pregnant women were
protected from such problems. An added danger was that if a pregnant
woman's cravings or fancies were not satisfied, these too could mark
the baby. This was taken so much for granted that everyone around
an expectant mother would be careful not to be the unwitting cause
of a baby being marked. A well-known way to remove birthmarks was
for the mother to lick it every day, but there were also more drastic
remedies, such as stroking with the hand of a recently dead man.

The notion of maternal impression is found all over the world, and has
been documented in virtually all ages. A well-known case is attributed to
the Greek physician Hippocrates (*c.*460–*c.*370 BC), in which he
reputedly saved the honour of a princess who had borne a black child
and was thus under sentence of death for adultery. He attributed the
fact to the painting of a Negro which was hung in her rooms and was
therefore in her sight throughout her pregnancy, and thus proved her
innocence. Indeed, the biblical Jacob was operating on the same principle when he set up striped wooden rods before his flocks to increase
the proportion of striped and speckled animals (Genesis 31:31–9).

The idea is still not completely exploded. In January 2002 an 86-year-
old man phoned the present author at Croydon Library, asking about
First World War Zeppelin raids. He said that as a child he had had
very shaky hands, and his handwriting had been atrocious. His mother
always said that this was because she was frightened by the Zeppelin
raid when she was expecting him, and he still believed it to be so.

The most widely known example of the belief in the strength of
pre-natal impressions was that if a pregnant woman met a hare her
child would be born with a hare-lip (cleft lip) or cleft palate.

> If a woman in an 'interesting condition' sees a hare in her path, she
> must immediately stop and make three rents in her under garment,
> or the child will be hare-shorn – i.e. have a cleft upper lip.
>
> Warwickshire (1875)

This tearing of the shift or skirt was widely accepted as the only way
to prevent the tragedy. The earliest reference to the term 'hare-lip' in
the *OED* is 1567, and it is clear that not only the cause but also the
remedy were already well known at that period.

'Monday's child'

An extremely well-known rhyme exists, even in the present day, which purports to predict a child's character or fate from the day on which it was born. Despite being reported from a wide range of places, over more than 160 years, the wording has remained remarkably stable. The version noted below from a 56-year-old woman in Surrey in 2001, who learnt it from her mother, is almost word-for-word the same as the first known version published in 1838:

> Monday's child is fair of face
> Tuesday's child is full of grace
> Wednesday's child is full of woe
> Thursday's child has far to go
> Friday's child is loving and giving
> Saturday's child works hard for a living
> But the child that is born on the Sabbath day
> Is bonny and blithe and good and gay.

It is not clear how seriously this was taken as a superstition, and those who print it do so without comment. It must be said that it has a 'bookish' air to it, as if it started life in some 'improving' children's book, but if such a publication were sufficiently popular to launch such a well-known rhyme, it is strange that it has not been identified. It is equally strange that if such a rhyme had been well known in previous centuries, nobody seems to mention it.

The idea that the day of birth might be significant is much older than the rhyme. Thomas Nashe, for example, comments in his *Terrors of the Night* (1594), 'I have heard aged mumping beldams ... tell what luck everyone should have by the day of the week he was born on', and the whole basis of astrology links birth and time in determining character. But the rhyme does not even fit with other beliefs about days of the week, most notably the almost universal notion that Friday was the most unlucky day, particularly for starting anything important.

babies born with a caul

Babies who are born with a section of the amniotic membrane, or caul, over their head and face have widely been regarded as being generally very lucky, and specifically immune from drowning through-out their life, at least while they keep the caul safe:

> A close connection of mine born in Worcestershire in 1906 came into this world with a caul . . . The circumstances of his birth did not inspire his choice of a career, nor until after his third escape did he learn the old superstition about children being born with cauls preserved from drowning. It is undoubtedly a coincidence that he has had three narrow shaves from a watery death.
>
> Worcestershire (1950)

In most cases, this immunity only lasted while the fortunate one (or his/her family) kept the caul safe. Nevertheless, some families were more than willing to sell the caul because the immunity was thus transferred to the buyer, and regular advertisements could be seen in newspapers and dock-side shop windows offering or requesting such items – particularly in times of war or other particular danger for sailors. An additional function of the caul is that if kept by the child's family it acts as an indicator of the well-being of its possessor when absent. The belief certainly dates from before 1500 in Britain, was reported frequently right into the late twentieth century, and may still be current.

'carrying up' the baby

A neat piece of symbolism, this very widespread custom was practised to ensure that a newborn baby 'went up in the world':

> When a child was taken from its mother and carried outside the bedroom for the first time after its birth, it was lucky to take it up stairs, and unlucky to take it down stairs. If there were no stairs in the house, the person who carried it generally ascended three steps of a ladder or temporary erection, and this, it was supposed, would bring prosperity to the child.   W. Scotland (1879)

In the absence of a step-ladder, the resourceful nurse would step on to a box or a chair.

This superstition is probably behind the comment in William Congreve's play *Love for Love* (1695), in a scene which includes refer-ences to many other omens and beliefs, when Jeremy says, 'and I came upstairs into the world, for I was born in a cellar', and it lasted well into the twentieth century.

babies' hands

In the symbolism of superstition, hands have an integral part to play in luck, and they are nearly always connected with money. This is the context for the widespread idea that one should not wash a baby's hand, for fear of washing away its luck, or future riches:

> I have often and very recently seen the creases in the palms of children's hands filled with dirt; to clean them before they were a year old would take away riches – they would live and die poor.
>
> Cornwall (1887)

In some versions it is only the right hand which matters, and some keep it unwashed only until the christening. Although reported widely, this belief has not been found earlier than the second half of the nineteenth century, whereas a different prognostication on babies' hands is demonstrably older.

> It was observed how infants held their hands for some time after birth. If they kept them closed it was a sure sign they would hold fast the money that came in their way, and the remark about such a child would have been heard, 'He (she)'ll be a grippie, that ane', or 'he'll be a gey grippie lad'. If, on the contrary, the hands were kept open, the money would go as fast as it came.
>
> Aberdeenshire (1895)

In essentially the same form, this idea was included in John Bulwer's treatise on hands, *Chirologia* (1644). It is still common for adults, when meeting a baby for the first time, to give it a coin 'for luck', and the humorous comments which are often made if the baby immediately grasps the coin tightly show that this idea of the prediction of future character is far from dead.

tempering the baby

A neat pun on the word 'temper', as verb and noun, led to a charming idea that the first person to kiss a baby was particularly important:

> A good-tempered person should be selected as the first to kiss the baby, as the good influence will persist through life. A lady told me that her old nurse was much disturbed because the wrong person had kissed and so 'tempered' the baby.   Norfolk (1929)

The handful of examples all come from East Anglia, but the belief is unlikely to be quite so regionally restricted.

wrapping the baby in old clothes

Some traditional nurses and midwives indulged in a custom of wrapping babies first in old clothes:

> A new-born child should be wrapped in something old, preferably an old flannel petticoat. An old-fashioned nurse told me she never liked to dress babies in new clothes for the first time, if she could avoid it. She always took an old flannel petticoat with her, to be the first garment worn by each baby she nursed.   Herefordshire (1912)

The reasons for this appear to vary considerably. It was possibly to avoid tempting fate by avowing pride in the new life, but sometimes the father's clothes were specifically chosen as a protection, or 'to make it strong' (Norfolk, 1929). In some reports, the clothes were specifically those of the opposite sex to the baby, which may have been to confuse the fairies or other ill-wishers, but it was also believed that this would make the child attractive to the opposite sex in later life. These traditions date at least to the eighteenth century.

baby's first visit

The principle of wishing luck at beginnings is strongly evident in traditions regulating what to do the first time a new baby is brought to visit you, or the first time you meet it elsewhere. In most cases in the past, the mother would not bring the baby to visit until she had been churched (first visit to church) and the baby christened. Highly symbolic items were then given. Egg, salt, and bread are the three items recommended in the two eighteenth-century references and in most of the early nineteenth-century sources, but by the later twentieth century this had dwindled to simply giving money. The need to follow tradition still remained very strong:

> The giving of gifts to a new-born child is usual . . . in rural Ulster . . . the gift tends to take the form of money. I was very surprised, although I should have known better when an old lady who had been in the habit of calling at my mother's house for a weekly alms, presented my baby daughter with a shilling to 'hansel her'. ('Hansel'

means to protect from evil or to bring luck.) The money is never handed to the parent; it is always placed in the child's hand.

N. Ireland (1951)

The custom is extremely widely recorded from the 1770s onwards, and was clearly common all over the British Isles. The feeling that a coin is appropriate 'for luck' is still very strong.

unchristened babies in danger

The sacramental rite of baptism, by which a baby is admitted into the Church, has long been popularly believed to have wider meaning and usefulness, and numerous unofficial traditions grew up around the ceremony. Unbaptized children were seen as in particular danger from witches, fairies, or others who might wish to harm them, because they did not yet have the protection afforded by God. The strength of these beliefs varied considerably, but could be taken very seriously:

> Baptism was administered as early as circumstances would permit, and for various reasons. Without this sacrament the child was peculiarly exposed to the danger of being carried off or changed by fairies. It could not be taken out of the house, at least to any great distance, or into a neighbour's, till it was baptised. It could not be called by its name till after it was baptised . . . Death might come and take away the young one, and if not baptised its name could not be written in the 'Book of Life' and heaven was closed against it . . . There was an undefinable sort of awe about unbaptised infants, as well as an idea of uncanniness in having them without baptism in the house.   N.E. Scotland (1874)

In a similar way, christening was believed to cure sick children – of both real diseases and character defects:

> Children who are ill-tempered before baptism will be good-tempered after they have been baptized. They will also sleep better and thrive better. In this respect baptism acts as a charm.

England (1895)

Moreover, water used in a christening was believed to have special properties – to cure and protect – for a wide range of problems, physical and supernatural.

baby must cry at the christening

One of the most widespread christening beliefs was that a baby should cry during the ceremony. This was taken as a sign that the Devil had been cast out, whereas it was unlucky if the baby remained silent. In the latter case it was also said the child would not live long – as being 'too good for this world'.

> I was lately present at a christening in Sussex, when a lady of the party, who was a godmother of the child, whispered in a voice of anxiety, 'The child never cried; why did not the nurse rouse it up?' After we had left the church, she said to her, 'Oh Nurse, why did not you pinch baby?' And, when the baby's good behaviour was afterwards commented upon, she observed, with a very serious air, 'I wish that he had cried'.   Sussex (1878)

The earliest reference dates from 1787, where the 'will not live' belief was already present, and similar fears were still being voiced nearly 200 years later. It is most likely that the basic idea originated with official church baptismal procedures. Earlier forms of christening in the Anglican, and continuing forms in the Catholic, Church specifically included an element of exorcism.

christen boys before girls

Another popular belief dictated that great care must be taken in christening babies to get them in the correct order:

> The belief prevails still in some parts of the Perthshire highlands, that when a boy and girl are presented for baptism, the parents must be particular to let the boy be christened before the girl, otherwise the boy will grow up in life without a beard.
>
> Perthshire (1876)

This would seem to be simply an example of the expected sexism of organized religions and traditional societies, and this view is possibly supported by an extract from Leofric's *Missal* of about 1050 which lays down the regulation for christening: 'The priest receives them from their parents, and they are baptised first males, then females.' But some twentieth-century informants said that it was girls who must come first, or they would get the boys' beards.

Apart from Leofric's *Missal*, we have no evidence of a concern with precedence before the very end of the eighteenth century, and this gap is too long for us to assume a definite connection and continuity in beliefs. Moreover, a handful of nineteenth- and twentieth-century references indicate a range of other concerns about the christening procedure, including further worries about relative position and about using the same water, especially if three children were presented at the same time.

christening piece

A widespread custom in Scotland dictated that the party returning from a christening should present the first person they meet with a 'christening piece' or 'bit', to ensure luck to the baby:

> Going along one of the principal streets of Edinburgh lately on a Sunday afternoon, I met a very respectably dressed female with an attendant (nurse) carrying an infant. They stopped me, and the former presented to me a paper bag. On expressing my surprise, she said, 'Oh! Sir, it is the christening bit' and explained that it was an old custom in Edinburgh on going with a child to be baptised to offer a 'christening bit' to the first person they met. Mine I found on getting home consisted of a biscuit, bit of cheese, and a bit of gingerbread.   Edinburgh (1871)

The basic shape of the custom was remarkably stable, although details varied considerably. In some cases it was the first adult met, others allowed children to be the recipient, while many insisted that the piece be given to the first person of the opposite sex to the baby in question. Published references confirm this to be an overwhelmingly Scottish and northern English custom, although there are, most intriguingly, a handful of references from Devon and Cornwall. The earliest reference is one from Glasgow in about 1820, but it was clearly already an established custom at that time, and it was still going strong in the 1950s.

churching

Churching, or the occasion of the first visit to church by a new mother after the birth of her baby, has excited controversy for much of the last 500 years. The basic problem has been whether the ceremonies carried out at the time should be viewed as 'purification' or 'thanksgiving'. After the Reformation, the churching rite was roundly condemned by a range of reformers as being both Popish and an unacceptable relic of Jewish religion. The idea of purification was anathema to the increasingly vocal puritan sects, so mainstream churchmen responded by attempting to redefine the ceremony as one of thanksgiving rather than ritual cleansing. The debate rumbled on for centuries, and while the ceremony was kept in existence, any reformer could use it as a stick to beat the establishment. On the other side, fundamentalists defended their position by quoting the Old Testament, which makes it quite clear that mothers are unclean for a specified period:

> If a woman have conceived seed, and born a man child: then she shall be unclean seven days; according to the days of the separation for her infirmity shall she be unclean ... And she shall then continue in the blood of her purifying three and thirty days; she shall touch no hallowed thing, nor come into the sanctuary, until the days of her purifying be fulfilled. But if she bear a maid child, then she shall be unclean two weeks.   Leviticus 12:2–8

A more recent controversy has emerged among historians who have debated the question of how churching should be viewed historically. At one extreme are those who see the whole business as an aspect of patriarchal tyranny which seeks to control and marginalize women at all times. At the other end of the spectrum are those who recognize that women enjoyed the period after childbirth as a predominantly female time, and regarded the churching itself as a time for female-centred celebration.

Given this background of official ambivalence and controversy, it is hardly surprising that there were many unofficial superstitions surrounding the time following a birth and the mother's activities and responsibilities. These were firmly rooted in local tradition, and were stringently imposed, at least in the nineteenth century. The most widespread rule was that the woman should not leave her house until she has been churched. If she did, she must not enter anyone else's house, as she would bring bad luck to her hosts:

> She must particularly refrain from entering another woman's house, for she will certainly bring misfortune of some kind, and if the

second woman is pregnant, she may cause a miscarriage. The rector of a poor parish in Oxford told me that this custom is rigidly observed there . . . the notion lingers that unchurched women are somehow dangerous and bringers of bad luck.   England (1955)

Given the restrictive nature of this belief, it is gratifying to read a story – probably apocryphal – that Irish women circumvented the prohibition by placing pieces of their house thatch in their hats so that they could claim to be still 'under their own roof' while out and about.

On her way to the church for the ceremony, the woman's behaviour was still prescribed by superstition. She should not look at the sky or even cross a road:

A woman in this village, when going to church for the first time after the birth of her child, keeps to the same side of the road, and no persuasions or threats would induce her to cross it.

Hampshire (1854)

There was also the astonishing idea that unchurched women who broke these codes of conduct were not even protected by the laws of the land and could be attacked, or even murdered, with impunity.

There is no clue in the official service laid down in the Anglican *Book of Common Prayer* to explain any of these popular beliefs, nor in the verses of Leviticus, but there may be in the words of Psalm 121, which, until the late seventeenth century, was recited as part of the ceremony: 'The sun shall not smite thee by day, nor the moon by night.' These may have been interpreted as an injunction to stay at home.

cradles and prams

Cradles, and later prams, which inherited their beliefs, are the subject of two widespread traditions.

First, couples expecting their first baby are strongly advised not to bring a new cradle or pram home before the baby has actually arrived. To do so will tempt fate and thus risk the baby's life:

I was so proud when I got my Silver Cross pram for my first. Mum and Nan had helped me pay it off weekly. But even when I'd paid for it, I never brought it home until I'd had the baby. You didn't then. It was like a sort of superstition. Just in case.   London (1950s)

This idea seems to be no older than the early twentieth century, but it was still being reported at the turn of the twenty-first. A contributor to the *Babyforum* Internet discussion list (May 2002) asked her fellow mums-to-be:

> Has anyone bought their pram and had it in the house before their baby was born? We've just got ours and the lady in the shop asked us if we wanted them to keep it till after the birth as it was unlucky to have it in the house.

Two people who replied wrote that they took no notice of this superstition, but both had a relative (mother-in-law and sister respectively) who certainly did believe in it.

Second, it has been considered very unlucky to rock an empty cradle, or push an empty pram, although the predicted consequences vary considerably; indeed they are virtual opposites – either it means that the cradle/pram will soon be filled with a new arrival, or it means that the current baby will die. The new arrival theory has been the most widespread:

> 'What a handsome cradle!' said a lady, going up to an old carved oaken one one day in a cottage at Berrington . . . 'Oh, but I suppose you won't like me to touch it.' 'Eh, dear! no, ma'am', responded the good woman of the house; 'I've had eleven already, and I've only been married fourteen years.'   Shropshire (1883)

The notion that rocking an empty cradle will cause the baby to die has been less widespread, and has also proved less durable. Neither of these meanings has been found before the nineteenth century, but the 'baby will die' appears from the Scottish borders about 1816, while the 'new baby' is first mentioned in the 1850s.

Several other traditions were reported less frequently, but were probably more widely known in their time:

> In Yorkshire, new parents were warned that a cradle must be paid for before the baby sleeps in it, otherwise it 'will end its days lacking the means to pay for its own coffin'.   Yorkshire (1898)

> The first-born of a family should never be put in a new cradle, or it will surely die. Any neighbour will lend a cradle rather than see the rule broken.   Co. Longford (1936)

baby's fingernails and hair

An extremely widespread superstition prohibited the cutting of a baby's fingernails and hair before it had reached a certain age – usually a year:

> It was considered very unlucky to weigh a baby or cut its nails before it was twelve months old. If this was done it would never grow strong and well; the prejudice still exists, and district nurses are looked upon with scant favour for bringing ill-luck on the infant. The nails, if cut, make the child light-fingered; they should be bitten, not cut.   Warwickshire (c.1930)

As in this example, it was permissible for the mother to bite the nails off, and in most cases the consequence of ignoring this injunction was that the child would grow up to be a thief – and this was taken perfectly seriously by many mothers. The basic superstition has been noted from all parts of the British Isles, and was apparently extremely well known from Victorian times onwards, although the first known references are only from the 1850s. It is unlikely to have been brand new at that time, considering that by 1851/2 it was already reported from the Orkneys to Dorset.

teething

Various remedies have been tried by parents and nurses to help babies who have trouble cutting their first teeth. Three main approaches have traditionally been recommended: placing items in bags to be worn around the baby's neck; rubbing the gums with particular materials; and necklaces made of minerals or plants.

Items placed in bags included woodlice and donkey's hairs – both of which were more often recommended for other ailments. Others used teeth, of humans or animals, and some young women apparently kept any teeth they lost to use for their future babies. John Aubrey commented that the Irish 'do use a wolves fang-tooth [holder] set in silver and gold for this purpose' (*Remaines*, 1686).

Necklaces could be made of various materials – glass beads, deadly nightshade berries, myrtle stems, henbane roots, elder, orris root, and so on – but the most widespread and oldest amulet was coral:

> Though coral doth properly preserve and fasten the teeth on men, yet it is used in children to make an easier passage for them; and

for that intent is worn about their necks. But whether this custom were not superstitiously founded, as presumed an amulet or defensative against fascination, is not beyond all doubt.

Thomas Browne, Pseudodoxia Epidemica (1672)

As Browne was aware, coral was also believed to be an effective protection against witchcraft, and it is not clear whether this aspect of its magical power, or its reputed practical effect directly upon the teeth and gums, contributed most to its widespread use, even to the present day. Several other sixteenth- and seventeenth-century writers also link coral and teething, and it was clearly well known at the time. They presumably got the idea direct from classical writers such as Pliny.

baby's first teeth

There is a range of traditional interpretations concerning a baby who is born with teeth, or who teethes early. In many cases, it means that the mother will soon fall pregnant again:

> Soon teeth soon toes – This means that if your baby's teeth begin to sprout early, you will soon have toes, i.e. another baby.

N. England (1850s)

However, a similar saying – 'Soon toothed, soon with God' – indicating an early death, was included in seventeenth-century proverb collections, and 'soon toothed, soon turfed' was still being quoted in the late nineteenth century. Even worse, some believed that such a baby would grow up to be a murderer. Another belief regarding children's teeth, reported only from the Midlands, northern England and Scotland since the mid nineteenth century, held that if a child's first tooth was in its upper jaw it was at best unlucky, and at worst a sign that it would not live long.

weighing the baby

A number of superstitions exist which warn that it is unwise to be too precise in counting or measuring, as it tempts fate to do so, and the same principle is involved in weighing:

> The prejudice against weighing babies before they are twelve months old is dying out fast under the influence of health visitors and clinics. It was formerly very strong, however, and there are still

women who dislike the practice. A member of the Oxfordshire Folklore Society was told by a district nurse in 1935 that a certain woman known to them both had refused to have her last baby weighed because an older child had 'gone funny', and she attributed this to his having been weighed too soon.   Oxfordshire (1957)

Where specified, the predicted result is usually that the child will die before the twelve months is over, or at best will be sickly or weak.

The superstition is nearly always voiced with regard to children, but the earliest reference, in 1709, refers to adults. Otherwise, the belief is only reported from the 1870s onwards, presumably because it was not common practice to weigh newborn babies before that time anyway. As indicated in the above quotation, the belief was still strong in the mid twentieth century, but was effectively killed by improvements in public healthcare which insisted on scientific measuring and recording of infants' details.

MARRIAGE

Given the propensity for superstitions to cluster around key points in people's lives, and beginning points especially, it is no surprise that weddings have attracted more than their fair share of beliefs. Almost anything that happens at a wedding can be interpreted as a sign of future prosperity, and dozens of superstitions have come and gone over the years.

'change the name'

Superstitions concerning weddings and marriage tend to be expressed in rhyme, and this has definitely helped them to be remembered, even long after anyone actually believes them. Many people know the following rhyme:

> If a lady's surname after marriage begin with the same letter as her maiden surname she will be very unlucky, for:

> > Change the name, but not the letter
> > Change for the worse, and not the better.
> > > Devon (1878)

The first known appearance of the belief is from the USA in 1853, and the belief was being recorded as indigenous to Britain by the mid 1860s.

wedding rings

The wedding ring has long been one of the central tangible symbols
of both the act of marriage and, by the type of extension common in
superstition, of future married life. Beliefs about the ring thus have
resonance for both the wedding ceremony and later points in the
married life of the couple in question. In Victorian times, there was
even a rule before the ceremony, since it was believed that it was
unlucky to try on the ring before the service.

Other beliefs include the notion that if the ring is dropped during
the ceremony, the marriage will be unhappy – on the usual superstitious principle that anything which starts badly is doomed to continue that way. This is such a basic principle in superstition that it is
no surprise that this is one of the oldest wedding superstitions, dating
from at least the seventeenth century and probably much earlier. Some
say that whichever of the bride or groom is responsible for dropping
the ring will die before the other.

It was also thought very unlucky for a woman to take her ring off once
married, for any reason, and even worse for her to break or lose it:

> Some thought the wedding ring must never be removed and if it
> accidentally happened, the husband should put the ring on again;
> other people said it was all right to remove the wedding ring after
> the birth of the first child.   Wiltshire (1975)

To balance these mostly negative attributes, wedding rings have
featured in love-divination processes involving wedding cake, which,
if placed under the pillow, allows the sleeper to dream of his/her
future partner. The cake's prophetic power is greatly increased if it is
combined with the ring:

> They made Agnes take off her ring, and I passed a great many
> pieces of cake through it for the benefit of those unmarried friends
> who wished to dream on it.   New South Wales (Scottish) (1844)

Versions of the wedding cake procedure were already well known in
the early eighteenth century, and are quite likely still practised.

'happy is the bride that the sun shines on'

The saying 'Happy [or Blessed] is the bride the sun shines on' is still regularly quoted in appropriate circumstances at weddings, and it has been proverbial since at least the seventeenth century. But there is plenty of evidence to show that in the past many believed quite literally in the sunshine as a positive omen. More rarely heard nowadays is the companion line about rain:

> Happy is the bride that the sun shines on
> Happy is the corpse that the rain rains on.
>
> Ireland (1865)

carrying the bride over the threshold

One of the wedding customs which has offended many modern minds, carrying the bride over the threshold is often assumed to be ancient, and rooted in male domination, but neither of these notions are supported by the evidence or, rather, the lack of it, as the history and development is unclear.

> It was considered very unlucky for a bride to place her feet on or near the threshold, and the lady, on her return from the marriage ceremony, was always carefully lifted over the threshold and into the house. The brides who were lifted were generally fortunate, but trouble was in store for the maiden who preferred walking into the house.   Wales (1909)

The custom can be definitely traced in Britain to the early nineteenth century, when Walter Scott described it in a note to his novel *Guy Mannering* (1815), and from that time on it is mentioned sporadically. Various unfounded guesses at meaning have been put forward, including the idea that it is a relic of bride capture, or that the threshold was a holy place which must not be defiled. Several other threshold beliefs and customs certainly existed, which may be relevant to an investigation of the origin of the carrying tradition. Some earlier sources mention a show of modest bridal reluctance to enter the house, as in Robert Herrick's *Hesperides* (1648), 'Now o'er the threshold force her in', but he does not mention lifting the bride. There was also the idea that whoever entered the house first would be master in the marriage. Another belief is the fear of bad luck for the marriage should the bride stumble on entering the new home. None of these can be shown to pre-date references to bride-lifting, however.

Nevertheless, there were unusually close beliefs in classical times. Plutarch (*c.* AD 46–120), for example, indicates not only that a similar custom existed in his time, but that its reason was already unclear:

> What should be the reason that they would not permit the new-wedded bride to pass herself over the door-sill or threshold when she is brought home to her husband's house, but they that accompany her lift her from the ground, and so convey her in?
>
> Plutarch, *Roman Questions*

It is hardly possible that the custom has survived uninterrupted in Britain since the first century, and it is most likely – but at present unproven – that it was introduced to this country by someone, or some group, familiar with classical sources.

the bride's bouquet

It is so much a part of the current traditional wedding for a bride to throw her bouquet to the assembled unmarrieds that it is difficult to remember that it was probably introduced into Britain, from America, within living memory. There have been a number of wedding customs designed to predict the next person – usually the next female – to get married. Throwing the stocking is probably the oldest and best documented, but another dictated that the first girl to secure a pin from the bride's dress would soon herself be wed. In earlier times, pieces of the bride's bouquet were also treasured:

> A flower from the bride's bouquet, secured before she is married, brings luck; I have seen more than one beautiful bouquet torn to pieces before the service began, through people snatching blossoms from it as the bride came into church and up the aisle.   Devon (1928)

Throwing is a recurrent theme – throwing old shoes, stockings, and so on. The modern custom thus very neatly combines three older elements – the next-to-be-married divination, throwing, and the luck of the bride's bouquet. It is not easy to pin down the date of the introduction of bouquet-throwing, but the key time seems to be the early 1950s. Ann Page's *Complete Guide to Wedding Etiquette* (1954) says, 'The custom of throwing the bouquet to the bridesmaids is a very old one.' She is completely wrong in her assessment of its age, but shows that it was already around at the time. Margot Lawrence's *Guide to Wedding Etiquette* of 1963 refers to the practice as

> a rather charming American tradition that is not very widely adopted here as yet, probably because English brides usually slip away quietly from the reception without any fuss.

wedding colours

For most people currently alive, the stereotypical bridal attire is a white dress, even if increasing numbers of brides choose not to follow this tradition. Nowadays, the term 'white wedding' does not simply describe the bride's dress, but the whole style of the event. Although there are records of brides wearing white in early times, it was only one of many colours which could be chosen, and it became an expected bridal colour only in the second half of the eighteenth century. It rapidly became the ideal to which many brides aspired, and has retained that reputation ever since. White also quickly took on the reputation as 'lucky', as well as fashionable, as is clear from a comment in Oliver Goldsmith's first comedy, *The Good Natured Man*, produced in 1768:

> I wish you could take the white and silver to be married in. It's the worst luck in the world in anything but white.

Increasing availability of cheap illustrated publications in the Victorian era brought high fashion into the homes of even the humblest of families, and raised expectations in brides' minds, even if economic reality kept them in check. Many of the key elements of what is now seen as the 'traditional' wedding were forged in that period. Throughout the nineteenth, and well into the twentieth century, the ideal of the white wedding was not readily attainable for much of the population, and most brides simply wore their best clothes, or if they bought a new dress made sure to buy something more practical than a dress worn once.

Apart from white, there is little evidence that colour was an important factor, and the strong impression is that fashion counted much more than tradition in this sphere, but there were two exceptions. Green was consistently branded as unlucky – for everyday wear as well as for weddings – from the later eighteenth century onwards. Black is not often mentioned specifically, but it is clear that as the colour of mourning it was usually avoided without comment. The ban on both these colours did not simply apply to the bride's dress, but to everyone at the wedding.

The widespread rhyme which covers most of the likely colours is a relatively modern invention:

> Married in white, you have chosen all right
> Married in grey, you will go far away
> Married in black, you will wish yourself back
> Married in red, you'd better be dead
> Married in green, ashamed to be seen
> Married in blue, you'll always be true
> Married in pearl, you'll live in a whirl
> Married in yellow, ashamed of the fellow
> Married in brown, you'll live out of town
> Married in pink, your spirits will sink.
>
> Highland Scotland (1926)

This is slightly longer than many, but there is remarkable stability across versions. Several versions were published in the 1920s and 1930s, but none has been found before that time.

throwing confetti, rice, etc.

The scattering of things over the bride and groom 'for luck' has a long history, and although the items have changed, the principle has remained the same. The earliest reference is in 1486, when Henry VII was showered with wheat by a baker's wife, who cried 'welcome and good luck', and the throwing of wheat at weddings was regularly reported from the sixteenth century onwards.

In the early 1870s, however, an apparently abrupt change took place. Reference was suddenly made to rice, and this quickly became the norm:

In Sussex I have seen wheat ... scattered over the bride and bridegroom as they left the church. No doubt rice, which seems to be becoming fashionable, is used with the same meaning as that attached to wheat. Its substitution for wheat is, probably, due to the fact that it is more easily obtained in an ordinary household.

Sussex (1873)

I never, in Ireland, saw rice sprinkled on the bride at parting, until
the 23rd of last October.   Ireland (1873)

Rice continued to be thrown until well into the twentieth century, but
its popularity was challenged and finally surpassed by the invention of
paper good-luck symbols. By the turn of the new century, the word
'confetti', named after the bonbons, real or imitation, thrown at Italian
carnivals, was being used at weddings in Britain. The paper symbols
gradually took over from rice, but until the Second World War confetti
and rice could both be found, separately or together.

Many writers assume that the throwing of wheat or rice was a
fertility gesture, but this interpretation was not made before the
Victorian folklorists started labelling everything in sight in this way.
Obviously, any wedding custom or tradition is open to a fertility
interpretation, but there is no evidence to support this as a general
rule. It is best to simply regard it as a good-luck gesture.

wedding curses

Not everyone wishes the bride and groom well on their wedding day,
and rival lovers had traditional ways of venting their anger or jealousy.

Psalm 109 to this day is looked upon as a means of destroying for
ever the fortunes of a young couple if read by a rival during the
marriage service.   Shropshire (1894)

This psalm is pretty powerful stuff when read with a vengeful eye. It
starts with 'Hold not thy peace, O God of my praise', and includes
lines such as 'For my love they are my adversaries. And they have
rewarded me evil for good, and hatred for my love. Set thou a wicked
man over him: and let Satan stand at his right hand.'

Other magical rites were possible:

If anyone at a marriage repeats the benediction after the priest, and
ties a knot at the mention of each of the three sacred names on a
handkerchief, or a piece of string, the marriage will be childless for
fifteen years, unless the knotted string is burnt in the meantime.
                                                          Aran Islands (1891–3)

Such practices are not mentioned often in the folklore literature, but
they clearly existed, for use when necessary.

who will be the dominant partner or the first to die?

Certain trivial occurrences on the wedding day, and after, were taken as indications of which of the newly-weds would be the dominant partner in years to come.

> As the married couple leave the church, if the woman puts her foot out of the door before the man, she will be master.   Devon (1928)

A similar idea lay behind the legend of St Kenelm's well in Cornwall, recorded in Robert Southey's popular poem 'The Well of St Keyne' (1798). In this story, bride and groom strive to gain the mastery by drinking the water first, but although the man rushes to the well as fast as he can after the ceremony, his bride has taken the precaution of having a bottle of the water with her at the church.

It was also said that certain plants, such as rosemary, sage, and parsley, grew best where women were the masters in the home.

Less cheerfully, trivial occurrences were used to predict which of the bride and groom would be the first to die:

> When the bride was being decked for the ceremony her maid bid her remember not to speak too loud in church, and, on being asked why, answered, 'Why, m'm, you know that them 'at speaks loudest dies first'.   Yorkshire (1980)

wedding parties must never meet funerals

For obvious reasons, it was accounted very unlucky for a wedding party to meet a funeral, and the fact that the same building usually catered for both events made this coincidence quite feasible:

> In March 1952, a burial at Caversham was preceded by a wedding. One of the mourners, arriving early, found the wedding-party still in the churchyard, taking photographs. The sexton was extremely agitated by this delay because, he said, it would be most unlucky if the bride saw the funeral. Eventually, he spoke to the best man who at once realised the urgency of the matter and hurried his party away.   Oxfordshire (1952)

For most, it was simply 'unlucky', but some said that it presaged a death of one of the wedding party – usually the bride or groom. It is surprising that such an obvious superstition does not seem to have a long history. The earliest reference so far located dates only from 1855, and although clearly quite widespread it only makes a moderate appearance in the documentary record.

'something old, something new'

A bride's dress on her wedding day should include 'Something old, something new, something borrowed, something blue'. This is one of the strongest wedding superstitions in modern times: there can be hardly an adult in Britain who does not know the rhyme, and a great many women abide by it even though few will believe it makes any real difference. The reasoning behind the 'old' or 'borrowed' items is that these will share in any existing luck by previous association if carefully chosen:

> It is widely accounted lucky to wear something on the wedding day which has already been worn by a happy bride at her wedding, and ladies consider it quite a compliment to be asked to lend their wedding veils to their friends for this purpose. Sometimes a lace veil has been worn in this way by successive generations.
>
> Shropshire (1883)

The full saying cannot be shown to be older than 1876, when a correspondent to *Notes & Queries* wrote to ask about its origin, and it did not become widely known until the twentieth century. Earlier references focus on one aspect or other, and it is probable that the rhyme was composed to incorporate existing but separate elements; so far it is only the 'blue' element which can be shown to have a long history.

throwing the stocking

In days before honeymoons, a high point of the wedding day was 'putting the bride and groom to bed', which was the excuse for a great deal of horseplay and engagement in traditional customs. The degree of refinement, or otherwise, depended on the company, but there was plenty of scope for, and tolerance of, rough play and ribaldry at all levels of society. One of the set-piece activities was 'throwing the stocking' – an example of one of the many customs at weddings which result in the selection of the person to be next married and therefore a precursor to the modern throwing of the bride's bouquet. There were many variations on the basic theme. One was for the bride to do the throwing:

> About the 'noon of night' the bride is put to bed by her maids, in the presence of as many spectators as the bed-room will contain, pressing, squeezing, standing upon tip-toe, and peeping over each other's heads for a glance of the blushing fair, who throws the stocking from her left leg over the right shoulder, and the person on whom it falls is to be first married.
>
> Scotland, *Edinburgh Magazine* (Nov. 1818)

In other versions, the guests did the throwing, and the idea was to hit the bride or groom as they sat up in bed. This custom was very widely known all over the British Isles, although the majority of references come from Scotland and northern England, which is presumably because it continued later in these areas. It was clearly well established by the seventeenth century, and the earliest reference dates from 1604, in a letter from Sir Dudley Carleton referring to the marriage of Sir Philip Herbert and Lady Susan Vere at Whitehall. The casual way he mentions 'casting off the bride's left hose' in a list of traditional ceremonies confirms that it must date back to the previous century at least. Nevertheless, the custom had faded out by the mid nineteenth century, falling victim to Victorian reforms and notions of decorum which laid the foundations for the modern wedding.

DEATH

death omens

The superstitious person, if so inclined, can find a death omen at every turn. Many things which happen in the natural world can be thus interpreted, but a wide range of occurrences are deemed to have a supernatural cause, and are thought to be infallible signs of coming death. These signs can be in the form of things seen or heard, and are usually symbolic rather than direct – loud knocks on the door, murmured voices, and so on. Only the widely known traditional ones are treated here; many others were specific to a community or even a particular family.

Under a variety of names, 'corpse candles' or 'death lights' were widespread death omens. They took the form of a light, like a ghostly candle flame, and appeared shortly before a death in the neighbourhood – often the night before the event. These lights were most often blue, and in some accounts the size and brightness indicated whether a man, woman, or child was to die, or the number of the flames corresponded to the number of victims. In the normal form of the story, the light appeared at the doomed person's house, and was then seen to make its way to the churchyard:

> A death-light has been described to me as a 'blue lowe' about three feet high, which leaves the house the moment death has taken place and traverses the road that the funeral will follow. It enters the church under the door, and stands on the exact spot where the coffin will stand, flooding the building with light. Out of the church it eventually comes, and takes its way to the spot where the grave

will be dug, and ends its career by sinking into the ground there.

Cumberland (1907)

The light was often seen to behave oddly, taking a detour across a field, for example, or standing motionless for a while at a particular spot. Its behaviour was always explained when the real funeral procession reached that spot and had to make the same pause or detour because of some natural obstruction. It was extremely unwise to try to interfere with a corpse candle, as those who did so could themselves soon sicken and die. Frequently, the candles simply marked the place of a future accident rather than the funeral route, especially if the death was by drowning.

The corpse candle is one of the few death omens which has its own legend of origin (at least in Wales):

> The origin of the corpse-candle is supposed to date back to the fifth century. St. David, the patron of Wales, earnestly prayed that the people he loved, and among whom he toiled, should have some kind of warning to prepare them for death. In a vision he was told that through his intercession the Welsh would never again find themselves unprepared; for always before such an event the people in the land of Dewi Sant would be forewarned by the dim light of mysterious tapers when and where death might be expected. St. David apparently prayed particularly for South Wales, because it is said that corpse-candles are seen more vividly and frequently there than in North Wales.   Wales (1909)

Whereas in modern times a death omen is viewed with horror, in certain religious contexts it can be seen as a welcome warning which provides notice of forthcoming events and the opportunity for the victim to prepare for a 'good death'.

A wide range of sounds have been interpreted as death omens, and their key elements are that they are sudden, not easily explained by natural causes, and although they can be heard clearly, nothing can be seen. Death warning sounds can be separated into several categories. First are those which are simply sudden, unexpected, unexplainable noises around the house or in its vicinity. Any suitably alarming sounds can be interpreted as death signs, especially in retrospect:

> Mr. L. of Maryport told me that in his own house, once when his father died and again when an uncle died, they heard a loud noise

of broken glass, as if a heavy chandelier had fallen. They had no
glass of any kind broken.   Cumberland (1909)

Second are more specific noises which are deemed to be natural sounds
of what will happen after the person is dead, but which occur out of
their proper time-frame – sounds of coffins being manufactured or
placed on chairs, of funeral carts, people gathering (footsteps, voices)
for the funeral, and so on.

These can take various forms:

> On another occasion she heard banging coming from the kitchen,
> so she went to investigate the noise. It appeared to come from two
> kitchen chairs, as she heard a bang on one chair, and then a bang
> on the other. The next day a neighbour came to borrow two chairs
> to lay a coffin on.   Mull (1992)

A third category includes a range of sounds which are neither random
nor naturalistic, but are traditionally known, and therefore understood,
in the community.

A specialized version of the death sound, which precedes and
announces a forthcoming death, is an unexplained knocking at the
door, window, sick person's bed-head, or anywhere else in the house.
In some cases it is a single sudden sound, but in the classic examples
it is three measured knocks, and therefore not amenable to naturalistic
explanation. Sometimes the sound is repeated three times during the
night, or on three successive nights:

> [My grandmother] had many other experiences such as three
> knocks which were premonitions of death. One night she was in
> bed in her cottage in Tiree and she heard three knocks at the door
> but when she got up to answer it there was nobody there. This
> happened three times that night and in the end she thought it must
> have been the wind. In the morning, however, she heard the
> three knocks again, so she went to the door, where she found her
> neighbour whose husband had just died, coming for help.
>
>   Mull (1992)

If there is a sick person in the house, the 'call' is usually for them,
otherwise it is taken to be an announcement of a relative's or neighbour's imminent demise. Additional sounds, such as voices, can also
be heard. The three knocks was first recorded by John Aubrey in 1696,

and although only rarely reported in the eighteenth century, numerous examples are available from the nineteenth and twentieth, from most parts of the British Isles.

One of the most widely acknowledged death omens is the sound of the deathwatch beetle. Certain wood-burrowing insects, of the *Anobiidae* family, such as the *Xestobium rufovillosum*, who make an audible clicking or ticking sound, have long been regarded as a warning of approaching death, and have been reported from all over Britain and Ireland since at least the late seventeenth century.

> Few ears have escaped the noise of the Dead-watch, that is, the little clicking sound heard often in many rooms, somewhat resem-bling that of a watch; and this is conceived to be of an evil omen or prediction of some person's death, wherein notwithstanding there is nothing of rational presage or just cause of terror unto melancholy and meticulous heads.   Thomas Browne, *Pseudodoxia Epidemica* (1672)

The belief has indeed been so common as to have been proverbial from the time of its first known mention, and has remained remarkably consistent throughout its history. Writers often simply list the belief with other well-known omens, such as a howling dog, without com-ment, as though further explanation is unnecessary: 'there is no end to the stories of ravens or deathwatches either; both are firmly believed in' (Essex, *The Monthly Packet*, 1862).

dying

Many people put off making a will, despite knowing how sensible it is to make one, as the thought makes them vaguely uneasy. This may simply be because they do not wish to be reminded of their own mortality, but there is plenty of evidence to show that many believed the act would in fact tempt fate and hasten their death, and it is likely that some still feel the same way. This notion has been around at least since the early seventeenth century, and is probably a lot older.

> Why, master Cole, what have you written here? You said you would write a letter, but methinks you have made a will . . . Tis true (quoth Cole) if it please God, and I trust this writing cannot shorten my daies.   Thomas Deloney, *Thomas of Reading* (1623)

It has been recorded sporadically ever since.

Unofficial euthanasia has no doubt always existed, whatever the view of the law or the official religion of the time. Two traditional methods are regularly mentioned in the literature, one of which, 'drawing the pillow', was certainly practised, while the other, smothering, was mostly apocryphal. Removing the pillow from under a dying person's head was widely seen as an act of mercy, to help the patient on their way and relieve their suffering:

> A doctor told me he had come across two instances where the death of a person, who was too slow in dying, was hastened by removing the pillow and allowing the sick person's head to fall back. On one occasion he reproached the old woman who had done it, and told her it was murder. 'Oh no, sir, it's not murder, it's what we call "drawing the pillow".'
>
> Norfolk (1929)

This practice was often linked with the notion that people could not die if their bed or pillow contained pigeon or game feathers. Removing the pillow, or removing the patient from the bed entirely, was seen as a way of ensuring that the release was not prolonged unnaturally. Most of the reports are from the nineteenth and twentieth centuries, but the method was certainly well known in the seventeenth, and probably long before:

> And in his next fit we may let him go,
> 'Tis but to pull the pillow from his head
>
> Ben Jonson, *Volpone* (1607)

'Smothering' was believed to be used in cases of animal infestation, rabies, and 'monstrous' births.

executions and suicides

Items associated with death by violence or execution have often, for some unknown reason, been prized as lucky, or as essential elements in cures. A piece of wood taken from a public gallows or gibbet and worn around the neck as an amulet, for example, was used as a cure for various ailments, including the ague and the toothache. Local legends frequently grew up around the sites of gibbets, which were often named after the last person to hang there, or a particularly famous occupant. Gibbets were disused from 1832, but their remains often lingered on in lonely, remote places.

A piece of hangman's or suicide's rope was also believed to have curative powers and was regarded as a lucky thing to possess:

> The instrument by which the unfortunate put an end to its life was eagerly sought after, as the possession of it, particularly the knot of the rope, if death was brought about by hanging, secured great worldly prosperity.   N.E. Scotland (1874)

Such an item was particularly prized by card-players.

The horror with which both official religion and local tradition held the act of suicide resulted in a range of beliefs and customs which seem barbaric to the modern eye. Until the 1820s, those found guilty of suicide in Britain were denied burial in consecrated ground and were interred by the public roadway (but not necessarily at a crossroads) with a wooden stake driven through their body. Thus the Parish Register of Pleasley, Derbyshire, simply states:

> Thomas Maule found hanging on a tree by the wayside after a drunken fit ... Same night at midnight buried at the highest crossroads with a stake in him.   Derbyshire (1573)

This treatment of suicides was officially sanctioned and widely followed, but it is unclear on what legal basis it rested. Sir James Fitzjames Stephen (*History of the Criminal Law of England*, 1883) could find no legal authority for the custom, or any earlier comment by legal historians. Stray references show that it was already in existence in the sixteenth century, and it is mentioned frequently from that time in a variety of sources, usually with no comment, simply as a matter of course.

It is likely that the stake and the unconsecrated burial were designed to enhance the deterrent and not from fears of the dead walking. The latter remains a possibility, of course, and it is quite feasible that at local level this is how it was viewed. Careless writers on the topic, however, have assumed that the stake was to prevent the body becoming a vampire, but there was virtually no vampire tradition in Britain until it was imported from eastern Europe in the eighteenth and nineteenth centuries by writers of gothic novels.

At local level, where the unfortunate person would have been known to many of the coroner's jury, feelings could run very high, and pulled in different directions. Any attempt to circumvent custom and bury the body in the churchyard could be met with violent opposition, while the friends and family of the deceased would sometimes disinter the body from beside the highway and, under cover of night, sneak it into a quiet part of the churchyard. By the early nineteenth century, public opinion was clearly moving towards a more compassionate and tolerant attitude to suicides, but until the law could be altered, little could be done to change the way things were done. The custom was finally abolished by Act of Parliament (4 Geo. 4, c.52, 1823), which made it unlawful for any coroner to order interment of a suicide in 'any public highway', and specifically banned the customary stake through the body. Suicides were henceforth to be buried in the churchyard or other burial-ground between nine and twelve at night, and without religious rites. The time limitation and the refusal of religious rites were both repealed in 1882 (45 & 46 Vic, c.19).

Many superstitions clustered around suicides and the peculiar nature of the burials. The presence of a buried body by the road predictably led to local ghost stories, but less obvious were tales which focused on the stake, which reportedly could grow into an eerie misshapen tree. There was a strong tradition that a suicide's body would not decompose until the time came when s/he would have died in the natural course of things, and there was also a widespread reluctance to touch a suicide's body – even to help retrieve a drowned body from the water, or to cut one down:

> Never touch a suicide – it's bad luck – so a person that has hung himself is allowed to hang until the police come.   Norfolk (1929)

the corpse

Anything untoward happening to a corpse is likely to be seen as ominous, and a corpse staying limp for longer than the usual time was formerly taken as a sign that another death would soon follow.

> In the case of my grandmother, aged eighty-eight, who was neither stiff nor cold the day she was buried, many were the solemn head-shakes and foretellings of what would follow. When an old relative, who had seen more than the allotted years of man, died six months later, many were the 'I told you so's' that went the round of the household.   Wiltshire (1893–5)

This notion was widely reported from the mid seventeenth century and into the twentieth, from most parts of Britain and Ireland, and it remained remarkably constant in form and meaning. A similar sign of a further death was when the eyes of a corpse would not close, although in the earliest report (1823), the open eyes were taken as a sign of a misspent life.

A death was also thought to follow if a corpse was left unburied on a Sunday (which must have happened quite frequently):

> It is an ominous sign if a corpse should be left unburied on Sunday, for this will mean that the death of another of the village community will occur 'before the week is out'. I have frequently heard this strange idea expressed with utmost sincerity and with a genuine belief in the inevitability of such a correlation of events.
>
> Sussex, *Sussex County Magazine* (1944)

Many people also had a horror of a grave being dug and left open on a Sunday, and most sextons would go to some lengths to avoid this happening. No real reason is given for these beliefs, although it takes little imagination to view an open grave as 'yawning' for another occupant. Nevertheless, they were widely known, at least in England, from the mid nineteenth century onwards.

touching the corpse

In times when most dead people were laid out in their home until the funeral, family, friends, and neighbours were expected to visit to 'pay their respects'. This involved viewing the body and, in many communities, touching it:

> To visit a corpse without touching it is running a grave risk; indeed, I have been practically commanded to touch it. If you refuse, your rest will be disturbed for long afterwards with dreams of the deceased and of death.   Cumberland (1907)

It is likely that the fear of dreaming about the deceased is a euphemism for being haunted by them. The contact itself was often ritualized, using thumb and forefinger, or the index finger, to touch the chin, cheek, or temple, and so on. Children were not exempted, and were often terrified by the ordeal. The custom was clearly extremely widespread, and it lasted well into the twentieth century. It is surprisingly late in appearing in the documentary record, with the earliest clear reference dating from only 1787. Nevertheless, some authorities seek to connect this belief with the similar one in which the wounds of a murder victim's corpse were thought to bleed anew if approached or touched by the murderer. This has a very long history in European cultures, and features in medieval tales such as the *Nibelunglied* (*c*.1200) and Chrétien de Troyes' *Ywain* (*c*.1200). In Britain, the belief had official sanction in King James I's *Daemonology* (1597):

> In a secret murder if the dead carcase be at any time thereafter handled by the murderer, it will gush out of blood, as if the blood were crying to heaven for revenge of the murder.

It continued to be fully trusted as a genuine proof of guilt throughout the seventeenth century, when it was frequently commented on as an example of God's way of ensuring that murderers would not escape justice. It was also used regularly as a dramatic device by playwrights of the time. The whole notion appears to have rapidly lost favour with the educated classes in the late seventeenth century, but it survived in the folk tradition until well into the twentieth century.

first and last burials in the churchyard

Only a handful of published references – oddly confined geographically to Scotland and the English West Country – document a belief that it was unfortunate to be first person buried in a new churchyard:

> There was great difficulty in bringing the new churchyard into use. No one would be the first to bury his dead there, for it was believed that the first corpse laid there was a teind [tithe] to the Evil One. At last a poor tramp who was found dead in the road was interred, and after this there was no further difficulty.   Aberdeenshire (1866)

This has the appearance of an ancient belief, but at present it cannot be dated earlier than the late nineteenth century.

Another superstition, reported almost exclusively from Ireland and Scotland, held that the person most recently buried in a churchyard had to undertake onerous tasks on behalf of those already buried, and this led to unseemly haste and even pitched battles between rival funeral parties to get their loved one buried first. The tasks were usually to fetch water for existing occupants, or:

> The watch of the graveyard – The person last buried had to keep watch over the graveyard till the next funeral came. This was

called *Faire Chlaidh*, the graveyard watch, kept by the spirits of the
departed.   Highland Scotland (1900)

The belief ran deep enough to arouse strong emotions. A fight which
took place near Dublin, for example, described in *The Times* (28 July
1835), led to a full-scale riot which resulted in the deaths of two
mourners and serious injury of many more. As with the first-burial
notion detailed above, this superstition appears to have the hallmark
of an ancient belief, but it can only be dated to the late eighteenth
century, and the majority of references are from the late nineteenth
and twentieth centuries.

treading on graves

It is hardly surprising that it was regarded as very unlucky to tread on
a grave:

> You should never, under any circumstances, walk upon a grave, or
> in any way tread upon it; it brings bad luck to do so, and is
> considered not only as a mark of disrespect to the person buried
> beneath your feet, but to all the dead that lie around.
>
> Lincolnshire (1908)

Pregnant women had to be particularly careful in this respect, or their
baby would be born with a club foot. This idea is certainly nothing
new, as Theophrastus' *Superstitious Man* (*c.*319 BC) was also careful
not to tread on a tombstone.

avoid burial on the north side of the churchyard

A widespread and persistent belief, reported from the mid sixteenth to
the late nineteenth century, held that the northern section of a churchyard was unsuitable for the burial of respectable Christians, and should
be reserved for strangers, paupers, suicides, excommunicated persons,
the unbaptized, and stillborn babies. It thus took on a sinister and
'unlucky' reputation and often remained mostly unused for centuries.

> I asked the sexton at Bradfield why, in a churchyard that was rather
> crowded with graves, there was no appearance of either mound or
> tombstone on the north side? His only answer was, 'It's mostly
> them 'at died i' t' workhus is buried at t' backside o' t' church'.
>
> Yorkshire (1851)

By the eighteenth century, this prejudice against a significant section of the churchyard was already causing problems in many country parishes, and local clergy began to try to overrule it, but success came only gradually. It was often believed that the ground to the north was unconsecrated, but there is no evidence anywhere that a particular area was ever officially omitted at the time of consecration. A lively correspondence in *Notes & Queries* in the 1850s, and again in 1899, brought to light numerous places where the prejudice had flourished, but also presented many examples of parishes in which it was apparently unknown, or where local factors conspired against it. In particular, correspondents pointed out that in places where the church was close to the southern boundary of the churchyard, or where the main approach from the local village was from the north, it was the southern side which was neglected and the north which was crowded with graves.

Nevertheless, the majority of older Christian churches in Britain are aligned on an east-west axis and the main door is normally on the south side, so the most plausible explanation for the custom is a pragmatic rather than spiritual or magical one. With a main door in the southern wall, parishioners will normally approach the church from the south, and the northern part of the churchyard is thus seen as, and was often called, the 'backside' of the church. Certainly, in Catholic times, it would be considered highly desirable to keep the memorials to the dead in constant view of churchgoers. In addition, the northern side would tend to be in the shadow of the church, and the southern side therefore sunnier – 'It would be so cold, sir . . . to be always lying where the sun would never shine on me' (*Notes & Queries*, 1851) – so the latter's character as the preferred side in local consciousness is understandable. It is clear that this has operated as a self-reinforcing circle – the ground which is popularly believed to be reserved for miscreants and strangers would be shunned by the families of deceased parishioners, and an already unpopular and unpopulated area would be an obvious place to bury any corpse whose character or religious standing was questionable.

Some writers have tried to prove a less obvious origin to the custom, and have assumed that there has always been a confirmed prejudice against the north. There are indeed sporadic references to the north being evil in Christian writing, but the notion does not seem to have been sufficiently widely known to found such a long-lasting and widespread tradition.

funerals

It hardly needs stressing that funerals have changed dramatically in Britain over the last hundred years, and one major consequence of these changes has been that people's personal contact with death has been minimized and placed at one remove. The potential for superstition and individual belief has thus narrowed considerably. In general, corpses are not kept in the home, friends and neighbours are not expected to visit and 'view the body', the coffin is not carried through the parish on bearers' shoulders, nor is it followed by mourners on foot, and, as cremation becomes increasingly more common, there is no graveside service. In former times, however, every part of the time between death and final burial was governed by a mixture of religion, law, etiquette, fashion, tradition, and superstition, and there were hundreds of beliefs in the final category. Only the most well known are included here, but a piece from Northern Ireland demonstrates some of the niceties involved.

In the funeral preparations there is also a code of behaviour which must be observed. When the coffin has been resting on chairs and is removed, the chairs must be knocked over or, if it had been laid on a bed, the bed must be shaken up. The coffin must always be taken out of the house feet-foremost, and it must be carried for a part of the journey to the graveyard on the shoulders of relatives and friends. The shortest distance for carrying is until the procession is out of sight of the home. There is a certain etiquette attached to carrying. The nearest blood relatives come first, insofar as height will permit, for obviously four men of roughly equal height are required. The rule must be strictly observed if family feuds are to be avoided. In-laws come after blood relatives, then friends and neighbours, and it is a delicate task to arrange these in correct order of precedence. It is considered to be altogether wrong to take short-cuts with a funeral, and care must be taken to avoid gaps in the procession, for a gap in a funeral is believed to be a sign that another death will occur shortly after. It is indecent for a funeral to hurry unless it is known that there is to be another burial in the same graveyard around the same time. In such a case it is essential to arrive first, for there is a belief that the last person to be buried must wait on the others in the graveyard. I once heard a woman ask her husband when he returned from her father's burial, if they had arrived at the burying-ground before another funeral. When she heard that they had, she sighed with relief and said, 'Thank God! I wouldn't have liked to think of my Da waiting on the like of thon!' It is unusual for women to attend funerals in Ulster. It is thought to be 'not their place'. In North Antrim I have never known women to sit down to the after-funeral meal with the men. In some old graveyards, Inishmurray for instance, the men are buried on one side and the women on the other.

N. Ireland (1951)

opening doors at funerals

Many actions were necessary once a death had occurred in the house: the clocks were stopped, mirrors and pictures were covered, the bees had to be told, and so on. Two superstitions involved open doors – the first when a person was dying, and the second at the time of the funeral. It was widely believed that, as near as possible to the time of someone's death, all windows and doors, or at least the windows of the death room or main door of the house, should be opened wide. It was thought this assisted the flight of the dead person's spirit, but it was also part of a more complex belief concerned with ensuring an 'easy death'. In many instances, it is recorded that people believed that closed doors and windows, and locks of cupboards, boxes, and so on, actually impeded or even prevented the natural course of death taking place, and failure to see to these details caused the unfortunate one to 'die hard' (endure a long, drawn-out death). The custom of opening doors and windows is presumed to be ancient, but the earliest clear reference so far found dates only from the early nineteenth century, in Walter Scott's novel *Guy Mannering*, published in 1815.

The second belief which connects death with an open door is concerned with the time that the coffin leaves the house for its final journey:

A few days ago the body of a gentleman in this neighbourhood was conveyed to the hearse, and while being placed in it, the door of the house, whether from design or inadvertence I know not, was closed before the friends came out to take their places in the coaches. An old lady, who was watching the proceedings, immediately exclaimed, 'God bless me! they have closed the door upon the corpse; there will be another death in that house before many days are over'. She was fully impressed with this belief, and unhappily this impression has been confirmed. Yorkshire (1850)

Again, the belief does not seem to have had a long history, as its first recorded instance is only from 1850, and the last is from the mid twentieth century.

unlucky to meet a funeral

It is hardly surprising that meeting such a reminder of human mortality as a funeral procession was regarded as at best unlucky, and most often as a sign of an impending death.

For a funeral to cross your path betokens either an approaching death in your family or a coming sorrow. Warwickshire (1875)

A number of ways were suggested for counteracting the evil influence of the encounter. Taking off your hat was recommended both as a mark of respect and a counter-charm, but the most regularly reported method was to turn and accompany the procession for a short time, thus, presumably, breaking the *meeting* part of the omen. In some communities, this was not regarded as optional, and was as important for those in the procession as for those meeting it. For obvious reasons, it was particularly unlucky for a wedding party to meet a funeral, and organizers would go to great lengths to avoid this happening.

The force of this belief has, of course, been severely weakened by developments in the way funerals are carried out, as the modern car-borne funeral has removed much of the personal aspect of the procession, and although a few older people may remove their hats briefly as a funeral cortège goes by, those not personally involved take little notice of its passing.

'blessed is the corpse the rain rains on'

'Happy is the bride the sun shines on' is still a well-known saying, but equally common in previous times was the corollary concerning funerals:

In Wales they say, 'Blessed are the dead that the rain rains on.'
Wales (1909)

It was generally believed that the soul of the deceased was thereby benefited, but how this was meant to work is not altogether clear. Some took it symbolically – the heavens were weeping in sympathy – but most sources do not explain, and it may simply be that rain for sorrow, and sunshine for joy, is a 'natural' human reaction. The idea was widely known and believed, and the earliest reference is in the play *The Puritan* (1607), four decades before the earliest known for the happy bride, although it is quite feasible that they came into being at the same time. The rain belief has not lasted so well, and is probably close to being completely forgotten.

the sin-eater

Our knowledge of the sin-eater, whose reported job it was to take away the sins of the departed by symbolically eating something at the funeral, commences with a description by antiquarian John Aubrey:

> In the County of Hereford was an old custom at funerals to hire poor people, who were to take upon them all the sins of the party deceased. One of them I remember lived in a cottage on Ross-high way. (He was a long, lean, ugly, lamentable poor rascal.) The manner was that when the corpse was brought out of the house and laid on the bier, a loaf of bread was brought out, and delivered to the sin-eater over the corpse, as also a mazer-bowl of maple (Gossips bowl) full of beer, which he was to drink up, and sixpence in money, in consideration whereof he took upon him (ipso facto) all the sins of the defunct, and freed him (or her) from walking after they were dead. *Remaines* (1686)

Aubrey's manuscript was not fully published until 1880, but his writings were recycled in a number of earlier nineteenth-century publications. Later writers took this description on face value, and made sweeping assumptions that the custom must be ancient, previously universal, and that any food-related beliefs or funeral customs must therefore be a survival of it. Heated controversies on this matter took place during the nineteenth century, when at least one leading folklorist attempted to argue that it was a survival of ancient ritual cannibalism, while other scholars pointed out the flimsy nature of the evidence for any such character or for any widespread custom of 'eating sins'. If the concept of sin-eating did exist, there is no need to look outside Christianity for origins. There are in fact plenty of strands in the history of Christian funeral practices which could have resulted in such a custom, and biblical references such as Hosea 4:8, 'They eat up the sin of my people', probably made the biggest contribution.

The Human Body

∽

PARTS OF THE BODY

Lucky Cutting your hair when the moon is waxing • Your right eye or hand itching • Throwing shed teeth on to the fire • White mark on the fingernails • Starting a journey with the right foot

Unlucky Letting pieces of your hair or nails fall into the wrong hands • People with red hair • People with crossed eyes or meeting eyebrows • Ringing in the ears

∽

ACTIONS

Lucky Saying 'bless you' when someone sneezes • Crossing fingers and legs

Unlucky Shuddering • Washing hands in the same water as someone else

PARTS OF THE BODY

hair

The two parts of the body which are routinely removed are hair and nails, and on the principle of sympathetic connection, it was formerly believed that what happened to them after removal could still vitally affect the body itself. Hair and nails could thus be used for good or evil – in cures or witchcraft – and beliefs about them were often interchangeable or combined. Many other beliefs reflected further concerns for the time and method of cutting, as well as the disposal of hair.

cutting hair

The most widespread belief about hair cutting was that it should be done at the waxing, not the waning of the moon, while another was that children's hair and fingernails must not be cut until they are at least twelve months old. A further group of superstitions was concerned with days on which it was not acceptable to carry out the operation. As with fingernails, Friday and Sunday were the days most often prohibited:

> Friday cut and Sunday shorn
> Better never have been born,
>
> Lancashire (1870)

but some Irish informants reported that Monday, too, was shunned, and to complicate matters, occasional references stated that cutting hair on Good Friday was beneficial. Many people were in deadly earnest in their concern for where any strands of their hair ended up:

> It was once believed that witches had the power to draw to them any person whose hair had fallen into their hands, and wise-women in the country used to advise girls to obtain a lock of hair of the man they wished to marry.   N. Ireland (1951)

Pieces of hair and nails still turn up in surviving examples of witch bottles and other receptacles in which the ingredients of witchcraft were placed. An additional concern was to keep hair out of the way of birds:

> Hair, too, should be carefully burnt. It is unlucky to throw it out of doors, as birds may weave it into their nests, and then the person to whom it belonged will suffer from headache.   Shropshire (1883)

But there was sharp disagreement about the wisdom of burning hair. While the English sources recommended it as the surest way of destroying the hair, most Irish writers viewed such behaviour with alarm. A simple form of divination, aimed at ascertaining whether a long life still lay ahead, was to take note of how your hair burns when thrown on the fire:

> If a person's hair burn brightly when thrown into the fire, it is a sign of longevity; the brighter the flame, the longer the life. On the other hand, if it smoulder away, and refuse to burn, it is a sign of approaching death.   Co. Durham (1866)

swallowing hair

It used to be firmly believed by many that if you swallowed a long hair it would wind around your heart and kill you, and the same thing was said of thread. The belief was quite widespread in the nineteenth and twentieth centuries, and was clearly not new even then:

> If I trust her, as she's a woman, let one of her long hairs wind about my heart, and be the end of me; which were a piteous lamentable tragedy, and might be entituled, 'A fair warning for all hair-bracelets'.   Thomas Middleton, *The Witch* (c.1615)

red hair

There was a long tradition of distrust of red-haired people in Britain, which showed itself in a number of linked superstitions, and which still survives in some contexts as a vague feeling that red hair is undesirable. The general prejudice held that red-haired people were devious, cruel, lascivious, unlucky, and generally untrustworthy:

> It seems to be generally supposed, by those who harbour the doctrine, that red-haired people are dissemblers, deceitful, and, in fact, not to be trusted like others whose hair is of a different colour; and I may add that I myself know persons who, on that account alone, never admit into their service any whose hair is thus objectionable.
> General (1853)

The dislike was widely manifest in the idea, particularly associated with fishermen and miners, that meeting a red-haired woman first thing in the morning or on the way to work was especially unlucky. In addition to their supposed character faults, red-haired children were said to be the result of their mother's infidelity, or of intercourse during menstruation, or to be descendants of the archetypal villains of English tradition, the Danes. The prejudice has a long history. Iona Opie and Moira Tatem identify three examples earlier than the mid fifteenth century, starting with the *Proverbs of Alfred* (*c.*1200), and it was simply taken for granted by seventeenth-century dramatists, in such lines as George Chapman's *Bussy D'Ambois* (1607), 'Worse than the poison of a red-haired man'. Several stock evil characters were popularly held to have had red hair (or at least a red beard), most notably Judas Iscariot, Cain, Mary Magdalene, and Shylock, and this fact is often cited as the origin of the superstitious feeling against the colour. This may be so, but it is more likely that these characters were assigned these attributes because of an existing prejudice.

your character in your hair

It was generally believed that certain characteristics of a person's hair would reveal elements of their general character. The most widespread example was the distrust of red-haired people, but for others, curly hair was also suspect. Such hair was seen as a sign of pride, whether naturally curly or revealed when tested in a traditional way:

Curly hair is a sign of pride. Nurse-maids teach their charges to draw a hair sharply between the nails of the fore-finger and thumb, to discover by its 'crinkling' or the reverse, whether the owner is of haughty temperament; and the writer of this note has more than once been saluted by unmannerly children with the cry 'Co'ly locks, my wo'd is n't she prood'.   Lincolnshire (1908)

This tradition does not show much stability, as several other interpretations were possible, for example that the person was flirtatious, would be rich or poor, or that the number of curls would reveal the number of husbands a woman would have. The general distrust of the curly meant that straight hair was often imbued with good qualities.

widow's peak

A widow's peak is a particular formation in the hair of a woman (or occasionally a man) which, when appearing suddenly, was formerly thought to foretell impending widowhood or that a future husband would not live long:

Mrs.—of Scawby was tidying up her bedroom, and as she dusted the mirror she caught sight of herself; she seemed 'somehow different' and paused to look at herself more closely. She saw that she had a curl over each temple, which she had never had before. She knew quite well what this omen meant. Within the fortnight her husband was brought home ill, and died soon after.   Lincolnshire (1936)

Others describe it as a lock or point of hair on the forehead. The term 'widow's peak', or earlier, 'widow's lock', has been in general currency since at least the mid sixteenth century, and the belief was presumably already present at that time.

ears and cheeks

A burning or tingling of the ear or cheek is by far the most widespread and oldest of the itching beliefs (see p. 88), and is the only one still heard on a regular basis. The basic meaning has remained remarkably constant for centuries, although certain details vary considerably:

Most people are familiar with the notion that when the right ear tingles some person is speaking well of one, but should the sensation be in the left ear then the opposite is the case.   Dumfriesshire (1890/91)

The designation of right for good and left for bad is generally agreed, but is far from universal, as a significant minority of authorities report the opposite, including John Melton in 1620. Others sidestep the issue by contrasting mundane with desirable, rather than good with bad:

> [From a servant girl, about nineteen years old] If your right ear burn, your mother is thinking of you; if your left ear, you are occupying your lover's thoughts.   Devon (1878)

Many versions continue 'but left or right is good at night'. Pinching your ear, biting your finger, cutting a piece off your apron, or tying a knot in it were all thought to make the talker bite their tongue, or develop a stammer.

Chaucer is the first to mention the belief in Britain (*Troilus and Criseyde*, c.1374), and it has been regularly recorded ever since in a wide variety of contexts in almost every quarter of the British Isles. It is still routinely expressed today, even if not meant literally. The belief is of even older vintage, however, and it is one of the few where the examples from classical times are genuinely similar in meaning to the modern ones. Pliny, for example, wrote, c. AD 77, 'according to an accepted belief absent people can divine by the ringing in their ears that they are the object of talk'.

ringing in the ear

A ringing in the ear can have more than one meaning. Since the eighteenth century at least it has been taken as a death omen, or at least a sign of bad news on the way:

> 'What a night of horrors!' murmured Joseph Poorgrass, waving his hands spasmodically, 'I've had the news-bell ringing in my left ear quite bad enough for a murder, and I've seen a magpie all alone!'
> Thomas Hardy, *Far from the Madding Crowd* (1874)

A later interpretation, however, was more cheerful:

> She had a 'singing' in her ears; when this occurs to one, one should at once ask for a number, and at once get it. One should then count the letters of the alphabet till one comes to the number given; the corresponding letter will be the initial letter of the name of the person one is destined to marry.   Oxfordshire (1865)

The ominous meaning was first reported by Daniel Defoe in the early eighteenth century, and was still being quoted, in milder form, in the mid twentieth. The divinatory number procedure was known from only 1865 onwards, but was still current in the 1980s.

eyebrows

Eyebrows which meet across the bridge of the nose have generally been held to be indicative of the character, or general fortune, of the person who bears them. The vast majority of references treat this feature as a very bad thing, but some disagree completely and claim it a very fortunate sign. The earliest reference is unequivocal:

> They whose haire of the eye-browes doe touch or meet together, of all other are the worst. They doe shew that hee or shee is a wicked person, and an enticer of servants, and given to unlawfull and naughty acts which Iohannes Indagnies saith, hee hath observed in old women being witches, which were led to bee burned, whose eye-browes were such.   Thomas Lupton, *A Thousand Notable Things* (1579)

Something like this was said by numerous sixteenth- and seventeenth-century writers, but the documentary record goes strangely quiet until the Victorian era, when meeting eyebrows again causes much comment. This resurgence was probably aided by popular fortune-telling books, many of which included a negative view of meeting eyebrows in their sections on physiognomy.

eyelashes

A simple wishing custom to be undertaken when an eyelash comes out:

> If an eyelash falls out, put it on the back of the hand, and wish, and the wish will come true.   Worcestershire (1909)

eyes

An itching eye usually meant laughter or tears, depending on the eye involved:

> A twitching in the eyelid is lucky; but you must not say when it comes nor when it goes. Right eye itching, a sign of laughter; but left over right, you'll cry before night.   Cornwall (1887)

The majority of later references follow the general right/good, left/ bad pattern of other beliefs, although occasionally the meanings are reversed. It is noticeable, however, that all the seventeenth- and eighteenth-century versions cite the left eye as good and the right as bad, and there seems to have been a reversal in meaning over time, which in turn may suggest that the relative attributes usually assigned to right and left are less stable and long-lasting than is often assumed. The belief is certainly as old as the early seventeenth century, as Shakespeare has Desdemona say, 'Mine eyes doth itch, Doth that bode weeping?' and it is reported sporadically into the twentieth century. There are also classical analogues, as in, 'My right eye itches now, and shall I see my love?' (Theocritus, *Idylls*, c.275 BC).

crossed eyes

Of the many people and animals which one was unlucky to meet first thing in the morning, or when starting on a journey, a person with crossed eyes was widely regarded as one of the worst, and the bad luck was intensified if it was a woman. Personal disability or deformity was routinely regarded as unlucky in the past, but there were exceptions. It was considered lucky to see and touch a hunchback, for example, and even the cross-eyed person was not universally shunned:

> They believe in a 'lucky look' from a person who squints, but it must be one glance, and have done with it. Should the look be repeated, or even prolonged, the good turns to evil, and they will have 'bad luck'. At Billingsgate Market, and at Faringdon Market as well, may be found any morning a half-silly ragged boy with a squint, who picks up many a half-penny by dispensing 'lucky looks' amongst the itinerant fishmongers and greengrocers, ere they begin their daily 'round'.   London (1880)

The general antipathy to cross-eyed people was extremely wide-spread in the British Isles in the last four centuries. Many early writers mention it, such as Thomas Lupton (1579), Reginald Scot (1584), and John Aubrey (1686), and the Chester monk Ranulf Higden does so even earlier, in his *Polychronicon* of about 1350. In this form it can be traced back to Pliny's *Natural History* (AD 77), and to a clear connection with the traditions of the evil eye.

teeth

The idea that teeth which are lost, either as milk-teeth or by extraction or accident, should be disposed of in traditionally sanctioned ways is found in most, if not all, European cultures and probably throughout most of the world. In Britain, the standard ceremony for shed teeth, which lasted from at least the late seventeenth to the late twentieth century, was for the tooth to be burnt, usually after covering it with salt, and often with an accompanying rhyme:

> Old tooth, new tooth
> Pray God send me a new tooth

We said this with the air of performing a serious rite. It was a tradition, and we followed it.   Derbyshire (*c.*1890)

Reasons for this procedure varied, and the result of non-compliance was sometimes simply given as 'being unlucky', but two more specific outcomes were commonly cited. The first was particularly apposite for children's milk-teeth, for, if the tooth were lost and a dog (or other animal) got hold of it, the replacement would grow like an animal's tooth. The second applied to adults – on the Day of Judgement we would all have to account for any missing body parts. Extracted teeth therefore either had to be ceremoniously burnt, or kept safely somewhere in the house. The earliest reference to the salt and fire ceremony occurs in 1686, in John Aubrey's manuscript collection of customs and beliefs, but it does not seem to be mentioned again until the early nineteenth century, when it is frequently recorded.

The twentieth century saw a marked change in the way children's milk-teeth were treated. From at least the 1920s, the idea existed that the fairies were interested in taking the teeth, in exchange for money, at least in some families. For much of that time it was simply 'the fairies' who would take the tooth, if left under the child's pillow (or occasionally elsewhere), but at some point after the Second World War the 'Tooth Fairy' became the staple character in the deal. As the fire-and-salt method was still being cited into the 1950s and 1960s, it overlapped for some decades with the fairies, and some children were well aware that different methods existed and endeavoured to use those which promised money in return, which must have given the fairies a distinct edge over older methods. It is usually assumed that the Tooth

Fairy character was introduced from America, and this may well be so, but research there has shown that the fairy connection has no longer history in the USA than in Britain – arising and gaining popularity at roughly the same time in both countries. Nowadays, the Tooth Fairy is ubiquitous on both sides of the Atlantic, and crops up in children's books, board games, advertisements, dental health campaigns, and political cartoons, without explanation. Newspaper columnists regularly lament how the silver sixpence given by the fairies of yesteryear became, by stages, a shilling, a half-crown, a pound coin, and so on.

There is general agreement that having a gap between your two front teeth is significant and predicts the possessor's future or character, but unfortunately there is no consensus as to its exact meaning. Most say it is fortunate in some way – you will be lucky, rich, or will travel far, and in the author's teenage years (1960s) it was reputed to be sexy. But in Victorian Scotland it meant that the possessor would be short-lived, while in Wales in 1909 that they would be rich. Reports appear fairly regularly from mid Victorian times, and it would seem to be yet another minor belief which emerged in the nineteenth century if it were not for two lines in the *Canterbury Tales* nearly 500 years earlier:

> She koude muchel of wandrynge by the weye
> Gat-tothed was she, soothly for to seye.
>
> Chaucer, *Canterbury Tales* (*c.*1387)

tongues

If you have a pimple or sore spot on your tongue, the general opinion is that you have been telling lies:

> It was bad enough to have a sore spot at the end of one's tongue without suffering the moral pain of being told that it was a proof that one had been telling 'stories'.
>
> Lincolnshire *Grantham Journal* (29 June 1878)

This idea was widely known in the early seventeenth century, as is shown by Shakespeare's 'If I prove honey-mouth'd, let my tongue blister' (*Winter's Tale*), and it has been regularly reported ever since. Much the same was said in classical times (e.g. Theocritus, *Idylls* 12, *c.*275 BC), which raises the possibility that it entered British tradition by direct translation from ancient Greek writings.

hands

The dominant symbolism of hands in the superstitions of Britain and Ireland is that they mean money – coming in or going out, depending on the context. Added to this is a range of beliefs concerning itching as predictive of future events:

> If the right hand itched, it signified that money would shortly be received by it; and if the left hand itched, that money would shortly have to be paid away.   W. Scotland (1879)

This idea was very widely known. An additional rhyme, apparently dating from the mid nineteenth century, gave further information:

> Rub it on wood
> It's sure to be good
> Rub it on brass
> It'll come to pass.
> Norfolk (c.1895)

The meaning is already in place when John Melton included it in his list of superstitions in 1620. A few years earlier, Shakespeare (*Julius Caesar*, 1599) had given evidence of a different meaning of the 'itchy palm', which, while still involving money, suggested avarice and corruption. Both interpretations can still be heard.

fingers

Apart from the widespread beliefs about fingernails and crossed fingers, a variety of other beliefs and customs have also been collected on the subject. As with many other body features, the size and shape of a person's fingers were thought to reveal major character traits. Long fingers, for example, were believed to show a disposition to thieving, but there was little agreement about crooked fingers: 'Crooked fingers indicate a crabbed disposition' (Aberdeenshire, 1895); 'One with crooked little fingers will be rich before death' (Hebrides, 1895).

Children seem to be especially fond of little fingers, as they feature in several of their customs. If two people say the same thing at the same time they should link little fingers and make a wish, and after a quarrel they can link fingers and chant something on the lines of

'Make up, make up, never do it again'. In Victorian times they had a custom of pinching each other's little fingers 'to see whether they could keep a secret or not'. It is suggested that this custom may help explain two obscure references in Shakespeare (*Henry IV Part 1*, 2:3 and *Winter's Tale* 1:2) which refer to fingers and truth, and pinching fingers, respectively.

It was thought by many in the nineteenth and even for much of the twentieth century that the forefinger, or index finger, of the right hand was poisonous, and must never be used in any medical treatment. Sources vary on which was the best finger to use instead: some recommend the middle finger, while others insist on the ring finger. In much older tradition, as evidenced from a fifteenth-century manuscript in Cambridge University, each finger had a name and supposed character. The ring finger was there called 'lecheman' (leechman, or doctor), but the index finger is called 'towcher' (toucher), and no mention is made of any bad qualities.

Occasional references indicate a divinatory procedure which involved cracking the joints of someone's fingers:

> We pulled each finger and the number of joints that cracked meant
> one had that number of sweethearts.   Sussex (*c.*1915)

In some versions the cracks predict the number of babies one would have in the future. Although recorded only a few times, this divination game is quite long-lived in that it was already in circulation in the 1750s, and still being reported 200 years later.

cutting fingernails

Superstitious minds of previous generations appear to have been obsessed with fingernails. The idea that finger- (and toe-) nails should be cut only on certain days was extremely widespread in British tradition, and has a recorded history of over 400 years. Details vary to a certain extent, but the strict prohibition of nail-cutting on Fridays and Sundays was almost universal, while the day singled out for lucky paring was most often Monday:

> If you cut your nails on Monday morning before breakfast you will
> receive a present before the week is out. Cut them at all on Friday
> and dire misfortune will follow.   Hampshire (1890)

Several references to nail-cutting have survived from the sixteenth and early seventeenth centuries, which attest to the belief's wide currency at that time.

The well-known rhyme, still often quoted, which enumerates each day of the week, is a relative newcomer, reported from only 1830 onwards. It varies little from version to version, which suggests a primarily literary rather than oral tradition:

> Cut them on a Monday, you cut them for health
> Cut them on a Tuesday you cut them for wealth
> Cut them on Wednesday you cut them for news
> Cut them on Thursday, a new pair of shoes
> Cut them on Friday you cut them for sorrow
> Cut them on Saturday see your true-love tomorrow
> Cut them on Sunday the devil will be with you all the week
>
> East Anglia (1830)

gifts on your fingernails

The small white specks which sometimes appear on the fingernails were widely believed to be significant and to betoken a forthcoming gift. So widespread was this notion that the specks were simply called 'gifts' in everyday language. Further information could be gleaned by which finger the mark appeared on:

> On the thumb, sure to come
> On the finger, sure to linger
> [Counting from the thumb]
> A friend, a foe, a letter to write
> And a journey to go.
>
> Wiltshire (1893–5)

Several seventeenth-century writers refer to such marks on the nails as predictive, in terms which show that the belief was already proverbial by that period. Ben Jonson is the earliest, in the play *The Alchemist* (1610), and Thomas Browne was sceptical about their meaning in his *Pseudodoxia Epidemica* (1652). John Melton (1620), however, provides a clue to wider nail beliefs: 'to have yellow speckles on the nails of one's hand is a great sign of death'.

feet

In the superstitious world of luck good and bad, a lucky or unlucky 'foot' can mean either the style of someone's foot per se or a person one meets at the start of a journey or who arrives at the house, as in first footing.

> I will not speak of ridiculous friets [superstitions], such as our meeting with a lucky or unlucky foot, when we are going about important business.   Highland Scotland (1685)

But the unfortunate person may indeed have gained this reputation because of something wrong with his/her feet, and flat-footed people were singled out as particularly unlucky. A bare-foot person was similarly shunned. Fear of meeting a bare-foot woman is first mentioned by Nigel de Longchamps in his *Mirror of Fools* (1180), but the flat-footed were apparently safe until the early seventeenth century. They were both still being avoided in the mid twentieth century. These concerns with feet are almost entirely restricted to Scotland, Isle of Man, and Ireland.

The general rule of right/good, left/bad, was translated into a concern with which foot was used first when setting out from home, or entering another:

> If you enter another man's house, with your 'skir' [left] foot foremost, you draw down evil on its inhabitants. If, therefore, you have carelessly done so, you must avert the mischief by going out, and making your entrance a second time with the right foot foremost.
>   N. England (1866)

Recorded examples of this belief are only spasmodic, but there is no doubt that it was generally known and followed by many from at least the seventeenth century and probably earlier. It was certainly known in classical times.

ACTIONS

itching

A sudden or persistent itch on any part of the body has long been held to have significance. The meanings given for some are well known and surprisingly stable over time, while for others there is little agreement. As can be seen below, the meaning is often relatively logical – as in the case of the foot, or the ear – but others are less clear, such as that given for a nose itch. At times there seems to be an element of parody – as in the reason for a back itch:

Hand – you will give or receive money
Ear – someone is talking about you
Foot – you will tread on strange ground
Eye – you will cry or laugh
Knee – you will kneel in a strange church
Elbow – you will have a strange bedfellow
Nose – you will be kissed, cursed, run into a gatepost, or shake
    hands with a fool
Stomach – you will eat pudding
Back – butter will be cheap when grass grows there

shuddering

A sudden shiver will often elicit the comment that 'someone is walking over my grave', and this has been the case for at least the last 250 years. It is not clear whether this has ever been a genuine belief, or simply a proverbial metaphor, but it has remained remarkably stable since its first recorded reference in Swift's *Polite Conversations* of 1738, and to be included in that work it must have been a well-known phrase of the time.

sneezing

The idea that a sneeze must be answered with a salutation from bystanders appears to be known across the whole of Europe, and may well be found all over the world. In modern Britain 'bless you' is the universal wording, but in earlier times there was more variation:

> We have a custom (yet in mode) that when one sneezes every one else puts off his hat and bows, and cries 'God bless ye Sir'. I have heard, or read a story that many years since, that sneezing was an epidemical disease, and very mortal, which caused this yet received custom.   John Aubrey, *Remaines* (1686)

The modern notion that we say 'bless you' because our ancestors believed they could 'sneeze out their soul' is simply guesswork and has no evidence to confirm or deny it. We do know, however, that the idea that the custom started with some great sickness has itself been traditional for many centuries. The earliest English reference to saluting a sneeze, Caxton's *Golden Legend* (1483), already included this notion. There are also antecedents to the blessing of sneezes from the classical period. Pliny, for example, asked 'Why do we say "good health" to those who sneeze?' in his *Natural History* of AD 77, so even at that early date the reason was not known.

People in Britain have also tried to read meaning into the number and situation of sneezes since at least the sixteenth century, and complex prognostications were attempted, but these have not lasted. A rhyme which purported to give meanings for sneezes on certain days ('Sneeze on a Monday, sneeze for danger', etc.) was noted a number of times in the nineteenth and twentieth centuries, with only minor variations. Similar day-of-the-week rhymes existed, concerning things as diverse as cutting fingernails to washing clothes, all first appearing in the 1830s or 1840s with a suspiciously literary flavour about them. In more recent times, a much simpler notion has sufficed:

One for a kiss
Two for a wish
Three for a letter
Four something better.

Norfolk (*c*.1895)

spitting

Spitting has occurred in a number of superstitious contexts – for luck, for protection, to counteract bad luck, to express contempt, to underline an oath, to seal a bargain, to effect a cure, and more. As recorded in 1911:

> Spitting for luck is still practised in countless ways; for instance, on money received or found; on a piece of coal; through a ladder; on a horseshoe; for a bad smell; on a finger, and touching the toes of the boots when a black-and-white horse is espied; on marbles or buttons whilst playing games with them, etc.

We may understand the situations, but we still do not know why spitting itself is the particular action which is required. Records show that one of the most widely reported contexts for 'spitting for luck' was to spit on money received. This could be done at any time, but was most prevalent when the money taken was the first of the day (a handsel), or when it formed a gift or gratuity. A key element here is that the spitting and the wishing ensured that more would follow. In many cases, the custom appears to be based on the idea that *receiving* anything, whether by bargain, gift, or simply by finding it, opened one up to ill-wishing, and that the spitting was thus protective against bad luck rather than to promote good. Spitting customs were extremely well known across the whole British Isles. The earliest reference is provided by John Aubrey (*Remaines*, 1686), but there is no reason to believe that the custom was new in his day.

crossing fingers and legs

Crossing the fingers is one of the most widely recognized luck gestures in modern Britain and Ireland, and it was no accident that the UK National Lottery adopted the symbol of the crossed fingers as their logo in the 1990s. In recent decades, the gesture has had several different, but linked, meanings, depending on the context. We cross our fingers for luck and to enhance the chances of success in some venture, although we often say 'I'll cross my fingers for you' rather than actually doing it. We also cross our fingers when telling a lie, in the hope that the gesture will negate the misdeed, and we are advised to cross our fingers for protection after we have walked under a ladder, seen a magpie, or tempted fate in some way.

Desmond Morris (*Gestures*, 1979) demonstrated that the gesture was virtually unknown elsewhere in Europe, and considering its ubiquity in Britain it is astonishing to learn that it does not seem to have been known before the late nineteenth century. The earliest clear reference comes from Hampshire as late as 1890: 'If you walk under a ladder, cross your fingers to avert bad luck.' Indeed, crossed legs are much older than crossed fingers as a good-luck gesture. In addition, long before crossed fingers are recorded, the most common gesture designed to protect against witches and other ill-wishers was to fold the thumb within the hand.

Sometime in the twentieth century, a popular explanation for the gesture was circulated which is still heard today. It explained that in the early days of Christianity, when followers were being persecuted, they used the crossed fingers as a secret gesture, to symbolize Christ's cross. Apart from the fact that the shape of crossed fingers bears no relation to the shape of a cross, the gesture's late appearance and severely restricted geographical spread combine to expose the explanation as groundless guesswork based simply on different meanings of the word 'cross'.

Well within living memory, in situations where crossing the fingers is not practical (e.g. when sitting an exam), many people have tried the expedient of crossing their legs for luck. Even today, it is also not unusual to hear someone speak of crossing the legs as an intensification of the crossed fingers. On present evidence, however, crossing the legs is considerably older than crossing the fingers, as it is reported regularly from the 1670s onwards, usually in the specific context of gambling – either lottery tickets or card-playing.

washing hands

A widespread belief held that it was unlucky for two people to use the same water to wash their hands, either at the same time or, more rarely, in succession. Where a specific result was prophesied, it was that they would quarrel:

> If a person wash in the water which another person has washed in, he and that person will quarrel before the day is out, unless the latter, before commencing his ablutions, takes the precaution of making the form of the cross with his finger on the water. Some, however, contend that the safest course is . . . [to] spit in the bowl, and some do both.   Northamptonshire (1851)

The two traditional remedies are mentioned here – making a cross on the water, or spitting in it. The belief was a popular one: it was collected from most parts of Britain and Ireland, particularly from the nineteenth century onwards. It was clearly in circulation in its current form in the seventeenth century; John Aubrey (*Remaines*, 1686), for example, notes:

> 'Tis an old received opinion that if two doe pisse together, they shall quarrell; or if two doe wash their hands together, they will quarrel.

It is difficult to see how such a superstition came about. In days before indoor plumbing, it must have been extremely common to share water for washing hands. A possible explanation is offered by Reginald Scot in his *Discoverie of Witchcraft* (1584). He gives a cure for the ague which specifically calls for two people to wash their hands together:

> More charmes for agues . . . Wash with the partie, and privilie saie this psalme 'Exaltabo te deus meus, rex, etc.'

If this was a common motif in cures, it is possible that it became considered as unlucky simply because it implied that the 'disease' would be transferred from the sufferer to the other hand-washer. If this cure existed before the Reformation (only a few years before Scot's time) it is likely to have involved making the sign of the cross. However, in the absence of more evidence, this is simply speculation.

A few informants have reported a similar belief that it was unlucky for two people to dry their hands on the same towel. One other belief about washing hands has been widely reported: if you washed them in water in which eggs have been boiled, you would get warts.

It may perhaps be thought that soap slipping out of one's hand would be too common an occurrence to be noteworthy, but there is more than one report from the nineteenth century that it was at best unlucky, and at worst meant a forthcoming death.

Domestic Superstitions

ॐ

IN AND AROUND THE HOUSE

Lucky Picking up a pin • Two spoons in a saucer • Finding a piece of coal • Turning your chair to turn your luck • Tripping up the stairs • Getting out of bed on the right side

Unlucky Entering and leaving a house by different doors • Turning a mattress on a Friday • Buying a broom in May • Turning the calendar to a new month before the old month is out • Leaving a single lighted candle alone in a room • Knives placed across each other • Passing anyone on the stairs • Breaking a mirror • Washing clothes on Good Friday

ॐ

FURTHER AFIELD

Lucky Nailing a horseshoe to a door • Finding a piece of iron • Finding a bent coin • Giving 'luck money'

Unlucky Walking under a ladder • Finding money

ॐ

CLOTHES AND ACCESSORIES

Lucky Wearing new clothes at Easter • Putting money in the pocket of new clothes • Throwing a shoe after someone

Unlucky Mending clothes while wearing them • Casting off winter clothes before the end of May • Wearing green at any time • Putting new shoes on a table • Opening an umbrella indoors

FOOD AND DRINK

Lucky Breaking empty eggshells • Marking dough with a cross before baking • Setting a hen on thirteen eggs • Burning salt to keep away witches • A tea stalk in your cup

Unlucky A loaf with a hole in it • Burning eggshells • Spilling salt • Helping someone to salt • Two people pouring tea from same pot

IN AND AROUND THE HOUSE

Numerous superstitions are concerned with particular aspects of houses, and what goes on in them. Records show that creatures coming into the house, such as bees, birds, or snakes, had particular meaning, as did cockerels crowing at the door, and it was believed that certain birds' nests (especially those of martins and swallows) should be left unmolested if they were attached to the house. A whole range of flowers must not be brought indoors, such as hawthorn, primroses, snowdrops, and daffodils. Seeing the new moon or a funeral procession through a window was unlucky, but doors and windows had to be opened in thunderstorms or when there was a death in the house. Which door to use was also governed by superstition:

> If anyone called at the house, mother always made them go out of
> the same door. You couldn't come in at the back door and leave at
> the front, that would bring bad luck.   Lincolnshire (*c*.1930s)

Nobody should open an umbrella, or shoulder a spade, in the house, and there were several beliefs about what could be done on the stairs.

Fires, beds, and other furniture had their own superstitions, and the house itself could be unlucky if numbered thirteen. The plant houseleek was encouraged to grow on the roof, as it protected the house from lightning, and various trees such as holly and rowan were considered lucky if planted near the house. You may still wish to nail a horseshoe to the door, or hang a holed stone somewhere for protection against the evil eye. You will certainly hope that the previous occupiers have not cursed the house with a fire of stones.

Dozens of other house-related beliefs have been recorded only a few times in the nineteenth and twentieth centuries, and an interesting group focuses on the act of moving into a new house. Clearly many people felt that this important step needed special attention and measures to promote good luck. The recorded beliefs are quite diverse, but are often similar to other symbolic actions at points of beginning. For example, the newcomers should not enter empty-handed but must carry certain items, such as coal or salt, with them, and visitors should similarly always bring something on their first visit. Others believed that when you went into a new house you should poke the fire for luck.

beds

Considering the importance of beds in people's daily lives, it is no surprise that they are more ruled by superstition than any other item of household furniture. Aspects covered by belief are many and various and are a curious mixture of the practical, the symbolic, and the magical. In addition to those detailed below, many other beliefs are bed-related: horseshoes and holed stones are hung above the bed for protection, Bibles and other lucky items placed under the pillow, and the dying can be helped on their way by a form of euthanasia called 'drawing the pillow'. Many love-divination procedures culminate in the participants retiring to bed – often backwards or in silence – primarily because the object of the exercise is usually to dream of the future spouse.

The first thing to get right is the orientation of the bed, which tradition dictates is essential for health and a good night's sleep. Unfortunately, there is no overall agreement as to which direction is best:

> There is, I have been told, a folk-belief that it is better to sleep lying north and south than lying east and west; in the former position perhaps one is supposed to roll over and over with the earth.   (1938)

> A bed should point to the east and west, and not to the north and south. Restlessness is caused by placing the bed in the direction of north to south.   Derbyshire (1895)

The majority of informants recommend north/south, and some claim that the earth's magnetic field makes it natural that our heads should point to the north. This latter explanation was already under discussion in the seventeenth century (e.g. Thomas Browne, *Pseudodoxia Epidemica*, 1646).

From the mid nineteenth century, a different concern over bed direction was widespread. It was believed essential to ensure that your bed was placed in line with the bedroom floorboards or beams of the room rather than across them. Failure to observe this rule would at best mean a bad night's sleep, or much worse:

> An old gossip in these parts, on being told by the mother of a dying child that her daughter's death was a very lingering one, went up to the sick chamber, and observing that the position of the bedstead was across the planks, instead of being parallel with them, assigned that as the reason for the patient's lingering death; so the bedstead's position was altered, and it is said the poor girl's death was both speedy and painless.   Kent? (1879)

Fitted carpets and plastered ceilings have made this belief redundant, and many people nowadays will be unaware of which way their bedroom floorboards run, even if they cared.

feathers in beds

A very widely reported belief held that the presence of pigeon or game-bird feathers in a pillow or mattress of a dying person prevented death occurring quickly, and caused them to 'die hard' (endure a long, drawn-out death).

> A few months ago a case occurred of an old woman who was dying 'very hard', as the saying is, when a neighbour suggested that probably there were pigeons' feathers in the pillow. It was immediately changed for one that was known to contain none, and the patient became quiet at once and did not very long survive.
>
> Berkshire (1889–91)

Although there are variations in the particular birds to be avoided, versions of the superstition are remarkably similar and are often supported by purportedly true anecdotes concerning instances known to the narrator. Taking somebody out of bed and putting them on the floor, or removing the pillow from under their head, to help them 'die easy' were both standard ways of showing compassion for the old and terminally ill, and existed independently of the feathers belief. In these narratives, however, they often provide a touch of unconscious humour, not lost on the folklorists who noted them down, 'he went off like a lamb' being almost a punchline in such reports:

> Dearee me, sir, you see there was partridge feathers in the bed, and folks can't die upon *geame* feathers no-how, and we thought as how he never *would* go, so we pulled the bed away, and then I just pinched his poor nose tight with one hand and shut his mouth close with t'other, and, poor dear! he went off like a lamb.
>
> Kent (1881)

The earliest clear reference dates from 1710, with a letter published in the *British Apollo* requesting information, and from then on the belief was noted regularly until well into the twentieth century. This is just the sort of motif to have appealed to the seventeenth-century dramatists, and its apparent absence from their plays could be taken as tentative evidence that it did not exist much before the first reference noted here. The superstition makes its most famous appearance in Emily Brontë's novel *Wuthering Heights* (1847): 'Ah they put pigeons' feathers in the pillows – no wonder I couldn't die!'

making the bed

Bed-making came in for more than its fair share of superstitions. Before the invention of sprung mattresses, beds needed a great deal more attention than they do in modern times. Feather beds in particular needed to be turned over and 'plumped up' every day, and 'turning the bed' was an onerous daily chore. It was widely believed that it was unlucky to turn your mattress on a Friday, and some also said Sunday as well:

> No bed was ever turned on Friday, and this custom brought a welcome release, a sigh of contentment to all bed-makers . . . and, of course, no bed was turned on Sunday. 'It's Friday, we mustn't turn the bed today', said one, and they pushed and tossed the feathers in the great feather beds, thankful that they could be left. It took some strength to turn those beds, and to puff the feathers till the whole thing rose like a balloon. To get the bed to settle down into a horizontal position afterwards was not easy, for we were not allowed to flatten it violently.   Derbyshire (1890s)

As it was often young women – as housewives or maidservants – who made the beds, the predicted misfortune often took the form of being unlucky in love, 'We shall turn away our sweethearts if we do' (Herefordshire, 1912), while others promised bad dreams for the occupant of the bed, or even early death. This mattress belief is known from only about 1835, and is reported from all over England but not, it seems, elsewhere in the British Isles. Dozens of variations on similar themes have been recorded.

getting out of bed

Much older superstitions showed great concern about how one got out of bed in the morning, as this would affect your fortune and your temperament for the rest of the day. 'You got out of the wrong side of the bed this morning' is still regularly said to someone who is unaccountably grumpy. The basic notion of rising properly goes back at least to the sixteenth century, but its exact nature varied considerably from person to person. In the earlier versions it tended to be a concern with getting out of the right (as opposed to left) side:

> It is unfortunate to rise out of bed on one's left side. It is a common saying when evil befalls a person, who seems to himself have rushed to meet it, 'I did not rise on my right hand today'.
>
> Highland Scotland (1900)

For others, it was getting out on to the right foot which mattered, and a third variation was to get in and out on the same side. The idea was already proverbial in the sixteenth century, appearing in two early plays, John Palsgrave's *Acolastus* (1540) and *Gammer Gurton's Needle* (1575).

brooms

Virtually all basic domestic items have had their superstitions, and brooms were no exception. A few beliefs were widely reported, but there were also many others, as, for example:

> If a girl strides over a besom-handle she will be a mother before she is a wife. If an unmarried woman has a child, people say 'She's jumped o'er t' besom' or 'She jumped o'er t' besom before she went t' church'. Mothers used to be particularly anxious that their

daughters should not stride over a broom, and mischievous boys have been known to leave brooms on door-steps, and such like places, so that girls might accidentally stride over them. In Sheffield, a woman of loose habits is called a 'beesom' or 'besom'.

Yorkshire (1895)

It was broadly believed to be extremely unlucky to buy a broom in May, or to use one bought in that month:

> Buy a broom in the month of May
> Sweep one of the house away.

Devon (1911)

This idea was still going strong in the second half of the twentieth century, as it was apparently well-known to door-to-door brush salesmen. No reason is given for this belief in any of the sources to hand, although the month of May is also unlucky in other contexts. There is certainly some confusion between the implement 'broom' and the plant 'broom', and the latter shares the widespread prejudice against being brought into the house with the hawthorn. There is no sign of these broom beliefs before the mid nineteenth century.

A handful of references from nineteenth-century Scotland reveal a tradition of throwing a broom after a person or animal to bring luck and break any possible ill-wishing. The motif of throwing for luck is also seen in the more widespread, and apparently much older, custom of throwing an old shoe.

calendars

Given the fundamental fear in the superstitious mind of actions which tempt fate, commercial products with dates – such as calendars and diaries – are an obvious problem. Occasionally recorded, but more widely known, is a set of linked beliefs which show this unease:

Calendars received about Christmas time should not be hung on the wall till the new year, as it is unlucky to do so. Birmingham (1934)

Nor should one turn to a new month before the old one is out. Surprisingly, the earliest known references come from only the 1930s, but the underlying notions are still being cited in the twenty-first century.

candles

Domestic candles were the subject of numerous superstitious beliefs, and many of these were so widely known as to be proverbial in the nineteenth century, although they have almost completely disappeared with changes in the technology of home lighting. The children's author Alison Uttley comments about her own childhood:

> As was natural in a candle-lit house, we had an intimate feeling for those soft yellow flames and the white candle. A spark flying from the flame meant a letter. A brightly glowing tip to the wick was a sweetheart in the candle. A tiny shred from the wick, falling into the cup of hot wax, was called a thief. A curl of wax rippling down the side of the candle was a winding-sheet.   Derbyshire (1890s)

Almost every possible combination of flame and wax could mean something:

> Winding-Sheet – a little projection of wax or tallow which, as the candle burns, gradually lengthens and winds round upon itself. It is a sign of the death of the person sitting opposite it.
>
> Lincolnshire (1877)

The earliest reference to this so far located is in the *British Apollo* (1708), but it is reported there as if it were already proverbial. It was in the nineteenth century that the belief became so well known that 'winding sheet' became the generally accepted word for such a formation.

A number of writers comment on a candle flame burning blue, although various interpretations were possible. In the earliest references, up to the late seventeenth century, the standard interpretation was that spirits or ghosts were near. Shakespeare alludes to this when, after a succession of ghosts has appeared to him, King Richard III observes, 'The lights burn blue. It is now dead midnight.' In the early nineteenth century, the meaning still held good, but it could be the wraith of the lover, summoned in a love-divination procedure which affected the flame. In some sources, however, a blue flame is simply described as a death omen.

three candles

The positioning of candles also caused comment or concern. Three lighted lamps or candles in a room were widely held to be ominous, but there was sharp disagreement as to meaning. Many informants maintained that it meant a death, and they would immediately blow one out if they found three candles burning together. Others, however, claimed it meant a wedding, and were thus happy to leave them alight. Even in the earliest known example, in Francis Kilvert's famous diary, the ambiguity of meaning is already evident:

> Three candles were burning on the kitchen table, and the cook said that the person who was nearest to the shortest candle would be married first. Some people put it, 'Will die first'. It seems to be an old saying about three lighted candles together, but it was quite new to me.   Cornwall (26 July 1870)

On balance, the unlucky interpretation wins on points.

single candle

There was no such ambiguity about a candle left alight in an unoccupied room:

> If a lighted candle is accidentally shut up in a pantry, it is a sure sign of death in the family soon. I asked Mrs. Z about this belief and she said, 'I went into my pantry and left a lighted candle there, and a month after my aunt died'.   Suffolk (1924)

chairs

Chairs appear in many superstitions, although none of these is as widely known as those concerning tables. Knocking over a chair as you rise from it seems an obvious candidate for superstitious interpretation, but the few references which have survived do not provide an agreed meaning. For some it was simply 'unlucky', for others it showed that the person concerned had not been telling the truth, but the earliest reference, found in Jonathan Swift's *Polite Conversation* (1738), states that s/he will not get married that year. In the nursing profession in the mid twentieth century it meant that an emergency case (or simply a new patient) would arrive soon.

For those of us brought up to replace their chairs on rising from the table, it may be surprising to learn that in several mid twentieth-century references this was considered an unfriendly act:

> When having a meal with an acquaintance, do not push your chair under the table when you get up, or you will not come there again for a meal.   Lincolnshire (1936)

The motif in question would seem to be the air of finality which the action entails.

When playing cards or other games of chance, a widespread notion is that one's luck can be improved by changing the situation or setting, in particular the chair in which one sits. Again, Swift provides the earliest reference (*Journal of a Modern Lady*, 1728), but 'Turn your chair and turn your luck' was still being said in the twentieth century. On the other hand, the same action could be interpreted in a different way:

> While talking thoughtlessly with a good woman, I carelessly turned a chair round two or three times; she was offended, and said it was a sign we should quarrel: and so it proved, for she never spoke friendly to me afterwards.   William Hone, *Year-Book* (1832)

clocks

The most widespread of clock beliefs connected a stopped clock with death, but in two relatively distinct ways – one in response to some mysterious power, and the other by the more prosaic intervention of a human being. In the former it was believed that a clock which stopped of its own accord was a sign of the death of a family member occurring at that very moment, either at home or at a distance, as described in 1864:

> A relative, describing to me the death of a parent, said the clock stopped just at the time of his decease: adding, the nurses said it was a usual occurrence. On making enquiry, I was told, the clock went well previously, and had gone well since – nothing to account for the stopping.

The doomed person could be any member of the family, although an especially strong link seemed to exist between the head of the household and the main clock of the house. On a higher level, several sovereigns are reputed to have left behind stopped clocks – George III,

William IV, and Queen Victoria, for example. Folklorist Charlotte
Burne commented drily:

> I have heard of this belief only in respect of grandfather clocks. The
> small, cheap, modern mantelshelf clock does not seem to know its
> duty in this respect.
>
> Shropshire (1938)

All the references are nineteenth and twentieth century; the belief was
sufficiently well known in Victorian times to inspire a tremendously
popular song, *Grandfather's Clock*, written by Henry Clay Work in 1875.

The other version held that clocks *should be stopped* as a mark of
respect when someone died:

> When the corpse is 'laid out', the death chamber is shrouded in
> white, the clock is stopped, and the looking-glass covered, to show
> that for the dead time is no more and earthly vanity departed.
>
> Co. Durham (1910)

The stopped clock was linked with the covered mirror and ornaments
in most accounts. As with the other clock beliefs, this has not been
found before the 1820s.

A clock striking the wrong hour, or otherwise misbehaving, can
even now upset the superstitious and be regarded as unlucky:

> I have often heard it said in the North Riding of Yorkshire, that, if
> a clock strike thirteen times instead of twelve, some member of the
> household will shortly die.
>
> Yorkshire (1892)

In these cases, it is the misbehaviour of the clock, rather than the
number thirteen, which is ominous.

A variety of beliefs were concerned with a clock striking while other,
seemingly innocuous, events were taking place. The most common
ones were connected with church clocks. In several places, the notion
was reported that if the clock chimed while a hymn was being sung
inside the church, or while other specific parts of the church service
were being performed, a death in the parish would soon follow. More
specifically, it was particularly unlucky for a bride and groom if the
clock struck during their wedding ceremony. None of these beliefs
were reported earlier than Victorian times. The fear of the chimes
coinciding with the wedding service seems to be exclusively northern
English, whereas for the others there is a preponderance of western
English and Welsh examples.

coal

A piece of coal has, for obvious reasons, been given a symbolic meaning in many contexts, especially those to do with hearth and home. Specific instances include giving a piece to occupants of a new house, to a newly married couple, putting some in a Christmas stocking, and, most commonly, being carried by New Year first footers.

> When visiting someone who has just moved into a new house, never go with your two hands the one length. Always take something to hansel the house. Coal is the luckiest.   Co. Tyrone (1972)

Less easily explained was a widespread set of beliefs that a piece of coal was, in itself, a lucky object. If found, it should be picked up and thrown over the shoulder (some say spit on it first), or put on the nearest fire. Several writers record pieces of coal being carried in pockets and purses, again for luck, and Iona and Peter Opie discovered children taking pieces of coal into exams and adults to driving tests. Although recorded from the 1870s onwards, these beliefs in coal as a lucky object appear to be much more common in the twentieth century, and have only recently begun to die out.

fires

The winding-sheet or letter in the candle were so familiar to all that they became well-known sayings in their own right, and the same thing happened with aspects of the domestic fire's behaviour, such as the 'stranger on the bar':

> If a piece of soot clings to the bar of a grate it is a sign that a stranger may be expected; and if it hangs down a long flake you can ascertain what day the stranger will come by clapping your hands close to it until it falls off by reason of the current of air thus created, whilst repeating at each stroke a day of the week.   Dorset (1922)

Further prognostication could be made from the size of the flake, and so on. First mentioned in the mid eighteenth century and lasting well into the twentieth, the belief is presumably now the victim of smokeless fuels and the demise of the domestic open fire.

Also well known was the meaning of a cinder falling from the fire:

> A cinder thrown out of the fire is eagerly examined, and if it is long
> and hollow, is called a coffin; if it is round, it is said to be a purse.
>
> Yorkshire *Leeds Mercury* (4 October 1879)

The earliest known reference is in 1727, in John Gay's poem 'The
Farmer's Wife and the Raven', but the belief was clearly already well
known at that time by the proverbial way in which it is mentioned. The
basic belief is remarkably stable over the years, although occasionally a
third shape (oval) was held to resemble a cradle and to predict a birth,
or the sound the cinder makes was significant: noiseless (funeral) or
clinking sound (money). As in other falling or spilling superstitions,
note was often taken of who the cinder flew towards, as they would
be the one for whom the omen was destined.

Part statement of social etiquette and part superstition, it was
previously a common saying that one should never poke another
person's fire – unless you had known them for seven years:

> we do not like strangers to stir our fires. This would only be done
> by a person of long-standing acquaintance, and is usually prefaced
> by the remark, 'May I poke your fire? I've known you seven years,
> I think'. And even though the hostess might assent, she would still
> think it not very good manners on the part of the other person.
>
> Co. Durham (1960)

This notion is reported only from England and Wales, and although
reasonably widespread, does not appear to date back further than the
late nineteenth century. Much more widely reported was another
belief that focused on the poker:

> If the fire does not burn well, and you want to 'draw it up', you should
> set the poker across the hearth, with the fore part leaning across the
> top bar of the grate, and you will have a good fire – if you wait long
> enough . . . I have seen the thing done scores of times.   Suffolk (1878)

While in the past some maintained hotly that it was a scientific
fact that this stratagem worked, with an explanation involving split
draughts, others were equally sure that it was practised to keep witches
or other evil powers away, by forming a cross between the vertical
poker and the horizontal bars of the grate. Either way, the custom
was certainly very common, and was already well known in the early
eighteenth century.

knives

In superstition, as in real life, knives are tricky things, and can have both negative and positive attributes in different contexts. While their sharpness can be dangerous – physically as well as symbolically – they can also be protective. Many of the knife beliefs can thus be seen as a combination of superstition, etiquette, tradition, and common-sense safety, but the negative beliefs surpass the positive in both number and popularity.

An extremely widespread superstition dictates that one must never make a gift of a knife, pair of scissors, or other sharp object, to another person, unless the recipient pays for it with a trifle. As reported in 1912:

> When lads and lasses gave their sweethearts scissors or knives, great care was taken that something should be passed in return – a kiss, a handkerchief, or a small coin. This custom was 'thought much of', and now and then a lass would give a knife, and refuse anything in return, on purpose to cut love. But I never knew a lad to do so.

There are abundant examples from all over the British Isles, including a letter from young Dorothy Osborne to her estranged lover in 1654:

> Did not you say once you knew where good French tweeses were to bee had? Send me a payer, they shall cutt noe love.

The origin is still unknown, but it is interesting to note that the three earliest examples – 1611, 1619, 1620 – are so close to each other that we can assume either that it was already well known at that time, or perhaps was fashionably new.

crossed knives

Another extremely widespread superstition maintains that knives (or occasionally knife and fork) laid across each other are very unlucky and presage at best a quarrel and at worst a death:

> The sight of accidentally crossed knives upon our luncheon table today caused a distinct shudder to run through my wife and grown-up daughters . . . The nearest one made a grab at the offending cutlery and at once carefully placed the knives parallel. Further, they almost simultaneously exclaimed, with evident concern,

'Crossed knives! dear me, how very unlucky'. This belief is general
throughout Devonshire.   Devon (1902)

The superstition is well reported across the whole of England, but is
recorded much less frequently in the other parts of the British Isles,
and it is something of a puzzle. For a start, it appears to contradict
two widespread motifs. Elsewhere in superstitious tradition, the sign
of the cross is always beneficial and protective, and so too is metal.
Nevertheless, as the most commonly predicted result of crossed knives
is a quarrel, and occasional informants state that other edged tools
such as sickles must also not be crossed, it has been argued that the
symbolism here invoked is the 'crossed swords' of battle. It has also
been suggested that before the Reformation it was normal to place
one's cutlery in a cross form (despite the fact that forks were not
generally used until the late seventeenth century), as a pious protection
and benediction of the meal. As with all such back-formed origin
theories, this sounds plausible enough, but is at best unproven and is
probably nonsense. Another nineteenth-century explanation was that
the crossed knives were branded as superstitious and therefore banned
by the revolutionaries of the French Revolution. This too can be
readily discounted, as a number of references pre-date that event by
many decades.

The picture is further clouded by disagreements over the etiquette
of knife handling at the table. Modern middle-class British table-
manners dictate that knife and fork be placed together, side by side,
to signify that one has finished eating, while if they are laid down
somewhat apart it signals that the meal continues. But this was once
far from universal:

In the Midland counties, when I was a lad, we used to leave our
knife and fork crossed on our plate when we desired a second 'help'
and side by side when we did not.   Midland England (1903)

The ban on crossed knives was already well known in the early
eighteenth century, as several writers make clear reference to it. The
only earlier reference, as discovered by Iona Opie and Moira Tatem,
is not so clear, and introduces the notion of witchcraft:

Some marks of witches altogether unwarrantable, as proceeding
from ignorance, humor, superstition ... are ... the sticking of
knives across, &c.   Gaule, *Select Cases of Conscience Touching Witches* (1646)

knives dropped and spun

If you drop a knife, it means that a man is coming to the house. The gas-man and a friend arriving almost immediately after this announcement on the occasion of such accident, fulfilled it to the great satisfaction of the speaker.   Devon (1926)

In most cases, a dropped knife means a man coming, a fork means a woman, and a spoon either a child or a fool. The notion of the dropped knife was formerly extremely widespread, being noted all the way from Cornwall to the Orkneys. The earliest mention is from Shropshire in 1873, and there are several other examples before the turn of the century, but the superstition did not seem to reach its full popularity until well into the twentieth century. Other aspects of a dropped knife include the belief that the person who drops it should not pick it up, a common motif for things dropped.

Lesser-known knife superstitions also abounded in the nineteenth and twentieth centuries. For example, a knife spinning round on the table could be good or bad, depending on whether it was deliberate or accidental:

If a knife turns round and stops with its point towards me (say when I'm washing up and put it on the table) I always dodge to one side out of its way.   Lancashire (1985)

mirrors, photographs, and pictures

There is no doubt that mirrors have an uncanny side in many people's minds, even today. A scene with the female victim in front of a mirror is almost a cliché of horror and thriller films, and in the past traditions about covering mirrors on a death occurring in the house, or gazing into a mirror at midnight on Hallowe'en to see the reflection of a future lover, worked on the same idea. But while this seems to explain some of our mirror beliefs, others appear to be based on different principles, and we must be careful not to simply presume a potential 'supernatural' basis for them all.

The idea that breaking a mirror means bad luck is one of the most common superstitions in Britain today. The first known reference dates from only 1777, but others follow soon after, and are very similar in content:

> To break a looking-glass is extremely unlucky; the party to whom
> it belongs will lose his best friend ... Breaking a looking-glass
> betokens a mortality in the family.
>
> Francis Grose, *Provincial Glossary* (1787)

The belief is clearly widespread through the nineteenth and twentieth
centuries, and most of the references continue to simply predict
unspecified bad luck or death of a family member with no elaboration.
The specific 'seven years bad luck', so common nowadays, appears
from only 1851 onwards, but still has the power to upset people:

> In February 1996 a young woman who was hurriedly packing her
> possessions (on the break-up of her marriage), heard the mirror on
> the inside of her vanity-case break. She burst into tears, saying 'As
> if I didn't have enough troubles – now I'm going to have seven
> years!'   Sussex (1996)

The underlying rationale of such a belief is not immediately clear, but
comparison with similar superstitions concerned with pictures and
photographs suggests the idea of a lasting personal connection between the mirror and its owner brought about by its ability to reflect
the person's image. If the reflection symbolizes the person, bad things
happening to one will influence the other. This is an attractively
simple theory, but is undermined by the fact that many of the early
sources specifically state that the breakage may predict the death
of someone else, not simply the owner or the one who causes the
breaking.

Not as well known as some of the other mirror superstitions, the
idea that it is unlucky for a baby to see itself in a mirror was reasonably
widespread from the mid nineteenth to the later twentieth century,
but is almost certainly forgotten now. The period of prohibition varied
from four months to two years, or before the child could walk, talk,
or had teeth. Similarly, the consequence varied from general bad luck
to contracting rickets, becoming cross-eyed, or having a hard time
teething. The underlying belief might have been to do with preventing
the child from being vain, but if the 'mirror = self' hypothesis is true,
then it could have been seen as tempting fate to give the mirror power
over the child's well-being.

When death occurred in a house, a number of traditionally sanctioned customs were carried out. One of these was covering any

mirrors or pictures in the room (or even in the whole house), a practice which was sometimes extended to all ornaments:

> The custom of covering, not looking-glasses only, but various articles in the apartment where the corpse is laid, was, and is even yet, a well-known custom in Scotland ... Different individuals have different whims ('frets' they call them); for example, I have heard of persons turning the face of a looking-glass to the wall on the occurrence of a death, while some turn the face of a portrait of the deceased in like fashion, should there chance to be one in the house.   Glasgow (1888)

The earliest known reference, from Orkney, is from the 1780s, but the custom is very well documented in the nineteenth and first half of the twentieth centuries. In the majority of instances where a reason is stated, the fear is expressed that anyone looking into a mirror at such a time, even if only accidentally, will see either an unspecified apparition or the dead person looking over their shoulder – clearly something to be avoided. Some informants offer a more symbolic interpretation that for the dead 'all vanity is over', or that they are beyond all everyday needs.

Another mirror superstition seems to be based on some form of scientific reasoning, even if a little misguided. In a thunderstorm, shiny or reflective objects or surfaces could attract lightning, and so must be covered or put away:

> At the first sign of a thunderstorm Mum had taught us to cover up the looking-glass and the water-jug with cloths, otherwise it was a direct invitation to have the house struck by lightning.
>
> London (1920s)

The belief was reported regularly through the twentieth century, from various parts of England, at least up to the 1980s.

It is possible that some of the underlying beliefs in mirror superstitions are related to those concerned with pictures and photographs. The sudden falling of a picture from the wall has been widely regarded as ominous, but although the broad pattern is similar, details vary from case to case. The strongest notion is that if the picture is a portrait then the person portrayed is definitely not long for this world. In other cases, a distinction is made between whether the glass is broken in the fall – if so, a death is expected soon in the family; if not,

simple bad luck is predicted. The earliest references are from the
seventeenth century, commencing with Heylin's *Life of William Laud*
(1668) in which the archbishop is described as finding a portrait of
himself fallen flat on the floor, and wondering if it is an omen.

The supposed close connection between a photograph or portrait
and its human subject is also reflected in a sense of unease which many
people in the past reportedly felt about having their photograph taken:

> To the present day they [Gypsies] fear – or affect to fear – the
> taking of their photographs . . . 'No, doctor, I ain't going to have
> you take my photygraph no more. I've had nought but ill-luck since
> you took me last year,' said a handsome old Romany woman. 'I'm
> sorry for that,' I said, 'because I've got some packets of your favourite
> 'Nosegay' baccy with me, that I meant to give you if . . .', 'Oh well,
> doctor,' she hastened to add, 'seeing as how 'tis you.'

> Sussex, *Sussex County Mag* (1939)

Reports of this belief are spread across England, Scotland, and Ireland,
but do not seem to have appeared before the mid nineteenth century.
It is tempting to argue that this dating reflects the invention and rise
of photography, and therefore the gradual spread of access to personal
photography across the populace. But the first reference, from Cam-
bridgeshire Gypsies in 1851, describes a violent objection to being
sketched.

ornaments

Many British homes in the past sported china ornaments of various
shapes and sizes, whose prime purpose was decorative and aesthetic.
Nevertheless, a few reports indicate ulterior motives and even claim
china dogs and flying ducks as good-luck objects. The one belief
which was more widely known concerned the placing of the ornament:

> It is a superstition in my family . . . that any ornament which has a
> face should be so placed that it is facing the door by which one
> normally enters the room. I am not sure whether it is so that one
> can see its face – or it can see yours. Not to do so is considered
> unlucky, and it was suggested that the death of my father in 1967
> was affected (or portended) by an ornament being accidentally
> turned round some weeks earlier. I presume that the very common
> ornament of a few years ago, the carved black elephant, either

caused a general superstition to be attached to a particular ornament, the elephant, or a particular superstition to become generalised.

London/Essex (1970)

None of these ornament beliefs has been found earlier than 1940.

pins

The humble pin features in a wide range of beliefs, both as central character and in walk-on parts, but the reason for its being there varies from case to case. In some superstitions, the pin's pointed nature symbolizes attack or defence. Pins have been used extensively in witchcraft, both for harming (e.g. sticking pins in effigies) and for counter-spells (sticking pins in the heart of a bewitched animal to get back at the witch, or placing pins in witch bottles). Its sharpness makes a pin dangerous to find if pointing towards you, and, as is commonly said of knives, to give one to someone is unlucky because it 'cuts the love' between you.

Pins can take on the attributes of a particular occasion: when they are taken from a bride's dress they can carry the power to help bring on another wedding. In dressmaking and tailoring, they can be good or bad, depending on the situation. They can be stuck into onions as part of love-divination ceremonies, or pointed at warts to help cure them, but they must not be taken on to a fishing trawler.

Pins are also symbols of insignificance – things are 'not worth a pin'. If one must give or leave something, a pin is the most nominal thing there is, a gesture. This is probably the reason behind the throwing of pins into wells.

Since at least early Victorian times, we have been exhorted in a very well-known rhyme not to pass by and leave a pin on the floor or in the street:

> See a pin and pick it up
> All the day you'll have good luck
> See a pin and let it lay
> You will have bad luck all day.
>
> Lincolnshire (1936)

The wording of the third and fourth lines varies considerably, but the point is always the same. In this case the meaning seems to be simply that of thrift – take care of the pennies and the pounds will look after themselves. Samuel Pepys recorded in his *Diary* for 2 January 1668, 'I see your majesty do not remember the old English proverb, "He that will not stoop for a pin, will never be worth a pound"', and more recently a Welsh proverb maintains: *Gwell plygu at bin, na phlygu at ddim* (It is better to bend down for a pin, than to bend down for nothing) (W. Wales, 1911).

The first known appearance of the rhyme is in 1842, and it is still regularly quoted today. Nevertheless, it is flatly contradicted by another, less common, maxim: 'Pick up a pin and you pick up poverty' (Norfolk, *c.*1895), or 'Pick up pins, pick up sorrow' (Shropshire, 1883). To complicate matters further, some sources claim that a pin is only lucky if its head is towards you. This variation is in line with beliefs about other sharp-edged finds, such as knives, and is much older than the common rhyme, as it is mentioned in William Congreve's play *Love for Love* (1695).

The sharpness of the pin seems to be at the root of a range of prohibitions regarding giving or lending them:

> Many north country people would not, on any account, lend another a pin. They will say, 'You may take one, but mind, I do not give it.'
>
> N. England (1866)

Others stipulate that you must not say 'thank you' for a pin. This may be another manifestation of the ban on sharp edges in gifts, but similar references from the eighteenth century could be taken to mean that the real worry then was that the recipient might put themselves into a witch's power:

> This very old woman had the reputation of a witch. There was not a maid in the parish that would take a pin of her, though she should offer a bag of money with it.   *Spectator* (14 July 1711)

Alternatively, this could simply mean 'wouldn't take even a trifle from a witch'.

Any item associated with weddings can take on a 'lucky' aspect, and pins used in wedding dresses are no exception:

> A bride, on her return from church, is often robbed of all the pins about her dress by the single women present, from the belief that whoever possess one of them will be married in the course of a year.
>
> Sussex (1878)

This belief was quite well known in the later nineteenth and twentieth centuries, but has presumably faded out with the use of pins in dresses. It may, however, be much older. Iona Opie and Moira Tatem reprint a piece describing the marriage of Mary Queen of Scots in 1565: 'She suffreth them that stood by, everie man that coulde approche to take owte a pyn [from her wedding gown].'

scissors

Dropping a pair of scissors has been deemed significant by many people since the late nineteenth century – especially by dressmakers and others for whom they are basic tools of the trade. There is little agreement, however, on the exact meaning, which varies from a visitor, a wedding, or even a death, but this depends on whether the points stick into the floor or not. The further notion that it is unlucky to pick up dropped items yourself also applies to other domestic items such as umbrellas and cutlery. Scissors are included in the general super-stition that one must never give a gift of a sharp object, such as a knife, to a friend unless s/he gives something back in exchange, such as a small coin. Otherwise, the transaction will 'cut the love' between you.

spades

A spade may be a perfectly innocent tool to most people, but to the superstitious mind its overwhelming characteristic has been its connection with the grave:

> If in your house a man shoulders a spade
> For you or your kinsfolk a grave is half made.
>> Warwickshire (1875)

In almost all the reported cases, the carrying 'on the shoulder' is the particularly ominous detail. This omen was only reported from a relatively restricted area of England, and only since the mid nineteenth century, but continued well into the twentieth century.

spoons

A wide range of domestic items are believed to take on significance if they are dropped. A dropped knife or fork means that a visitor will arrive soon. A spoon is also sometimes included in this meaning, but it can also mean bad news or a disappointment, and, again in common with other dropping beliefs, the item must be picked up by someone else or bad luck will follow. None of these cutlery superstitions seems to be older than the late nineteenth century.

Another widespread domestic superstition holds that two spoons in somebody's saucer presages a wedding. This meaning is the most commonly reported, but considering the simple nature of the belief, a surprising number of variants have been recorded. These are all concerned with marriage and pregnancy.

> Two spoons in a cup: one woman'll become pregnant
> Two spoons in a saucer means a wedding.
>
> Lincolnshire (1992)

In common with many domestic superstitions, this one seems to be a Victorian invention: there is no sign of it before 1872. It has lasted well, however, and is still regularly quoted in appropriate circumstances.

stairs

Three well-known superstitions focus on the stairs. The most widespread, still often quoted, warns that it is unlucky to pass someone on the stairs:

> A lady from the country ascending the stairs of a house in the neighbourhood of Bedford Square, saw another lady, occupying apartments in the house, in the act of descending the same flight. The first-named lady, a visitor, stood on one side to allow the lodger to pass her. 'No thank you', said the latter; 'I never pass anyone on the stairs; it would be unlucky'. On this, the speaker retreated to her own rooms until the visitor had passed.   London (1890)

The majority of references simply give 'bad luck' as the result, but one or two suggest that it means a quarrel or a parting. On the available evidence, this notion is surprisingly recent, as the first known reference is only from 1865.

Demonstrably older is a concern with stumbling or tripping on the stairs, but with two very different meanings for the two directions of travel.

> But then I stumbled coming down stairs, and met a weasel; bad omens those.   William Congreve, *Love for Love* (1695)

> If a girl stumbles when going upstairs, it is a sign that she will
> marry shortly, but she must not look back after stumbling or the
> omen will not be fulfilled.   Oxfordshire (1952)

Stumbling down is reported less often, perhaps because it is so obviously unfortunate that many people do not regard it as a superstition
at all. Tripping up the stairs – by accident, of course – has been
reported regularly, with a remarkably consistent meaning of a coming
wedding, since its first appearance in the humorous survey of superstitions published in the *Connoisseur* in 1755.

tablecloths, sheets, etc.

The dominant superstition regarding tablecloths and sheets is the fear
of finding a 'coffin' shape created in the centre when it is unfolded:

> Recently, a Stratford lady of considerable mental attainment assured
> the writer that, before her husband died, for some weeks the
> newly-washed table linen showed a 'diamond' in the centre, and
> however carefully the cloth was folded it could not be avoided. The
> trouble ceased with his death.   Warwickshire (c.1930)

The belief has a relatively short recorded history – starting only in
1868 – but it was still well known in the late twentieth century,
although clearly losing its power to cause real concern.

tables

In the domestic sphere, a major superstitious concern since the 1890s
has been the bad luck consequent to placing certain items on the table.
The most often-quoted culprits are shoes, followed by bellows and
umbrellas, but a few reports include other things such as lanterns,
dustpans, and saucepans. This concern was widely reported in the
twentieth century, and in the case of shoes is still well known, but it
cannot be shown to be much more than 100 years old. Other concerns
with tables seem to be similarly recent. Sitting on a table, for example,
means you will never get married, but the idea that shaking hands
over a table brings a quarrel is reported from at least the early 1870s.

washing

The domestic wash-day has had its share of superstition, although the most widespread beliefs are simply concerned with when, rather than how, the washing is carried out. Records show that there were several days in the year when washing was forbidden, most commonly New Year's Day and Good Friday, but Holy Innocents' Day and Ascension Day were sometimes mentioned. The ban on Good Friday washing is supported by a story about Jesus Christ:

> Blessed is the woman who bakes on Good Friday, and five Fridays afterwards. The cursed is the woman who washes on Good Friday and five Fridays afterwards. The reason given for this is: When our Lord was going to be crucified He went to a woman's house to ask for succour. She was washing, and threw soap-suds at Him; then He went to another woman's house, she was baking, and gave Him a cake. He cursed in the one case and blessed in the other.
>
> Berkshire (1902)

In a number of versions, clothes put out to dry on Good Friday were found spotted with blood, or worse, the very soap-suds turned red. As with all these washing prohibitions, the risk was also that you would 'wash one of the family away'.

Two aspects of these traditions emerge from the references which have so far come to light. Firstly, they are surprisingly recent – no report before 1836, and the majority from the twentieth century. Secondly, they are all from England (apart from one example from Guernsey). The New Year and Holy Innocents versions are particularly restricted, all coming from the West Country. A specialized version of the no-washing rule has been found in fishing communities; not only are such families more likely to abide by the interdiction against washing on particular days, but many also have the added washing ban on the day their men set sail, as the symbolic connection between washing and being 'washed away' is too close for comfort.

In addition to the restrictions on washing on certain days in the year, there was a rhyme which dictated which days were suitable for the job:

> They who wash on Monday, have all the week to dry
> They who wash on Tuesday, are not so much awry

> They who wash on Wednesday, are not so had as the morrow
> They who wash on Thursday, wash for sorrow
> They who wash on Friday, wash in haste and need
> They who wash on Saturday, Oh they are sluts indeed.
>
> Bedfordshire, *Bedfordshire Magazine* (1954)

Versions vary little, and it is not clear how well known the rhyme was. The earliest known example dates from only the 1840s – about the same time that similar day-by-day rhymes about fingernail cutting and sneezing appeared. In addition, a handful of twentieth-century references specifically prohibit washing blankets in May, either because they will shrink, or more ominously, because someone will die.

The perils of the domestic wash-day are not solely confined to when the work is done:

> The woman who wets her apron very much, or splashes the water
> much about, will have a drunken husband.   Wales (1909)

The symbolism is fairly obvious, but the main surprise here is that this was still being said (by a young student) in the 1980s.

FURTHER AFIELD

horseshoes

The horseshoe is without doubt the most instantly recognizable graphic symbol of good luck in Britain and Ireland today. Horseshoe shapes appear routinely on good-luck cards, confetti and other wedding paraphernalia, brooches, charm bracelets and other jewellery, advertisements, and anywhere that the concept of luck needs to be graphically represented. We all understand it at a glance, and it is challenged in the good-luck context only by the shamrock/clover and crossed fingers. Everybody knows that it is lucky to nail a horseshoe to your door, and many still do so, but less well known today is the notion that it is lucky to *find* a horseshoe. Indeed, many of the earlier references make it clear that it is only a shoe that has been accidentally found that is worth nailing to the door or keeping for luck, as noted here in 1942:

> Horse-shoes that are found by the owner have ten times the power
> of those acquired in other ways, while one that is bought is useless.

Some even maintain that the found shoe must still have some nails in it, and many thought it was lucky to carry the shoe, or something associated with it, around with them. The earliest reference to the luck of finding a horseshoe dates from a late fourteenth-century manuscript (C. R. Rypon MS Harl. 4894, quoted Opie and Tatem) – 200 years before the first mention of nailing shoes up for protection, and on this evidence it is quite possible that the latter was simply a development of the former. The earliest reference to nailing a shoe on the door appeared in the late sixteenth century, but it was clearly already in general use:

> To shew you how to prevent and cure all mischiefs wrought by these charms and witchcrafts ... One principal way is to nail a horse shoe at the inside of the outmost threshold of your house, and so you shall be sure no witch will have power to enter thereinto. And if you mark it, you shall found that rule observed in many country houses.   Reginald Scot, *Discoverie of Witchcraft* (1584)

This meaning of a barrier to witches remained remarkably constant until the late nineteenth century when it began to degenerate into the colourless 'for luck' meaning it has for most people today.

There has been continued controversy about the right way to hang the horseshoe for at least 300 years. There is no definitive answer, as both ways have had their stalwart defenders. The earliest known description, in Joseph Blagrave's *Astrological Practice* (1671), maintains that the heel (the open prongs) must be upwards, and, on balance, most subsequent writers have agreed. This is certainly the most common way up nowadays, but is still far from universal. Furthermore, examples of graphical imagery from the past confirm that the symbol was regularly displayed with prongs down, especially when the design included an illustration within the shoe. In this debate, the champions of the 'prongs up' position have long used the mnemonic, first floated in the nineteenth century, that the luck runs out of the ends if it is put up the wrong way. This, however, is countered by saying that with the prongs upwards, the Devil sits in the shoe.

No remotely convincing reason for the faith in horseshoes has been forthcoming, although plenty of unconvincing ones have been proposed, ranging from the crescent moon of ancient Egyptian religion, a cult of horse-worship in pagan Britain, or the shoe representing the horned god – which one would have thought would attract witches rather than repel them. Apart from their complete lack of supporting evidence, one problem of explanations which extrapolate backwards is that they presume that it was the shape, or the connection with the horse, which was originally important, but what evidence there is indicates that it was primarily the metal which was valued.

iron

Finding and picking up a piece of metal in the road was regarded as lucky, especially if it was a horseshoe, of course. What was done with the metal once it was found varied from person to person; some took it home, or carried it about with them for luck:

> Picking up scraps of iron – I knew this custom as a regular thing in Derbyshire when a lad, and have known many others in various places do the same. One I know who had quite a collection of odd nails – horseshoe nails mostly – and bits of iron.   Derbyshire (1905)

But others actually thought it was unlucky to take old iron into the house. Some went through a little ritual, similar to that used in other contexts with things picked up in the street, of throwing it over their shoulder for luck. The idea that it is lucky to find a horseshoe was so well known that it effectively eclipsed the idea that finding any piece of iron was fortunate, even though the latter may have been the basis of the former. Iron has a very positive reputation in British superstition, but it is not clear why. In some contexts, including as a horseshoe, it had protective qualities – against fairies and witches – and this may simply explain why it was lucky to find it.

The earliest reference to finding iron is in the same source as that for the lucky horseshoe, the Harleian manuscript of the late fourteenth century which says 'iron nails are among the lucky finds' (quoted in Opie and Tatem), and it is mentioned regularly in seventeenth-century sources.

It was generally agreed that both witches and fairies disliked iron, and could be kept at bay by its presence. Apart from hanging a horseshoe on the door or wall, various other strategies were adopted to capitalize on this protective quality. Iron was regularly deposited in places thought particularly vulnerable to ill-wishing, such as the stable or the dairy, or at times of danger such as childbirth, or at sea.

> And a piece of iron should be sewn in the infant's clothes, and kept there till after the baptism.   Ireland (1888)

The earliest clear reference is in one of Robert Herrick's poems, 'Another Charme for Stables', published in 1648 while he was living in Devon, which advised the reader to hang up metal tools such as shears to keep the horses from being hag-ridden. This antipathy to iron felt by witches and fairies has never been satisfactorily explained, but was widely known, at least from the seventeenth to mid twentieth centuries. A late Victorian explanation, which still appears regularly in popular works on superstition, was that when the use of iron was first discovered most people were so in awe of it that they regarded it as a sacred substance. This was, of course, pure speculation, with no shred of evidence, nor even any probability, to support it. The idea that a superstition can have lasted, virtually intact, from the beginning of the Iron Age to the present day is hardly credible.

walking under ladders

The prohibition against walking under a ladder is one of the most widespread superstitions of modern Britain. It is unlikely that any adult does not know it – even if they do not believe it – and it is routinely acted upon even by many who profess not to be superstitious. The fact that it is one of the few well-known beliefs to have a genuine pragmatic value ensures that believers and sceptics alike have an interest in observing it, a frame of mind gently spoofed by the magazine *Punch* (1 January 1881):

> It is considered unfortunate by some people to go underneath a ladder. These are the people on whom workmen have dropped pots of paint and molten lead. Others consider it unfortunate to pass outside a ladder. These are they who have stepped off the pavement into the road and have been run over by traction-engines.

Several predicted results of walking under ladders have been given over the years. The earliest reference states simply that 'it may prevent your being married that year', and although this is not the most commonly cited result in later years, it was still being claimed by some informants in late Victorian times:

> Some few years ago I was walking with some friends along the streets of a considerable Midland town, when we reached a ladder reared against a house. We were a party of four; a young lady and a gentleman walking in front, a married lady and myself following. The two former walked straight on, unheeding. I, from force of habit, almost mechanically stepped into the roadway, and my companion followed me, exclaiming as she did so in horrified tones, 'Oh, Grace has walked under a ladder! Don't tell her, don't tell her!'

'Why not?' I asked innocently. 'What, don't you know? She'll never
be married now!'
                                                          Shropshire (1883)

Later references predicted that the careless pedestrian would end up
on the gallows. Nevertheless, the majority of historical sources, and
virtually everyone in modern times, simply state it is unlucky.

There are also several traditional ways of avoiding the ill luck.
Spitting is one (often specifically between the rungs of the offending
ladder, or a set number of times), and crossing your fingers is another;
both of which are regularly used in other protective contexts. More
modern prescriptions include details such as 'Don't speak till you see
a four-legged animal', or:

If you must pass under a ladder, cross your fingers and wish. The
unsophisticated spit; and if you are walking with someone wait for
him to speak first, and any ill luck that may be coming will fall on
his head.
                                                          Co. Durham (1910)

In popular tradition, there are three main contenders for the origin
of the ladder superstition. The one which appears to be the most
modern, and is certainly the most obtuse, is that the ladder, floor, and
wall form a triangle, and as Christians revere the Trinity, walking
through would be disrespectful. This explanation, which sounds like
one of the fanciful origin-explanations invented by journalists in the
1970s, was in fact already in circulation by the early 1930s. It is
suggested, for example, by Charles Igglesden in 1932. There is not the
slightest shred of evidence to support it, and it can be dismissed
unreservedly. The other two have at least the distinction of being
plausible and fitting with what we know of the workings of superstition
in general. One is that each ladder is symbolic of the ladder raised to
take Jesus Christ off the Cross, under which, some say, the Devil
lurked either glorying in his triumph or attempting to prevent the
removal. The other is that in some designs of gallows (depicted in
many popular prints), a ladder is shown leaning at an angle, up which
those about to die must climb. However, none of these suggestions is
supported by the earliest reference, which specifically claims the action
as detrimental to matrimonial opportunities, with which the crucifixion or the gallows would seem to have nothing in common.

The belief is so ubiquitous nowadays that it is difficult to imagine
a time when it was not so well known. But in later Victorian times, it

appears that some were unaware of its significance. Flora Thompson, that excellent observer of Oxfordshire village life, specifically states that she did not come across the belief in her youth, and Alexander Polson, writing of Highland Scotland at the turn of the twentieth century, comments, 'Neither was it thought unlucky to walk under a ladder'. The available documentary record therefore suggests that the ladder belief, from a slow start in the later eighteenth century, took time to achieve its total market penetration in the late twentieth.

money

For the superstitious person, the business of buying and selling was a delicate situation fraught with the threat of displeasure which could turn into ill-wishing and retribution. This was especially true for those selling animals, which are naturally subject to sudden illnesses and death, while their bad points can be disguised, their history concealed, and any subsequent fault blamed on the seller. The three most widespread traditions involved in buying and selling were handselling, spitting on hands and money received, and the giving of luck money.

At a market, or any other venue where selling takes place, the theory of handselling is that the first money taken is lucky and sets up good fortune for the day, but another belief – that it is unlucky to turn away the first offer of the day – complicated matters, as in this account from 1880:

> In the street market places, amongst the stall-keepers, it is reckoned to be nothing else than ruinous to turn away a 'first bid' for an article. It brings bad luck on the day's selling, and it is better to get the 'hansel' (as the first sale is called) over, even at a loss . . . And when he has taken hansel money, he would as soon think of throwing it into the road, as putting it into his pocket without first 'spitting on it'.

The transaction itself involves a certain degree of trust, but both sides must try to get advantage over the other. By praising an item too much, a seller would tempt fate and risk bad luck. If the buyer criticized the item, in order to lower the price, s/he had to add a ritualistic phrase to make it clear that no ill-wishing was intended. Reginald Scot shows that this was already the case in the 1580s:

You shall not hear a butcher or horsecourser cheapen a bullock or
a jade, but if he buy him not, he saith 'God save him'; if he do
forget it, and the horse or bullock chance to die, the fault is imputed
to the chapman.   Reginald Scot, *Discoverie of Witchcraft* (1584)

The customs described were formerly common all over the British
Isles, but there have also been many local variations. A reference from
Co. Tyrone in 1972 shows that even if you had no plans to sell an
animal, you were still potentially subject to superstition:

If somebody offers you a price for an animal you haven't put up for
sale, then take it because you won't get any more good out of the
animal. It has been blinked and will die.

luck money

One of the several traditions which covered the exchange of money,
the 'luck penny' or 'luck money' was given back to the buyer after s/he
had paid for the purchase, 'for luck':

A few years ago I sold a venerable carriage . . . to a young innkeeper
in East Lancashire for wedding and funeral purposes. In handing
me the money he asked for 'something back for luck' in such a
serious and formal manner . . . When he received my florin he
held it in the palm of his hand with some solemnity, and then
ceremoniously covered it with saliva before putting it in his pocket.
                                                          Lancashire (1903)

The amount given back was covered by loose, locally understood rules,
and was sometimes as much subject to bargaining as the purchase
price itself. The system was widely practised and deeply entrenched,
but it was open to abuse, and by the late nineteenth century was being
actively discouraged by farmers and businessmen, who regarded it as
an unofficial tax on their dealings. The concept of 'luck money' is
sometimes confused with that of 'earnest money' or 'God's penny'.
These are different ways of describing what was in effect a binding
deposit given before a sale or bargain, such as from a farmer to a farm
worker to secure his services for the coming term.

The notion of 'handselling' was also important in other contexts. If
one bought a new suit, for example, the tailor would place a small coin
in one of the pockets, to ensure that the wearer would always have

money. The same principle is still often in operation when giving a purse or wallet as a present:

> Another thing is that if a person bought a new bag or a new case or a new purse bag, the person that would have bought it for another person they would always put sixpence in it for good luck or for a 'hansel' because it was an old custom that when anybody would be giving a present of a purse it was the custom that they should put something in for luck.   Co. Wexford (1938)

Records show that even after the newness had worn off, it continued to be unlucky to allow any such receptacle to be empty, and references from the sixteenth century onwards reveal an idea that an empty purse or pocket was at risk of being occupied by the Devil himself. This idea was still being quoted over 300 years later:

> At an inquest held lately at Roydon, Essex, on the body of a man found on the line, a police constable stated that all the money he found on the deceased was one halfpenny, whereupon one of the jury said, 'They say that's to keep the devil out'.   Essex (1882)

finding money

To many people it may seem strange that finding money could have been regarded as unlucky, but such a belief is well attested from the sixteenth century until well into living memory. The earlier references simply state that finding, and keeping, money was unlucky, but later informants discriminate between circumstances and suggest protective strategies such as spitting on it.

> A sixpence is regarded by many as the most unlucky coin that can be found. Many people absolutely refuse to pick up a sixpence which has been lost. An instance is given in which some person picked up this unlucky coin in the road, and no end of illness followed on the daring act.   Cumberland (1907)

The one kind of money which was definitely lucky to find was 'crooked' money, also referred to as 'bowed' or 'bent'. Such coins have long been regarded as lucky pieces across Britain, and have been widely carried or worn to ensure good fortune or protect against bad. At least as early as the mid sixteenth century, bowed coins were being given to people by well-wishers 'for luck', and the practice was well known in the literature of the time. Even earlier, in the medieval period, bent coins were regularly offered to saints to accompany a vow, mark a pilgrimage, or request a cure.

From the early nineteenth century onwards, many reports focus on coins with holes in them:

> Mr Hooley [famous financier] asserts himself free from super-stition, but in point of fact he has one fad. Believing in the luck-bringing qualities of threepenny pieces with holes pierced in them, he gave his bankers a standing order to collect them for him, and used to give some to his friends, always carrying a lot of loose ones in his pocket.
> Cambridgeshire (1899)

The exact denomination does not seem to matter, although sixpences were mentioned more often than other coins.

Money also features in a wide variety of other beliefs, often ones concerned with the symbolic nature of beginnings: first footers should carry money when entering the house at New Year, one should turn over one's money when seeing a new moon, or when you hear a cuckoo for the first time, and so on. Not many superstitions promise good luck, but those that do often focus on money, as, for example, beliefs surrounding the tiny 'money-spider' and a certain shape of cinder falling from a fire, called a 'purse' by believers.

CLOTHES AND ACCESSORIES

Clothes feature in a very wide variety of superstitions, old and new, trivial and deadly serious. Thus, Sylvia Lovat Corbridge (born 1906), remembering her childhood in Lancashire:

> I would snatch a thread from a friend's dress because it would bring me a letter later in the day. On the rare occasions I wore anything green (even if it were only the leaf of the flower in my hat), I would solemnly put a piece of black material on my head when I came in, to make sure I would not wear mourning because, as everyone knew, black followed green . . . If I put my underslip on inside out, then it must not be changed that day, unless I wanted to miss my chance of receiving an unexpected present.

Accidental occurrences usually mean bad luck in British superstition, but as the above quote shows, one extremely widespread and long-lasting belief accounts it lucky to put an item of clothing on inside out, or back to front, as long as it is done accidentally and not put right when discovered.

> A retired schoolmistress reports that a child in her class arrived at school one morning very distressed as she had fallen and broken her wrist. 'I put my pinafore on inside out, and changed it back', she said, 'I didn't ought to have done it, did I?'   Dorset (1961–2)

The lucky interpretation has been steadily reported with little alteration since at least the eighteenth century (e.g. in William Congreve's *Love for Love*, 1695), but it is clear that other interpretations have been available:

> He that receiveth a mischance, will consider whether he . . . put on his shirt in the morning the contrary wyse.
>
> Reginald Scot, *Discoverie of Witchcraft* (1584)

Records show that other accidents happening to clothes were worthy of comment. If a woman's apron came undone, or fell off, the standard response was that her sweetheart must be thinking of her. This meaning was widely recorded from the 1860s to at least the 1950s, although other interpretations were occasionally recorded. In earlier days, when men and women wore garters which were tied with ribbons, similar things were said about that item coming undone. In the twentieth century, a woman's petticoat showing beneath her dress could elicit the comment 'Your father likes you more than your mother', presumably on the premise that a properly caring mother would notice and rectify the problem.

mending and mourning

It has been generally agreed, since at least 1850, that to mend clothes while wearing them brings bad luck, although the exact nature of the misfortune varies considerably, from 'evil will be spoken of you' to 'you'll never grow rich'.

Strict rules about mourning clothes have almost completely disappeared in recent decades, but up to the mid twentieth century there was a complex, well-nuanced code which most people at least tried to follow, and, not surprisingly, several widespread superstitions existed. Mourning clothes should not be kept in the house when not in use, and particular care was taken not to tempt fate by using them at any other time: 'If you put a widow's bonnet on you will become a widow yourself' (Derbyshire, 1895). Even in times of hardship, many people would not accept the clothes of anyone who had recently died, because it was generally believed that a dead person's clothes wore out very quickly, as the body rotted in the ground. The first known reference to this notion dates only from the mid nineteenth century, but it was still being quoted in the 1980s.

new clothes

The wearing of a new item of clothing for the first time was governed by a host of traditional rules. Many of these were concerned with notions of the importance of beginnings to future luck, such as the widespread custom of handselling new clothes by putting money in the pocket:

It was an old custom long ago with tailors to put either a penny or a half-penny in the pockets of the suit he would have made. Some say it was to hansel the suit. Others say that the person that would wear the suit would always have luck . . . Many people used not to go to a tailor that would not put something in the pockets of the suit. Co. Wexford (1938)

In other contexts, 'handselling' has a much longer history, but references to this new-clothes superstition have so far been found back to the second half of the nineteenth century only, although the idea was still being expressed in the 1950s. People wearing new clothes could also be greeted in a variety of ways:

It is proper to greet your friends with a pinch when they make their first appearance in new clothes . . . The kindly saying of one dear old lady, 'I wish you health to wear it, strength to tear it, and money to buy another with', formed a much pleasanter reception than the pinching. Shropshire (1883)

Tradition also dictated that new clothes should be worn at certain points in the year, to ensure future prosperity, and failure to do so would be punished by birds dropping on you. Whitsun, New Year, and Christmas Day are sometimes mentioned in this context, but Easter was the most popular time, and although reported widely in the nineteenth century, the custom was certainly not then a new one. Samuel Pepys wrote in 1662 of getting his wife new clothes 'against Easter', and in *Romeo and Juliet* (1597) Mercutio says, 'Didst thou not fall out with a tailor for wearing his new doublet before Easter?'

'ne'er cast a clout till May is out'

In the past, the decision when to stop wearing winter clothes was taken seriously. The ubiquitous phrase 'Cast ne'er [or Ne'er cast] a clout till May is out', first recorded in 1732, still causes controversy as to whether it means the month or the hawthorn plant, popularly called 'may'. Modern popular opinion appears to tend towards the plant, but this seems to be a relatively recent interpretation, and an examination of the phrase's history shows that it is definitely wrong. Other beliefs and sayings also focused on when to stop wearing particular clothes. A Sunday or Good Friday was usually thought best, because one therefore had the congregation's prayers as protection.

Dozens of other clothes-related beliefs were reported only once or twice during the last hundred years or so, but it is never clear how widespread these might have been – or even how seriously they were taken. For example:

> My wife was recently told by an old Hertfordshire woman that she should never iron the tail of a shirt, because by so doing she would be ironing the money out of it.   Herefordshire (1928)

bad luck to wear green

Apart from black, with its funeral associations, green is the only colour to be consistently regarded as unlucky across the British Isles. The strongest prohibition focused on clothes:

> The other day I heard a well-educated Hull lady say she had only had three green dresses during her lifetime, and in each instance she had had to put them aside to wear mourning for those dear to her. Never again, she said, would she appear in green, which she linked so closely with death.   Yorkshire (1901)

The colour was particularly unlucky for weddings, which was summed up in the oft-quoted phrase 'Green is forsaken and yellow is foresworn'. The dislike of the colour also manifested itself in other areas in the twentieth century. Many everyday items came under the ban, as in this comment overheard in 1962:

> A chemist giving orders for hot-water bottles said, 'For heaven's sake don't send any more green ones. Folk don't want them. Superstition I suppose. I've still ten left.'

Similarly, green cars are still proverbially difficult to sell.

This superstition is usually presumed to be ancient, but there is no evidence to support this idea. The earliest known reference describes a Yorkshire wedding, in the *Gentleman's Magazine* of 1793, although the wording implies that it was already well entrenched. The belief does not seem to feature in the prolific writings of the seventeenth- and eighteen-century dramatists, where one would certainly expect to find it if it did exist at that time, nor in any earlier published material so far located. There are numerous mentions of green clothing, without any perceptible hint of a bad reputation.

A number of informants stated that the reason for green's bad reputation was that it was the favourite colour of the fairies, and they resented mortals wearing it. This notion reads like a modern invented origin, because there is little evidence that fairies were particularly partial to green, but it was already in circulation in Scotland in the early nineteenth century, and by the twentieth century had become the orthodox explanation.

handkerchiefs

A few miscellaneous traditions centre on the humble handkerchief, although none is very widely recorded:

> It is very unlucky, I am told, to put your clean handkerchief into your pocket folded up. It should always be opened before being put into that receptacle.   Midland England, *Midland Garner* (1884)

Many people still claim that tying a knot in your handkerchief helps you to remember something, but this in itself is not always sufficient:

> Some years ago I mentioned to a friend that, though I often tied a knot in my handkerchief in order to remember something, I generally forgot what the thing was I had wanted to remember. 'Oh!' said he, 'you should whisper "rabbits" three times into the knot as you tie it. Then you'll remember.' I have met other persons acquainted with this custom, but not very many.
>
> Gloucester, *Saturday Westminster Gazette* (5 April 1919)

That the knotting is no recent innovation is demonstrated by a reference from the thirteenth-century work of advice to women about to become religious recluses:

> a man ties a knot in his girdle to remember a thing; but our Lord, in order never to forget us, made a mark of piercing in both His hands.   *Ancren Riwle* (c.1230)

The natural association between handkerchiefs and crying also resulted in another tradition that it was unlucky to borrow or give one. This was reported as still current in the 1980s, and many years earlier William Drummond referred to a handkerchief as an 'ominous present' and a 'gift miserable' in his *Poems* of *c.*1614.

shoes

A very wide range of beliefs focused on shoes in one way or another. By far the most common of those still current dictates that they must not be placed on a table:

> It is unlucky to put boots on the table, but the ill-luck may be counteracted by spitting on the soles. Some years ago, after examining and condemning a pair of narrow-toed boots in a ploughman's house, I placed them on the table and the ploughman's wife immediately removed them, saying: 'Would ye hae strife in the hoose afore nicht?' Aberdeenshire (1914)

Most references stipulate *new* shoes, and the penalty varies. Simple ill luck or a quarrel are the most often quoted, but some versions predict 'you'll never marry', or even imminent death. The spitting antidote is rarely reported, and more usually people insist that the person who is unwise enough to put the shoes on the table must be the one to remove them.

No plausible explanation has been offered for this superstition; it has been proposed that shoes on the table suggest a corpse lying there, but there is no evidence to support this, and it is by no means an ancient belief, as the first known reference dates from only 1869. Nevertheless, it is still widely known and followed:

> [Oxfam shop worker] A customer came up to me with a pair of slippers, hesitated, and said 'I suppose a counter isn't really a table'. I was puzzled and she explained that her mother had trained her never to put shoes on a table. So then I understood and reassured her – but even so I noticed that she passed the slippers to me hand-to-hand for me to bag up, so that it was I, not her, who put them down on the counter in order to take her money. Sussex (2001)

throwing a shoe for luck

From at least the sixteenth century to the middle of the twentieth, a standard way of wishing somebody good luck on a journey or for a new undertaking was to throw an old shoe after them. This was already proverbial in the first known mention by John Heywood (*Proverbs*, 1546) and was probably old even by his time, but by the 1820s it was increasingly described as primarily a wedding custom:

> The bride went straight away to her carriage. Someone thrust an old white pair of satin shoes into my hand with which I made an ineffectual shot at the post boy, and someone else behind me missed the carriage altogether and gave me with an old shoe a terrific blow on the back of the head.   Wiltshire, Francis Kilvert, *Diary* (1 January 1873)

The connection survived for a while in the custom of tying old shoes to the back of the newly-weds' car.

A more minor superstition, recorded since the 1840s, is still being said:

> Somebody walked past and their shoes squeaked. My colleague commented, 'My grandma used to say that if you have squeaky shoes it means you haven't paid for them.'   London (3 July 2002)

This can be compared to beliefs that a thread or pin left in clothes means that the tailor has not been paid.

The desire for a good beginning is a very powerful force in superstition, and putting your shoes on correctly is an important way of avoiding misfortune for the day. The general rule of right means good and left means bad applies here, as elsewhere, but is far from universal. Indeed, some informants specifically state the opposite. Occasionally, too, putting the left shoe on first is a prescription to prevent toothache.

umbrellas

The umbrella features in several superstitions which were previously well known, but which were mostly simply extensions of other beliefs about dropping things or putting them on tables or beds. Nevertheless, the one belief devoted entirely to the umbrella – that it must not be opened indoors – is one of the top ten most well-known superstitions of the present day. Even though it is a relatively simple belief, and it cannot be proved to be much more than 120 years old, there is still evidence that the belief has undergone change in its time. Most present-day informants simply claim it leads to bad luck, but earlier authorities, as here, were more likely to maintain that it meant death:

> If you open an umbrella in the house and hold it over your head, there will be a death in the house before the year is out.   Worcestershire (1909)

Only a minority of modern believers cite the part about 'holding it over your head'. No remotely sensible suggestion has been made as to why an umbrella indoors is considered so bad, although it could be argued that the belief is simply an example of the basic principle of 'appropriate categories' – outdoor items should not be brought indoors. The belief is essentially a twentieth-century phenomenon, with no sign of it yet before the 1880s. Umbrellas only became widely used in the early nineteenth century, which would seem to preclude any ancient origin, but this does not stop the origin-theorists from having a go. An explanation is in circulation at the time of writing which must take the prize, against stiff opposition, for the silliest theory of origin yet proposed for a current superstition. It explains that umbrellas were designed not to keep the rain off, but to provide shade from the sun. As the sun was worshipped at that time, putting an umbrella up indoors was an insult to the sun-god, and thus invited retribution. A less ambitious explanation at least has the virtue of simplicity, and has the hallmark of an evocative explanation given to children:

> We believed that goblins hid inside the umbrella and when it was
> opened the goblins would fly out.   Lincolnshire (1992)

An umbrella is one of the many items, such as shoes and bellows, which must not be placed on a table, for fear of bad luck or a quarrel, and, more rarely, the same is said about putting one on a bed. Umbrellas also share certain characteristics with other everyday items such as walking sticks, gloves and knives:

> In 1930 I dropped my umbrella in a train and was told by a
> country-woman in the compartment that I must not pick it up
> myself or I should have bad luck. In 1932 I dropped a parcel and
> was told by another country-woman the same thing.   Devon (1933)

This belief cannot be shown to be any earlier than the first decade of the twentieth century.

FOOD AND DRINK

bread

Most staple domestic items such as bread, fire, and candles have dual roles which straddle the practical and symbolic worlds, making them the ideal breeding ground for superstition. Thus bread can be simply a basic food or can be seen as a symbol of food essential for life, and by extension as a symbol of plenty.

The way the bread behaves while being made can therefore take on an importance beyond the family diet; for example, it can be blessed and used in official religious ritual, it can be presented to a newborn baby to ensure that it never lacks food, and it can be carried by a New Year first footer.

the hollow loaf

If a loaf was found to have a hole in it, this was interpreted as a grave or coffin, and indicated that someone close to the family would die soon.

> Then Granny cut me a slice of bread and butter and told me to go to bed. She looked at the loaf then and saw there was a big hole in the centre of it. She dropped the knife and said, 'Dear me, a coffin it is'. She went all white and trembly and the others looked frightened too. Then they spoke about the people they knew who were ill and wondered which one was going to die.   Wales (c.1870)

This idea is reported widely, at least in England and Wales, from about the 1870s, but occasionally it was said to foretell a pregnancy rather than a death. Less commonly recorded, from about the same

time, is the belief that if a loaf broke apart, either in baking or when
being sliced, it was considered an unlucky omen, but the exact meaning
varied from person to person.

It was regarded as particularly unlucky, even evil, to burn bread.
This appears to be a combination of the practical 'never waste food'
mentality and a feeling for the symbolic nature of bread, with even
crumbs being included in the prohibition, as recorded here in 1901:

> If a child threw crumbs in the fire the old-fashioned mother lifted
> a warning finger and said, 'If you throw crumbs in the fire you are
> feeding the devil.'

This belief was quite widely known, first noted in the 1880s, but it was
essentially a twentieth-century superstition, still being quoted in the
1980s.

crossing your bread

Marking bread with a cross during the bread-making process was a
widely reported custom, in England at least, throughout the nineteenth and well into the twentieth century:

> In Shropshire we always make a cross on the flour after putting it
> to rise for baking, also on the malt in mashing up for brewing. It's
> to keep it from being bewitched.   Shropshire (1875)

Some said it was to stop the Devil sitting on it, while in Yorkshire,
this action was called 'crossing the witches out'. It is usually assumed
that this tradition is a relic of pre-Reformation days, when making a
sign of the cross would have been commonplace when preparing and
eating food. This may be so, as the custom certainly existed in the
seventeenth century – it is mentioned by both the poet Robert Herrick
(1648) and the antiquarian John Aubrey (1686). But the only evidence
from before the mid seventeenth century is in negative form. For
example, in the time of Henry III (1252) bakers throughout Essex and
Hereford were forbidden by a royal mandate to mark the bread they
sold with the sign of the cross (*Close Rolls*) and the *Book of Common
Prayer* of 1549 insisted that the bread used in the rite of Communion
should be 'without any manner of print'.

An odd sort of belief, which in some versions sounds more like a
social cliché than a superstition:

> When you offer someone the last slice of bread-and-butter, or the
> last cake, on the plate, you say 'Which will you have, a handsome
> husband or a thousand a year?' and the other person usually says 'A
> thousand a year, and then I'll get the handsome husband as well'.
>
> Dorset (*c.*1935)

This is apparently still said in some quarters, but its meaning eludes
us.

eggs

Eggs seem to have more than their fair share of superstitions, which
cover the whole period from pre-production to their appearance on
the family table, and they also feature in love-divination procedures.
There have been numerous local beliefs, but the following were widely
known.

Witches like to use eggshells as boats, to go to sea and wreck real
ships, and for this reason anyone who eats a boiled egg must be careful
to break the shell afterwards:

> As soon as a Devonian has eaten a boiled egg, he thrusts a spoon
> through the end of the shell, opposite the one at which it was begun
> to be eaten. When I enquired why this was done, the reply given
> was: 'Tu keep they baggering witches vrom agwaine to zay in a
> egg-boat'. It is supposed that the witches appropriate the unbroken
> shells to sail out to sea to brew storms.   Devon (1892)

This custom is reported with little variation across Britain, although
in areas where fairies are more feared than witches it is they whose
machinations must be foiled. The idea of witches using shells as boats
goes back to at least the 1580s, as attested by Reginald Scot's *Discoverie
of Witchcraft*, and has been regularly reported ever since. Most of the
later informants imply that witches used the shells in some direct way
to go to sea, and why they did not simply get their own eggs for such
uses is not explained. However, at the root of the superstition may be
the notion that the eggs were used symbolically – placed in a tub of water
to represent ships, and the tub then agitated to cause a real storm at sea.

> Wells Parish Register: December 1583 – Perished upon the west
> coast, coming from Spain, Richard Waller [and thirteen others]
> whose deaths were brought to pass by the detestable working of an

execrable witch of Kings Lynn, whose name was Mother Gabley, by the boiling or rather labouring of certain eggs in a pail full of cold water, afterward approved sufficiently at the arraignment of ye said witch.   Norfolk *Norfolk Archaeology* (1859)

A different concern about eggshells was based on the idea of a sympathetic connection between objects which were once connected but have now been separated. If you burnt milk, for example, your cows would cease to produce, and on the same principle, if you burnt eggshells your hens would stop laying. A minor egg superstition prohibited taking eggs into, or out of, the house after sunset, and some egg-sellers refused to trade after dark. No explanation, rational or otherwise, is offered. The earliest known reference is from 1853, but it was still being said in the 1980s.

odd number of eggs

'Why does every old woman hold it as an indispensable rule to set her hen upon an odd number of eggs?' asked a correspondent to the *Gentleman's Magazine* in 1796. Unfortunately, no one wrote in to explain why, but he was correct in his assessment, and the custom was widely reported throughout the nineteenth and twentieth centuries:

> It's a strange queer thing, but an even number o' eggs (12 instead of
> 11 or 13) never hatches nowt but stags (cockerels).   Lincolnshire (1936)

The idea that odd numbers are lucky and even ones unlucky is a general rule in British superstitions, but many informants agreed that thirteen was the best number for eggs, and this is contrary to the modern general rule which holds this the unluckiest number of all. It is noticeable, however, that the earlier references all simply recommend an odd number, and it is only from the 1880s onwards – the same time as thirteen was beginning to be generally quoted as unlucky – that thirteen is singled out as desirable.

The earliest British reference is provided by John Aubrey (1686), who states, 'And our house-wives, in setting of their egges under the hen, do lay an odd number'; he also quotes Pliny, who devoted many pages to the lore and care of poultry, saying 'An odd number should be put under the hen' (*Natural History*, AD 77).

salt

Many superstitions are elusive because we lack basic information about their history and development and must rely on scattered references in which key factors are absent or obscure. In the case of salt and the superstitions in which it features, however, there is plenty of information, but firm conclusions are still elusive. There is no doubt that salt has been an extremely valuable commodity throughout recorded history. Whole empires have been founded on trade in it, wars have been fought to gain control of it, everybody needed it in one way or another. It made food preservation possible, and it was used to preserve the dead. There is also no doubt that in various civilizations, including those of the British Isles, salt was used in symbolic, magical, and religious ways. But how widely known these beliefs were, when they started, and how they fitted together is extremely difficult to fathom. The most widespread British superstition, that it is unlucky to spill salt, does not obviously mesh with any of these areas, and we must avoid the usual facile formula 'Salt was used in religious rites, therefore it was holy, therefore it was sacrilegious to waste it.'

The main problem is that it is not always easy to separate the symbolic and the magical from the mundane. Indeed, in this context they may be inseparable. Salt was burnt to counteract the power of witches, while in other reports it was simply placed in a baby's cradle for the same ends. Salt brought in by a first footer or given to a baby on its first visit to someone's house is apparently symbolic of the necessities of life, but any of the principals in these superstitious customs may also have had the anti-witchcraft motif in their heads, even if only as an added extra. Context is vital:

> The spilling of salt is not here always considered unlucky, nor is it yet by many; indeed, such a belief would be very awkward for those who cure fish.   Highland Scotland (1926)

The bad luck consequent on spilling salt is one of the best-known superstitions in the British Isles today. It is likely that every adult knows it, even if they do not believe it.

> If salt be accidentally overturned, it is unlucky for the person *towards* whom it falls. But if that person, without hesitation or remark, take up a single pinch of salt between the finger and thumb of his right

hand, and cast it over his left shoulder, the threatened misfortune
will be averted.   Lincolnshire, *Gentleman's Magazine* (1833)

The belief has been around for over 400 years, but there have been
some changes in that time. According to the available evidence – and
we have more for this superstition than for most others – the history
and development of the belief is interesting, but inconclusive. The
earliest recorded example is from Reginald Scot's *Discoverie of Witchcraft* of 1584:

> Amongst us there be manie women, and effinat men (marie papists
> alwaies, as by their superstition may appeere) that make great
> divinations upon the shedding of salt, wine, etc.

The next two references – from 1587 and 1597 – follow soon afterwards,
and we can take this as evidence that it was already well known at the
time, or perhaps that it was new and 'in fashion'. From then on it is
reported regularly up to the present day. One essential feature of the
earlier references, as shown in the first quotation above, which has
now been forgotten, is that it was unlucky for the person *towards*
whom the salt fell, not the person who spilt it. This belief is mentioned
regularly up to about 1833, but then seems to disappear. Another
change is that earlier references often threatened an argument or
quarrel as the result of the spillage, whereas it is now universally simply
bad luck. Occasional references in the late nineteenth century said
that every grain of spilt salt represented a tear to be cried later.

The modern way to avoid the promised ill luck is to throw a pinch over
your shoulder (most people stipulate the left shoulder). An alternative
method was to throw a pinch into the fire. This is first mentioned in 1711
but a later reference (1771) combines the two and instructs the salt spiller
to throw it *over their shoulder into the fire*. The fire motif continued to be
cited occasionally into the 1880s, but the shoulder motif is quoted far
more often. One modern explanation of the shoulder action is that the
Devil sits on your left shoulder, and the salt will blind him. This motif
of the devil sitting on the shoulder is very recent, and was probably
invented simply to explain the throwing. Many writers also confidently
state that the salt-spilling superstition originated at the Last Supper, at
which, we are told, Judas Iscariot upset the salt, and it was henceforth
deemed unlucky. It is repeatedly claimed that Leonardo Da Vinci's
painting of the Last Supper shows this, but it does not. This origin

explanation about Judas Iscariot was already current in 1865, when *Notes & Queries* contributors discussed the matter, but it has nothing in its favour, and, as usual, does not explain the 1,500-year gap between the supposed origin and the first verifiable reference. There appears to be no precedent for this superstition in the classical era. The real origin therefore remains unknown. The ban on spilling salt seems to have applied only to *accidental* spillages. There are several other traditions in which salt was thrown (e.g. in welcome, like confetti, or into the fire to cast spells or protect) or scattered in new houses.

burning salt

Salt was deliberately burnt in a variety of contexts, usually concerned with casting spells or protecting against ill-wishing by others.

> The power of a witch is supposed to be destroyed by sprinkling salt into the fire nine mornings in succession. The person who sprinkles the salt must be the one affected by the supposed witchcraft, and as the salt drops down must repeat, 'Salt! salt! I put thee into the fire, and may the person who has bewitched me neither eat, drink, nor sleep until the spell is broken'.   Lancashire (1873)

A handful of nineteenth-century informants indicated a custom of sprinkling salt, which was later burned, on the doorstep after an unwelcome visitor had left, to ensure that they did not come again, and salt was also sprinkled on a tooth before it was thrown on to the fire. In a few reports, salt was cast on the fire after an ill-omened action had been carried out, to counteract the bad luck. Burning salt does not appear in the literature before the 1830s, although salt as generally protective against witchcraft is demonstrably older.

salt protects

Salt also had a symbolic protective role in a range of contexts. In some writings, such as by Reginald Scot (1584) and John Aubrey (1686), it was specifically consecrated salt, like holy water, which was useful against witchcraft, but later sources speak of salt as effective in its own right. Two things which needed protection were newborn babies and calves:

> It was customary to place a small bag of salt in the cradle until the babe was baptised, to protect the babe from witches.   Wales (1909)

The use of salt in religious and magical rites is amply recorded in early history, and there are numerous examples in classical and biblical sources. For example, the protection of babies mentioned above, and the use of salt in baptism, may be based on a literal reading of Ezekiel 15:8:

> And as for thy nativity, in the day thou wast born thy navel was not cut, neither wast thou washed in water to supple thee; thou wast not salted at all nor swaddled at all.

'help to salt, help to sorrow'

Widely reported in the second half of the nineteenth century, the idea that to help someone else to salt at the meal-table, or elsewhere, would bring bad luck to them gave rise to a well-known saying – 'Help me to salt, help me to sorrow.' It is not clear how this could have developed, but on present evidence it is a relative latecomer on the scene. It is likely that Addison did not know of it when he wrote his satirical *Superstitious Man* piece in 1711, as his hostess berates him for spilling the salt, not for passing it to her. The first known reference is from 1787, but it seems well established by its second appearance in Berkshire in 1830, and it was still being reported into the late twentieth century.

In times when corpses were routinely kept in the house for the interval between death and burial, various conventions and rituals were followed, on both the practical and symbolic level. A widespread practice was to place a dish of salt on the breast of the corpse as soon as possible after death, and it remained there until the body was placed in the coffin. Where a reason for the practice was stated, informants gave overwhelmingly practical explanations: it would keep the body from swelling, keep the body sweet, and so on. Nevertheless, the preservative qualities of salt also made it an ideal symbol of eternity, and a few informants specifically stated that the salt helped to keep away evil spirits. The latter, despite being in decided minority, has been taken up and magnified by many writers on superstition who have presumed a magical impetus to the whole proceeding, but this is not borne out by the mass of the evidence.

The connection between salt and death is not hard to explain on the practical level. All communities would have been familiar with salt as a preservative of meat and fish. It was also used in earlier times as the basic ingredient for embalming and semi-embalming processes necessary when bodies were to be kept on show, or transported some distance before burial. This type of treatment would necessarily be restricted to the rich and famous, and is unlikely to have engendered the salt-on-the-breast custom. Nevertheless, it may have contributed to a popular connection between salt and death.

The practice of placing salt on a corpse was extremely widespread, being reported from every quarter of Britain and Ireland, from its first mention in the Scottish Highlands in 1771 till well into the twentieth century.

The supposed close connection between this custom and the use of salt in other ways in the presence of the deceased, assumed by some authorities, has also led to unwarranted speculation on ancient magical origins. Superficial similarities with mourners eating bread and salt, which took place in some communities, and the figure of the sin-eater do not shed any light on the origin or development of the bowl of salt.

tea

Superstition looms large in the business of making the tea, which was a far more complex and demanding process in the past than it is today. Nevertheless, the bulk of the beliefs surrounding tea are relatively non-threatening, and although there is certainly generic bad luck awaiting the unwary, there is little promised death and destruction, and mostly it is a matter of weddings, strangers, letters, and, at worst, a family quarrel or 'ginger-headed twins'. In addition to the widespread beliefs treated here, a host of others have been recorded occasionally.

Like so many other trivial domestic happenings, a stalk or leaf of tea floating in your cup indicates the coming of a stranger, or at least a visitor, and there is a set routine to learn more about him or her:

> A stalk swimming in your tea shows that a stranger is coming, it is placed on the back of the hand and the wrist patted. If it should fall at the first pat the stranger will arrive that day, if, at the second pat, on the second day and so on. You then repeat the operation to ascertain the hour . . . If the stalk be a hard one the stranger will be a man, if soft a woman. If the stranger be not welcome to come, the tea stalk must not be placed on the hand, but should be taken out of the teacup and thrown under the table.   Berkshire (1888)

Details vary remarkably little, although there are minor refinements. The belief was extremely well known, and the 'stalk in the cup' was almost as proverbial as the 'stranger on the bar' and the 'stranger in the candle'. It appears a little earlier than other tea traditions (apart from tea-leaf reading), and is first found in Glasgow about 1820. It was probably not brand new then, as only ten years later Mary Mitford could mention it in passing, as if everyone would understand, 'Who . . . searches the tea-cups for coming visitors?' (Berkshire, 1830).

tea-making rituals

If you accidentally leave the lid off the pot when making tea, it also means a stranger will call soon. This meaning is quite stable across most versions, spanning the years between the 1850s and the 1980s, although there are occasional variations. No rational suggestion has been made as to the origin of this belief, and nor is there ever likely to be one, but it is probably still said in some households. Another apparently meaningless tea superstition is that bubbles on the surface of your tea-cup are significant in some way. The most common prediction, which is still heard today, is that it means money coming to you, but there is little agreement overall as to precise meaning, The earliest known version, from 1832, claims that bubbles denote 'kisses', while another maintains that bubbles in the centre mean money, and those at the side, kisses.

Moreover, it is bad luck for two people (usually specifically women) to pour tea from the same pot:

> This evening as I was about to take the teapot from 'the neat-handed Phyllis' who looks after my wants, she – then pouring the hot water from it – said, 'It's bad luck for two to pour out of a pot, isn't it, sir?'
>
> Worcestershire (1885)

This is the earliest version, but later informants claim that it will result in a pregnancy, or even that one of the women will have 'ginger-haired twins', and the latter meaning is still heard. Other domestic beliefs warn against two people doing the same thing, such as washing hands in the same bowl, or drying them on the same towel.

The Occult

❧

PREDICTING THE FUTURE

Finding lost items Sieve and shears divination • Bible and key divination

Finding love Blade-bone divination • Tea-leaf reading

Foretelling future events 'tinker, tailor' • Pulling a wishbone

❧

CHARMS AND CURSES

Protective Abracadabra • Holed stones • Red thread • Dead man's hand • Touching iron and wood

Threatening Evil eye • Hag-riding • Hand of Glory • Nightmares • Fire of stones • Turning the stones

❧

LUCKY AND UNLUCKY NUMBERS

Lucky Odd numbers • Seventh son or daughter

Unlucky Counting • Even numbers • Thirteen • 666

PREDICTING THE FUTURE

The vast majority of divinatory procedures which have been recorded are concerned with future love prospects. Nevertheless, those who wished to ask questions about general future prosperity, or about specifics such as who was to die in the coming year or the whereabouts of stolen property, also had their traditional methods.

almanacs

Almanacs were cheap annual publications, produced in large quantities for mass sale. They contained a wealth of practical information, including a calendar, tide tables, lists of markets and fairs, historical chronology, and medical advice, but also weather lore, the phases of the moon, simplified astrology, and predictions for the coming year. In times of major unrest, as in the second half of the seventeenth century, they also participated in the great political and religious controversies of the day, but for most of their existence they filled a more humble role.

> The faith which some of our country folk place in almanacular prognostications is quite implicit. These annual publications are held in great esteem. There is nothing like a good comet year for the sale of them. On such occasions alarmist predictions are wont to swell the pages of these productions. And not a few of the more nervous portion of the community well-nigh tremble and quake with fear.
> Yorkshire (1911)

At a time when the printed word was still a mystery to much of the population, almanacs were sold in huge quantities, and even in the

1660s probably one in three families in England owned one. The leading titles became household names – *Raphael's*, *Zadkiel's*, *Old Moore's* – and in the late nineteenth century *Old Moore's* alone could sell a million copies. Almanacs provided much support for beliefs and superstitions, and they were the main way in which simplified astrology was disseminated among the labouring classes.

ash-riddling

A divination custom carried out at New Year or St Mark's Eve (24/25 April), designed to indicate who if any one in the household is destined to die in the following year:

> The last thing done on the last day of the year was to 'rist' the fire, that is, cover up the live coals with the ashes. The whole was made as smooth and neat as possible. The first thing on New Year's morning was to examine if there was in the ashes any mark like the shape of a human foot with the toes pointing towards the door. If there was such a mark, one was to be removed from the family before the year was run.   N.E. Scotland (1881)

A common detail, missing in this description, is that the ashes were sieved, or riddled – hence the usual name of the custom – ash-riddling. All the examples found are from Scotland, Isle of Man, and northern England.

Bible dipping

One of several unofficial uses of the Bible for divination purposes involved opening the book at random and interpreting the first verse which met the eye, to guide or predict future action or fate. The activity was often called 'dipping', and was typically carried out on the morning of New Year's Day:

> Opening the Bible on [New Year's Day] is a practice still in use in some parts of Somerset, and much credit is attached to it. It is usually set about with some solemnity before breakfast. The Holy Book is laid on the table unopened, and the parties who wish to consult it open it in succession. They are not allowed to choose any particular part of the book, but must open it at random. In whatever portion of the sacred volume this may happen to be, the inquirer is

to place his finger on any chapter contained in the two open pages, but without perusing its contents. This part of Scripture is then read aloud, and commented on by the people assembled, and from it they form their conclusions as to the happiness or misery that will ensue during the coming year.   Somerset (1877)

Dipping could also be done at other times – at the start of a journey or important enterprise, or in time of perplexity or doubt. Reported instances are all from nineteenth-century England, but there is no reason to think it was a strictly English custom, nor that it did not exist before and after that time.

Bible and key divination

The Bible and key could be used for answering any question, but its two main purposes were to find stolen or lost property and for love divination.

Many old people when they have lost anything, and suspect it to be stolen, take the fore-door key of their dwelling, and, in order to find out the thief, tie this key to the Bible, placing it very carefully on the eighteenth verse of the fiftieth psalm. Two persons must then hold up the book by the bow of the key, and first repeat the name of the suspected thief, and then the verse from the psalm. If the Bible moves, the suspected person is considered guilty; if it does not move, innocent.   Devon (1838)

Most informants named a particular passage for the key to rest on, which was also recited, but there is no overall agreement which one, and those chosen sometimes seem only tangentially relevant to the subject in question. Psalm 50:18, mentioned above, reads 'When thou sawest a thief, then thou consentedest with him, and hast been partaker with adulterers', which at least starts on the right lines. Ruth 4:4 is another verse recommended for the recovery of stolen goods: 'And I thought to advertise thee, saying buy it before the inhabitants and before the elders of my people. If thou wilt redeem it, redeem it; but if thou wilt not redeem it, then tell me that I may know, for there is none to redeem it beside thee.' For love divination, Ruth 1:16 was the favourite piece: 'And Ruth said, Intreat me not to leave thee, or to return from following after thee, for whither thou goest, I will go; and where thou lodgest, I will lodge.' This appears to be relevant, if one ignores its original context, as Ruth is here talking to her mother-in-law rather than her lover. Another popular passage was the Song of Solomon 8:6–7, which certainly seems to the point: 'Set me a seal upon thine heart, as a seal upon thine arm; for love is strong as death; jealousy is cruel as the grave; the coals thereof are coals of fire which hath a most vehement flame. Many waters cannot quench love, neither can the floods drown it, if a man would give all the substance of his house for love, it would utterly be contemned.'

The earlier references are all concerned with discovering thieves. The first is Mannyng's *Handlyng Synne* (1303), which talks of 'men turning the psalter', and Reginald Scot gives a good sceptical description in his *Discoverie of Witchcraft* (1584). As a love divination the procedure lasted well into the mid twentieth century.

It is clear that procedures such as the sieve and shears (see p. 160) and the Bible and key were of limited value as objective enquiries to find an unknown miscreant, but were an excellent way of confirming the suspicions already held by the aggrieved parties or their agents, precisely because they were open to manipulation, conscious or otherwise. Suspicions thus confirmed were sometimes correct anyway. It is obvious, however, that this system only operated effectively if criminal and victim lived in the same community.

blade-bone divination

A form of divination which used the shoulder-blade of a sheep, or occasionally another animal, thoroughly cleaned, to predict future events:

> The shoulder-blade of a black sheep was procured by the inquirer into future events, and with this he went to some reputed seer, who held the bone lengthwise before him and in the direction of the greatest length of the island. In this position the seer began to read the bone from some marks that he saw in it, and then oracularly declared what events to individuals or families were to happen. It is not very far distant that there were a host of believers in this method of prophecy.   Isle of Lewis (1895)

The earliest mention of the blade-bone procedure occurs in 1188, with a detailed description by Gerald of Wales. He writes of the Flemings, who had emigrated to Wales in the time of Henry I (1100–35). Other early writers also mention the procedure. Chaucer, for example, knew of it, as in the *Parson's Tale* (*c*.1395) he wrote of conjuration 'in the shoulder-bone of a sheep'. But it is difficult to sort out the literary from the popular traditions. It is clear that most of the earlier writers were quoting from Gerald, and their testimony cannot therefore be taken as independent evidence of the existence of the custom. Nevertheless, from the 1680s onwards, we find the divination described as prevalent in the Scottish Highlands, and a new literary tradition is set up, in which the earlier writers are quoted by the later ones. A similar bone was used in a love-divination procedure, designed to reveal a future spouse or to persuade a reluctant lover, but in contrast to the long history of the complex general divination, the love version has not been found before the mid nineteenth century.

dreams

The idea that dreams foretell the future, or report what is happening many miles away, is obviously not restricted to Britain and Ireland nor to the modern period. The subject is too broad, and examples too numerous, to do more than sketch a few lines of enquiry. A recurrent theme in British sources is that 'dreams go by contraries', so that to dream of a wedding, for example, signifies a death. This notion was already current in the classical era, as it is clearly stated in Apuleius' *Golden Ass* (*c*. AD 150), and it has been evident in many references in Britain since at least the fifteenth century. Nevertheless, the Saxon manuscript of dream prognostications of *c*.1050 published in Oswald Cockayne's *Leechdoms* (1866) provides a long list of meanings, including a number which appear to be based on the principle of opposites, but these are a minority, and the rest are either too obscure for classification or definitely based on obvious similarities rather than contrasts. Nearly all of the 'prophetic dreams' recorded in later sources, although couched in symbolic terms, were interpreted literally, and popular dream-books were full of meanings which were clearly not governed by the rule of opposites. It is difficult to avoid the conclusion reached by Hannah More in her moralistic tale about a swindling fortune-teller:

> Rachel was also a famous interpreter of dreams ... She had a cunning way of getting herself off when any of her prophecies failed. When she explained a dream according to the natural appearance of

things, and it did not come to pass, then she would get out of that
scrape by saying that this sort of dreams went by contraries.

Tawney Rachel (c.1810)

There are many interpretations of specific items and situations appearing in dreams, but only a handful turn up often enough to be definitely
labelled 'traditional'.

The symbolism of prophetic dreams is usually easy to understand –
at least once the outcome is known. They are normally told as simple
tales, and are all the more convincing for it:

> Over fifty years have elapsed since Mrs. A. received this symbolic
> intimation of trouble to come, but it has always been a tradition in
> the family. She dreamt she was walking with her two little girls, K.
> and M., in a beautiful wood full of violets which she could smell as
> well as see. Suddenly two men sprang out from behind the trees,
> snatched up M., and made off with her. Mrs. A. ran after them
> and begged them to give her back the child, and take K. instead;
> for she felt that one of them had to be taken. They did as she asked,
> and the dream ended. Neither of the children was known to be
> unwell at the time, but K. died that day week.   Isle of Man (1963)

Dream books were produced in large quantities and sold cheaply
by itinerant packmen in rural areas and in local shops and stalls in
towns. In addition to dream interpretations, many included other
fortune-telling material – how to read cards, tea-leaves, moles, basic
astrology, palmistry, and so on. They were extremely popular, but
it is unclear how lasting was their effect on traditional beliefs
about dreams. The published folklore collections contain a range
of traditional dream meanings, but in nothing like the numbers
which appear in the books, and there is apparently little real corre-
lation between the two genres at the level of individual meanings.
Dictionaries of dreams are still in print.

porch watching

'Watching' in the church porch was a superstitious custom which was
widely known and talked about, if not actually often practised:

> St. Mark's Eve . . . the watching in the church porch. It was, and
> in some places is, believed that any one watching for one hour

before and one hour after midnight in the church porch would learn who in the parish would die in the coming year. As the clock struck the hour of midnight a procession would pass into the church, infants unable to walk would roll in, those who were to be very sick, but recover, would come out again, after a stay correspond-ing to the duration of their illness, but those who were to die would not appear again. Those who were to be married during the same period also put in an appearance; they walk in couples and speedily reappear. If the watcher falls asleep, he will die himself during the year.   East Anglia (1885)

The proper night for the custom varies from account to account, but it usually took place on St Mark's Eve (24/25 April), and although details vary, the overall shape is nearly always the same. The custom certainly dates from at least the turn of the seventeenth century, and the essential elements are already in place in the first known reference:

Katherine Foxegale, of Walesbie, presented 26 July at East Retford . . . 'For watchinge upon Saint Markes even at nighte laste in the church porche to presage by divelishe demonstracion the deathe of somme neighbours within this yeere.   Nottingham (1608)

It was reported frequently right up to the early twentieth century, but most of the later references are couched in terms of what 'used to be done'.

second sight

Second sight is the usual English name for a power of seeing into the future, possessed typically by certain people in the Gaelic Highlands and Islands of Scotland, but also by others elsewhere. It was first noticed by the outside world in the late seventeenth century, and has since attracted a great deal of popular and scholarly attention; much material on the subject already exists.

The second sight is a singular faculty of seeing an otherwise invisible object, without any previous means used by the person that sees it for that end; the vision makes such a lively impression upon the seers, that they neither see nor think of anything else, except the vision, as long as it continues; and then they appear pensive or jovial, according to the object which was represented to them.   Western Isles (1703)

This is one of the earliest published descriptions, written by Martin Martin after a trip to the Western Isles about 1695. The matter was clearly in the air at that time, as George Sinclair had mentioned it in 1685, Robert Kirk had published his thoughts on the matter in 1691, and John Aubrey in 1696. Samuel Pepys corresponded with Lord Reay on the subject in 1699, and Royal Society member Robert Boyle had been interested in it from about 1678 to his death in 1691.

Second sight quickly developed into a battleground of belief. Investigators such as Kirk and Boyle were concerned to prove its existence, to help counter what they saw as dangerous ideas which threatened to deny the possibility of the supernatural and spiritual world completely. They foresaw that such a sceptical view would soon reach the conclusion that even religion itself was false. For others a little later, such as Boswell and Johnson, who visited the Hebrides in 1773, the Islands of Scotland were among the last unspoilt places where the inhabitants were wild but free of the cant and enervating artifice of contemporary 'civilization', and the possible existence of such supernatural powers was terribly romantic. Novelists were happy to use the motif in their tales, but some writers, like Thomas Pennant, thought the whole notion 'founded on impudence and nurtured by folly' (*A Tour in Scotland*, 1774).

Many Scottish writers accepted the reality of second sight in their quest to identify and preserve true Scottish or Gaelic customs and values against the colonizing onslaught of the dominant English language and culture. Second sight was something special which separated the Highlanders from their neighbours, and acceptance became necessary for any true patriot, even if their otherwise sceptical view of the world would incline them towards disbelief. Hence Alistair Macgregor, addressing the Caledonian Medical Society in 1899, could say:

> It is fortunate that this article dealing with the subject of Second Sight appears in the journal of a society, the majority of whose members are Scottish-born – otherwise I fear it would meet with scant courtesy ... Hence my fellow-Caledonians – partly from national sentiment, and partly perhaps from having had themselves some experience of second sight, personally or from hearsay – may be expected to have more sympathy with a dissertation on a supernatural belief indigenous to their native country than they would have had it been an alien.

Debate on the second-sight phenomenon has been particularly vulnerable to these religious and politico-social pressures and it is even now
difficult to avoid them.

From the earliest accounts onwards, there was disagreement over
whether or not the faculty of second sight was hereditary, and believers
found themselves in a dilemma. The power was clearly not possessed
by every child of every acknowledged seer, but the hereditary principle
was vital to the view that the second sight contributes strongly to the
'specialness' of Highland society. The consensus has therefore been
reached that the faculty must be hereditary, but does not manifest
itself in every generation. The non-believer would argue that this very
convenient answer means that any random person who claims to have
the power can be slotted into the hereditary scheme by assuming a
gifted ancestor somewhere in the past.

There has also been debate about the fundamental nature of the
second-sight gift. Some, like George Sinclair, a professor of philos-
ophy in the College of Glasgow, assumed it was the Devil's work:

> I am undoubtedly informed, that men and women in the Highlands
> can discern fatality approaching others, by seeing them in waters,
> or with winding sheets about them . . . It is not improbable, but
> that such preternatural knowledge comes first by a compact with
> the devil, and is derived downward by succession to their posterity,
> many of such I suppose are innocent, and have this sight against
> their will and inclination.   *Satan's Invisible World Discovered* (1685)

But the majority of writers stressed the anguish that many seers felt,
and claimed that most of them would be free of the gift if they could
achieve release. Descriptions of what the seers actually experience vary
considerably. Most accounts focus on sight, but smell and sound can
also play a part. Earlier accounts focused on 'sad and dismal' topics,
although the occasional vision foresaw a wedding or other happy
event. But it is far from clear what should properly be included in a
definition of second sight. Many of the descriptions include standard
omens found all over the British Isles such as death knocks, corpse
candles, wraiths, and phantom funerals. The only general way in
which second sight appears to be different from other visions and
portents is that it is a personal gift which happens regularly to the
seer, rather than being a random or one-off phenomenon. But earlier
descriptions provide another key difference, in that they involved a

structured symbolism which governed what was 'seen' and how it was interpreted. So, for example, a death was forecast by the seer having a vision of the doomed person wrapped in a shroud, and the higher up the body the shroud appeared, the sooner the death would occur.

sieve and shears

A relatively complex divinatory procedure involving a sieve and a pair of shears was used to discover thieves or lost items, and occasionally for love divination. As with the related Bible and key, the process relied on the power of inanimate objects to react to the naming of the culprit:

> Sticke a paire of sheeres in the rind of a sive, and let two persons set the top of each of their forefingers upon the upper part of the sheeres, holding it with the sive up from the ground steddilie, and ask Peter and Paule whether B or C hath stolen the thing lost, and at the nomination of the guiltie person, the sive will turne round.
>
> Reginald Scot, *Discoverie of Witchcraft* (1584)

Essentially the same procedure was still being used in the nineteenth century. Scot's description is the earliest known in Britain, but other references come thick and fast soon afterwards and throughout the seventeenth century. It was sufficiently well known at the time for writers such as Ben Jonson (1612) and John Melton (1620) to refer to it in passing, and a technical term for the process, 'coscinomancy', was current by at least 1603 (Christopher Heydon, *A Defence of Judiciall Astrologie*). Indeed, it was already in apparent everyday use in 1602 when two Shetlanders were accused of witchcraft.

Unusually for such a complex procedure, these British examples are very close to those reported from classical times. The Greek pastoral poet Theocritus provides the first reference (*Idylls*, c.275 BC). Reginald Scot was already aware that 'This is a great practise in all countries', and it is probable that the procedure was introduced into Britain by writers such as him, quoting continental European sources which were in turn based on classical writings. Despite these respectable historical antecedents, however, the sieve and shears was not reported often after the turn of the nineteenth century, and was certainly far less common in later years than the Bible and key.

tea-leaf reading

Reading the tea-leaves is nowadays a cliché of popular fortune-telling, but there is evidence that it was taken quite seriously in the past, and has been widely popular for nearly 300 years. The earliest three references come so close together, 1726 to 1731, that the obvious conclusion is that it was fashionably new at that time. The first is an advertisement in *Dublin Weekly Journal* (1726) for the 'famous Mrs. Cherry' who professed to be expert at the 'occult science of tossing of coffee grounds', and five years later a contributor to the *Gentleman's Magazine* described seeing it in practice:

> a lady and her company in close cabal over their coffee; the rest very intent upon one, who by her dress and intelligence he guessed was a tire-woman; to which she added the secret of divining by coffee-grounds; she was then in full inspiration, and with much solemnity observing the atoms round the cup; on one hand sat a widow, on the other a married lady, both attentive to the predictions given of their future fate. The lady (his acquaintance), though married, was no less earnest in contemplating her cup than the other two. They assured him that every cast of the cup is a picture of all one's life to come; and every transaction and circumstance is delineated with the exactest certainty.

Most of these early references refer to coffee grounds, but tea-leaf reading gradually became the norm. Nearly all the available descriptions stress that the natural audience for tea-leaf readings was overwhelmingly female, and primarily concerned with love and matrimonial prospects. Instructions for reading the leaves were published regularly throughout the nineteenth and twentieth centuries in small books devoted to the subject and also in others on fortune-telling, dreams, and so on. Modern examples of the genre still sell in sufficient numbers to keep them in print.

'tinker, tailor'

The extremely well-known fortune-telling rhyme, used mainly by children while counting fruit stones, buttons, beads on a necklace, spikelets on rye grass, or anything else close to hand, and thereby foretelling their own destiny, or that of their future husband:

Tinker, tailor, soldier, sailor,
Rich man, poor man, beggarman, thief.

Oxfordshire (1920s)

This is a standard version, but the exact words have varied considerably over the years. For matrimonial prospects, the items can be counted again to ascertain the wedding vehicle, clothes, and, most importantly, when:

Coach, carriage, wheelbarrow; Silk, satin, cotton, rags; This year, next year, sometime, or now, never.   Wiltshire (1893–5)

The earliest clear version is published in Moor's dictionary of *Suffolk Words and Phrases* in 1823, although if he was reporting his own childhood, that would set it back to the 1770s. In another context, however, the line 'A soldier and a sailor, a tinker and a taylor' had already appeared in Congreve's play *Love for Love* in 1695.

wishbones

When modern people take the furcula, or forked breastbone, of a bird they have just eaten and break it between them for a wish, they are indulging in an abbreviated version of a custom which dates back to at least the seventeenth century. In earlier versions, the procedure was usually more complex, and was often concerned with marriage prospects rather than wishes:

M got me to break a marriage-bone with him. I got the longest piece. I was then instructed to break it in two and offer both pieces as in drawing lots. I did this, and M got the longest piece. This he broke and offered me my choice, which resulted in my getting the longest piece and so I am the first to be married, as it falls to the one who gets the best in three chances.   Argyllshire (1901)

CHARMS AND CURSES

charms and charming

The word 'charm' has various meanings in modern English, but for present purposes it means a set of words which, when spoken or written down in the correct way, and with or without accompanying action by the charmer, have power in themselves to effect change or bring about action in the physical world. Thus a charm against bleeding will be expected to stop the flow of blood, against a toothache to stop the pain. Charms can be curative, as in these examples, or protective – to prevent overlooking or ill-wishing when churning butter, for example – or vindictive. When written down and worn or carried about the person, the charm becomes an amulet, and charms can be handwritten or printed.

> I have known people who wore written charms, sewed into the necks of their coats, if men, and into the headbands of petticoats if women ... These talismans were so generally and thoroughly believed in, and so numerous and apparently well-attested were the evidences of their beneficial effects, that in years not long past, medical men believed in their efficacy, and promulgated various theories to account for it. W. Scotland (1879)

The vast majority of recorded charms are overtly Christian, sometimes detailing an incident in the lives of Jesus, Mary, or the disciples. Alternatively, they simply draw on appropriate religious images such as the 'crown of thorns' when extracting a thorn, or as in this cure for the ague from 1751:

When Jesus saw the cross, whereon his body should be crucified, his body shook, and the Jewes asked him had he the ague? He answered and said, 'Whosoever keepeth this in mind or writing shall not be troubled with fever or ague; so, Lord, help thy servant trusting in thee. Then say the Lord's prayer. This is to be read before it is folded, then knotted and not opened after.'

Although they usually directly invoke God in the form of 'In the name of the Father', charms are not often addressed directly to God as prayers would be.

Records show that while the charmer concentrated on such matters as warts and toothaches, there was little to lose, but more serious consequences could easily arise, as, for example, the case of poor Thomas Ryder, a farm labourer from Cornwood, in Devon. He bled to death while local charmers attempted to stop the blood from his wounds instead of taking him to hospital (*Daily Telegraph*, 7 July 1887).

In most parts of Britain, at local level, there were amateur charmers who would undertake cures for free, but there were also many professional 'cunning men and women' who made a living from such activities. While certain people, such as seventh sons and posthumous children (those born after the death of their father), had charming powers in themselves, they still had to learn the appropriate words, and other ordinary people could acquire power simply by being taught the words of the charm and the technique. A common tradition stated that men could only successfully pass on a charm to a woman, and vice versa.

The belief in charms was extremely widespread and long-lasting. The Christian Church waged a continuing battle against their use, as most churchmen assumed that charms worked because the Devil or other spirits were behind them, despite their overtly godly tone. The pre-Reformation Church had, indeed, sanctioned the use of verbal formulae and written prayers, but was never successful in teaching the mass of the people the difference between official and unofficial 'charms'.

cunning men and women

Cunning men or women were widespread names for those local characters who professed to be expert in the occult sciences of discovering and countering witchcraft, divining the future, and so on, and whose services were at the disposal of anyone with the money to buy them. The terminology was elastic and regional, and such people could also be called wise men and women, conjurors, wizards, white witches, healers, charmers, or simply witches. Under any name, they were a regular feature of village and small-town life for centuries, and the majority of the populace would be well aware of who claimed powers in what context, and who could be paid for occult assistance when necessary. Even into the late nineteenth century, belief in witch-craft was not a minor aberration but a major element in community life. The standard fare for the average cunning man or woman would include fortune-telling, by various means, the location of lost or stolen property, love magic (whereby recalcitrant lovers could be brought to heel), the identification of spells cast upon the client and his/her goods, and measures to counter them, and magical healing techniques.

Gross superstition – A case was brought before the Plymouth bench of magistrates on Tuesday, showing the extent to which superstition lingers in Devon. The prisoner was Mary Catherine Murray, respectably dressed, aged about 50, and the charge was that of imposing upon Thomas Rendle by means of a piece of parchment called a 'charm'. The prosecutor is a labourer living at Modbury who out of the small earnings of about 10s. a week had managed to scrape together a few pounds. His wife was taken ill, and he thought she was 'ill-wished'. Hearing of the powers of the prisoner, who lived at 18 William Street, Plymouth, and whose reputation as a healer of those bewitched had spread as far as Modbury, he went and consulted her. She said his wife would have to go and see the planets, and gather certain herbs in the churchyard for 21 nights. The prisoner charged him one guinea for her advice, and afterwards received from him £3 for powders and a 'skin'. The skin was to be worn round the neck, and must be put on for the first time on a Sunday. The powders were to be burnt in the fire – one in the morning and the other in the evening, beginning also on the Sunday; and there was also some medicine in bottles. When the last powder was burnt, the prisoner ordered that the 91st psalm should be read. The prisoner expressed her belief in her powers and she was remanded, bail being refused.

Devon, *The Times* (13 December 1867)

Much of our information about such activities in the nineteenth century comes from narratives collected by folklorists, which are often good stories, but in themselves already traditional and filtered, and the characters already semi-legendary. An alternative view is gleaned from local newspapers, such as the one above, which tend to focus on court cases but give a more accurate picture of who and what was involved. It must be understood that the modern romantic view of these local practitioners as harmless eccentrics possessed of secret herbal knowledge which modern civilization foolishly ignores is seriously misleading. Countless people were tricked into spending their life savings on charms and nostrums, were persuaded that a neighbour had bewitched them, and were bullied and frightened by people whose main expertise was to identify and profit from human weakness.

cursing

The ability to curse someone effectively has presumably been part of the stock-in-trade of every aspiring witch, wizard, and cunning man or woman in all ages and cultures, and much of their power over their neighbours and customers must have depended on their reputation in this area. This power also necessarily required secrecy, as there would be no market for their services if everyone could do the same thing. Some curses, however, were available to all and sundry, and apparently needed no more special power than the necessary degree of anger and spite.

> A curious incident took place once at Penallt. A woman and her daughter had been turned out of their house, which had made them furious. Soon afterwards the older woman died, and while her corpse was being carried to church the daughter suddenly drew a slipper from under her apron and struck with it three times at the coffin, exclaiming as she did so, 'Mother, I'm here, fulfilling your commands!', and with that she threw the slipper into an orchard close by belonging to those people who had turned them out. And for long after that the farm never prospered and no one could stay there, though by this time the curse appears to have been removed, as the present inhabitants are doing well.   Monmouthshire (1905)

Scorned lovers had opportunity for revenge at the wedding of their former sweethearts. Folklorist Ella Leather reported an incident in which a jilted girl confronted her ex-lover as he left the church with his new bride and threw a handful of rue at him, saying 'May you rue this day as long as you live.' But a number of descriptions include the motif that a curse uttered lightly, or performed badly, rebounds upon the curser:

Any person can pray that his enemy be dead, if he wishes to repeat Psalm 109 ['Hold not thy peace, O God of my praise . . .'] every night and morning for a whole year. If he misses one night or morning, he must certainly die himself.   Wales (1909)

abracadabra

Long before the word 'abracadabra' became the stereotypical phrase of the stage magician, it was believed to be a powerful charm against ague, toothache, and various other ailments. Written repeatedly on a piece of parchment as an inverted triangle, with each line omitting some letters, and hung round the neck, it acted as an amulet:

> To cure an ague – Write this following spell in parchment, and wear it about your neck. It was to be writ triangularly. With this spell, one of Wells, hath cured above a hundred of the ague.
>
> John Aubrey, *Miscellanies* (1696)

Aubrey's is the first known example in English, but he claims that it was already in use. Within a year it was also published by John Durant, and there is little doubt that it was introduced to British tradition directly by some such translator of classical works, probably only a short time before Aubrey. The word is first found in a Latin poem by Q. Severus Sammonicus, physician to the Emperor Caracalla in the second century AD, where it was already recommended to be hung round the neck as a protective charm. The inverted triangle, it has been suggested, symbolized – or physically forced – the disease to diminish as the letters do in the charm.

The origin of the word is unknown, but this has not prevented numerous guesses that it is a secret word for a god, or the name of a demon. Astrologers and would-be sorcerers in Britain and abroad, from early modern times to the present day, have been fascinated by words which can be written in geometric shapes, especially if they can be read in various directions, believing that such words must have special powers. In essentially the same form, the amulet was still being reported in the twentieth century.

fire of stones curse

A powerful procedure, usually carried out by tenants forced to leave a farm against their will, involved placing a curse on the land by building a fire of stones:

> The plaintiff (if I may use the term) collects from the surrounding fields as many boulders as will fill the principal hearth of the holding he is being compelled to surrender. These he piles in the manner of turf sods arranged for firing; and then, kneeling down, prays that until the heap burns, may every kind of sweat, bad luck, and misfortune attend the landlord and his family, to untold generations. Rising, he takes the stones in armfuls and hurls them here and there, in loch, pool, bog-hole of stream, so that by no possibility could the collection be recovered.   Co. Fermanagh (1875)

Some details vary, but the essential core is the same. In some accounts the stones are left in the fireplace, to increase the dramatic effect, and to ensure that the incoming occupant will be in no doubt as to what has been done.

Examples have been noted from various parts of Ireland, and one or two from Scotland. Although curses such as this have an archaic feel, there seems to be no record of this one before the 1820s, and it was still being talked about, if not actually carried out, in Ireland in the later twentieth century.

turning the stones curse

'Turning the stones' was a way of inflicting a potent curse on anyone you wished to harm. The method was widely reported in parts of Ireland, although it was more often referred to than described:

> Near Black Lion, at the extreme north of Co. Cavan, there is a cursing stone. It is a large horizontal slab, with twelve or thirteen bullans or basins cut in it, and in each bullan save one, there is a large round stone. The curser takes up one of the stones and places it in the empty basin – and so on, one after another, till have been gone over. During the movement he is cursing his enemy, and if he removes all the stones without letting one of them slip (no easy operation on account of their form), his curses will have effect, but not otherwise. If he lets one slip, the curses will return on his own head.   Co. Cavan (1894)

Although assumed to be ancient, this procedure does not seem to have been described before the mid nineteenth century.

dead man's hand

A widespread belief held that a certain cure for wens, goitre, scrofula, tumours, and other swellings or skin complaints, was to stroke the affected place with a corpse's hand. In most cases, the hand of an executed criminal, or a suicide, was preferred:

> The body of a suicide who hanged himself in Heselden Dene was laid in an outhouse awaiting the coroner's inquest. The wife of a pitman at Castle Eden Colliery, suffering from a wen in the neck, following the advice given her by a 'wise woman' went alone, and lay all night in the outhouse with the hand of the corpse on her wen. She was assured that the hand of a suicide was an infallible cure.   Northumberland (1860/62)

In the days of public hanging (abolished 1868), the hangman carried on a lucrative trade charging people for the use of the dead hand, and there was often a queue of afflicted persons willing to pay for the privilege. The principles at work here are not clear, as the belief is open to a number of interpretations, all of them speculative and lacking in solid evidence. The simplest suggestion, backed by one or two references, is that this is an example of the widespread belief in the transference of disease – as the hand mouldered the affliction would disappear.

The belief is well attested in the British Isles from at least the 1590s onwards, and was very widely reported well into the twentieth century, although by the latter time it was passing rapidly into memory culture. Exactly the same belief was known in classical times, as reported, for example, by Pliny in his *Natural History* (AD 77):

> We are assured that the hand of a person carried off by premature death cures by a touch scrofulous sores, diseased parotid glands, and throat affections.

Indeed, this description is so close as to pose the question whether it was introduced to Britain by sixteenth-century scholars who were so keen on classical sources.

effigies (image magic)

The idea that someone can be harmed by an ill-wisher mistreating an image made in his/her likeness has a long history, and is found in most human cultures. This 'image magic' has been widely reported in Britain and Ireland, and although there are variations on the basic theme, the degree of stability is remarkable considering its longevity and wide distribution. There are records of the use of such effigies for malevolent purposes in Britain from the tenth century onwards, and numerous condemnations in early laws and penitentials. Early examples were usually documented because they were aimed at harming the sovereign or others of the ruling classes and were thus treated as high treason, and there is no doubt that kings and queens until the seventeenth century took such matters very seriously.

The key variables of the custom can be categorized as follows: (1) the materials used; (2) fashioning the image; (3) the inclusion of something of the victim or christening it with the victim's name; (4) mistreating it – usually with pins or nails, but also twisting or malforming – to cause illness or pain; (5) accompanying rituals or words; (6) destroying the effigy – burning, melting, dissolving, burying, rotting.

The two most common materials were wax and clay, probably because these were readily available and the operator had the choice to destroy them quickly or slowly, as required. If something intimately connected with the victim (e.g. hair or nail parings) could not be obtained, an alternative way to link the image and the victim was to enact some sort of ceremony naming the effigy after its human counterpart. A significant feature in several of the early cases was that the perpetrator managed to find a corrupt priest to christen the image, and this added considerably to its power.

The words that the ill-wishers used to accompany their image-work were not usually recorded, but Psalm 68, which was sometimes mentioned, certainly seems ideal for the job:

> As smoke is driven away, so drive them away; as wax melteth before the fire, so let the wicked perish in the presence of God.

Images could also be made for purposes other than direct harm, including the promotion of love, or at least infatuation. At village level, local witches and cunning men and women were always available to help to persuade a reluctant lover, but again the best-documented cases are those involving the rich and famous. Indeed, it seems that whenever anyone powerful wished to disentangle themselves from a previous marriage or liaison, they could claim that they had been bewitched in this way.

elf-shooting

It is generally agreed that the theory of medicine prevalent in the early Middle Ages in Britain, as evidenced by surviving manuscripts, was almost entirely based on classical and Christian sources. Very little can be shown to have survived from earlier periods of either Anglo-Saxon or British history. One exception to this rule is the concept of illness being caused by direct malevolent action by supernatural beings – elves or fairies – commonly called being 'elf-shot'. This could happen to humans, but was most common in large farm animals, particularly horses and cattle:

> The stone arrow heads of the old inhabitants of this island, are supposed to be weapons shot by fairies at cattle, to which are attributed any disorders they have: in order to effect a cure, the cow is to be touched by an elf-shot, or made to drink the water in which one has been dropped.   Hebrides (1771)

Cures usually involved soaking these arrowheads in water and giving the patient the water to drink. A regular alternative was to place silver money – if possible coins with crosses on them – into water, and to give this 'silver water' to the patient. As befitted a disease with a supernatural cause, elf-shot could only be diagnosed by a local cunning man or recognized healer. A regular method of diagnosis was to measure the afflicted animal several times, and if it was found to be getting smaller, a confident diagnosis could be made.

The idea was certainly current in many areas throughout the nineteenth and well into the twentieth century. Nevertheless, the history and development of this belief is still unclear, and we are faced with a couple of unsolved problems. The condition of being elf-shot is mentioned in a matter-of-fact tone in a number of medieval Saxon manuscripts (*see* Cockayne, *Leechdoms*, 1864–6). But the next available reference turns up in the 1660s. So what happened in the intervening six or seven hundred years? Is it safe to assume the existence of a direct tradition, surviving from generation to generation over that time, without any documentary evidence?

The second problem is concerned with distribution. Experts on medieval medicine such as Wilfrid Bonser and Charles Singer agree that the elf-shot concept is a survival of the Teutonic heritage of England, and was brought to its shores by Anglo-Saxon invaders and settlers. But the distribution of the belief in later years was predominantly in Scotland and Ireland, which, broadly speaking, are not known for their Teutonic roots.

the evil eye

The notion that certain people can harm other humans, animals, and even inanimate objects, simply by looking at them, is found in many cultures throughout the world but is not, it seems, universal. It has certainly been extremely widespread in Europe at least since classical times, and it also has biblical sanction. The best-known European evil-eye beliefs flourished around the Mediterranean – in particular Italy and Greece – but there was also a strong tradition in northern Europe (in which Britain and Ireland shared), which differed markedly from its southern counterpart. In contrast to the Mediterranean model, the evil eye in Britain is in many respects only a part of the general belief in witchcraft. Several of the vernacular terms for ill-wishing or witchcraft demonstrate the importance of eyes in the business of bewitchment – overlooking, blinking, eye-biting, and so on. Casting a spell by looking at something or someone was merely one of the weapons in the witch's arsenal. But some people had simply inherited it:

> In a district of North Antrim there is living at the present time a family, members of which are thought to possess the power to 'blink' cattle. No one will show them young animals, nor indeed any animal if they can avoid it. Other neighbours are taken to see the new foal or the litter of young pigs, but never a member of this family.   N. Ireland (1951)

Indeed, there are stories of people who were mortified to find that they had the power, and who always made sure they avoided causing damage by carefully regulating where their gaze fell. The first glance each morning was the most dangerous. Where the evil eye was used deliberately to do harm, it could fall on anyone who displeased the possessor, but certain areas of life seemed particularly prone to attack – babies, new animals, milking, and butter-making. Where babies and farm animals were concerned, the overriding emotional context was usually envy – anything which might incite another's envy was at risk. In the same context, people were careful not to praise things – if they praised their own they were tempting fate, if they praised others' they were suspected of wishing ill in the guise of honeyed words.

> You must bless the baby in praising it for there is danger from one's evil eye. The evil eye is peculiarly apt to fall on babies.
>
> Highland Scotland (1887/88)

A number of protective measures and remedies were available, although again these were the same as were used for other types of ill-wishing. Holed stones, horseshoes, pieces of rowan, and red thread were all recommended, but there is no sign of the elaborate system of gestures, amulets, and protective icons which are characteristic of Mediterranean and Middle Eastern traditions.

The phrase 'evil eye' occurs regularly in English at least from AD 1000 (*OED*), but it is not always clear whether it refers to the supernatural power or to a more generalized description of a facial expression or vindictive mood. James I certainly referred to the occult power when he used the term in his *Daemonologie* (1597), but Reginald Scot, writing a few years earlier, in the 1580s, called it 'eye-biting', while in Scotland, 'Ill eye' and 'Canny eye' were also widely used.

hag-riding

When horses were found sweating, exhausted, and frightened in their stables in the morning, it was automatically assumed that they had been 'hag-ridden'. The most widespread method of protection was to hang up a stone with a natural hole in it – thus often called a 'hag-stone', and another method was to ensure the presence of iron, which also deterred witches:

> Hang up hooks, and sheers to scare
> Hence the hag, that rides the mare.
> Robert Herrick, *Hesperides* (1648)

The juxtaposition of notions of night attacks and witches or evil spirits has wrought a fusion between the hag-riding attacks on animals in stable and byre, and attacks of the nightmare, which were predominately aimed at humans in their beds.

the Hand of Glory

The Hand of Glory was known in various forms across Europe from at least the Middle Ages onwards. It was the severed hand of an executed criminal which, once prepared with appropriate occult rites and ingredients, could be used for various nefarious purposes. In British stories it was invariably used to induce sleep while burglars made away with people's goods. The hand was anointed with fat (often gruesomely human fat) and the fingers lighted like candles or, alternatively, the hand was simply made to hold a candle. Once the candle, or fingers, were lit, everyone in the house (except the thief) would fall into an enchanted sleep. A human hand, reputedly used as a Hand of Glory, is one of the most popular items in Whitby Museum, Yorkshire.

A small handful of Hand of Glory stories were reported in Britain in the late nineteenth century, which were heavily influenced by European tales. These were copied and repeated by folklorists, and freely adapted by novelists, to become very well known in the literature, and they are still reproduced regularly on occult websites. But there are indications of older traditions of a similar nature which are far less well known. For example, a report of a coroner's inquest in Maidstone, Kent, in 1440 was told:

> Take . . . the arm of a dead man that has lain in the earth nine days and nine nights, and put in the dead hand a burning candle, and go to a place wherever thou wilt and though there be therein an hundred people, they that sleep shall sleep and they that wake shall not move whatever you do.
>
> *Bulletin of the Institute of Historical Research* (1963)

And 200 years later, the antiquarian John Aubrey wrote:

> a story that was generally believed when I was a schoolboy (before the civil warres) that thieves, when they broke open a house, would putt a candle into a deadman's hand: and then the people in the chamber would not awake.   *Remaines* (1686)

The derivation and history of the name 'Hand of Glory' is itself confused. First used in English around 1707, it is a mis-translation of the medieval French *maindegloire*, meaning a 'mandrake'. But the name 'Hand of Glory' was too evocative to be confined to such a grisly past, and it has now been appropriated by jewellery makers who market silver or pewter pendants in the shape of hands, on the Internet. In August 2002, one was described as to be worn 'for tranquillity and good health, and peace of mind', for only $4.95. A very far cry from the original.

holed stones

Stones with a natural hole in them were prized as lucky and protective. They could be hung up to protect a building against witchcraft, or carried on the person to ward off an evil eye, but the two most widely reported uses were to hang them in a stable to protect the horses against being ridden in the night by witches (hag-ridden), or on the bedstead to protect humans against the nightmare. The latter was not simply a bad dream:

> A stone with a hole in it, hung at the bed's head, will prevent the night-mare; it is therefore called a hag-stone, from that disorder, which is occasioned by a hag, or witch, sitting on the stomach of the party afflicted. It also prevents witches riding horses; for which purpose it is often tied to a stable key.
>
> Francis Grose, *Provincial Glossary* (1787)

The specific evils which the stone could counter varied from place to place, but were nearly always on the theme of what harm others (witches, fairies, malignant neighbours) could do to your home, family, trade, or stock. A holed stone was valued for its intrinsic power, and there is no evidence that it needed any special treatment or preparation before use, although some clearly believed that it only began to work once the string had been threaded through the hole for it to hang on. A number of sources indicate that the stone was most powerful if it was found by chance, or presented as a gift.

In Britain, the documentary record commences in the seventeenth century, but it was clearly already well known by then. Holed stone traditions were extremely common in much of the British Isles, and they were apparently well known as amulets, or curing stones, across most of Europe.

the horseman's word

In arable farming areas in the nineteenth century, the workers who handled the horses were the acknowledged aristocrats of the agricultural workforce, possessing skills which their employers could not match nor easily do without. The horsemen were proud of their status and jealous of their rights, and in northeast Scotland one result was a semi-secret trade society called the Horseman's Word. This was partly modelled on the Freemasons, but also on a previous trade organization called the Miller's Word. Members of the Horseman's Word had to undergo initiation ceremonies, which often parodied religious rites, had to swear oaths of secrecy and brotherhood, and generally behaved as all men-only working-class social groups did, and do. Members encouraged outsiders in the idea that the horsemen possessed secret magical charms and procedures for controlling horses, but it is clear that what was really shared, apart from drink and comradeship, were genuine skills rather than magic potions. The society also functioned to a certain degree as a trade union, and young horse-workers were keen to be accepted into its ranks.

References to the horseman's word in England are almost entirely confined to the eastern counties, particularly Suffolk, and in contrast to the Scottish evidence are vague concerning any organized fraternity. It is unlikely that any such organization really existed there, and most reports emphasize the supposed magical rite which the novice had to undertake to obtain the magical item – a frog or toad's bone – which would be the basis of his power. This ceremony explains why skilled horse-workers were often called 'toadmen'. Basic skills included 'drawing' a horse, working successfully with untrained or dangerous animals, working horses without reins or commands, and, most spectacularly, rendering horses immobile. As suggested, the horse-handling skills were a combination of experience and body-language, although some authorities suggested that the men used secret concoctions of herbs which acted on the animal's acute sense of smell. But the real mystery which featured in many of the stories was the power of the 'word' – the supposed magical charm which could be whispered in the horse's ear, and which was imparted to members of the fraternity only.

Long before the formation of the Horseman's Word societies, certain individuals had reputations as uncannily good horse-handlers, and some of the earlier references identify these as 'whisperers'. The earliest concerns John Young, a Sussex 'horse courser' in 1648, who could 'tame the fiercest bull, or the wildest horse, by whispering in its ear' (Méric Casaubon's *Treatise Proving Spirits*, 1672). Another seventeenth-century example demonstrates that the immobilization motif was already in force:

In Renfrewshire, Thomas Lindsay, a young lad apprehended on a charge of witchcraft, in 1664, boasted that he would for a halfpenny make a horse stand still in the plough, at the word of command by turning himself widdershins or contrary to the course of the sun.

Francis Grant, *Narratives of the Sufferings of a Young Girl* (1698)

preventing nightmares

The modern meaning of 'nightmare' as simply a bad dream obscures an earlier, more specific meaning, and there is also historical confusion with a different phenomenon called hag-riding. The original 'nightmare' referred to a distressing night-time condition whereby a sleeper feels a huge weight on his/her chest, suffocating and immobilizing at the same time. This was presumed to be an attack by an evil creature called an incubus or, in Old English, a 'maere' or 'mara'. The similarity in words, and the metaphor of being 'ridden' by the spirit, suggested a connection with real 'mares', and the night-maere became a nightmare. A further step connects this spirit-riding with the phenomenon of 'hag-riding' proper, or witches riding real horses during the night and leaving them sweating and exhausted in their stables in the morning.

Various methods were recommended for keeping the nightmare at bay, all of which were also used in other protective contexts:

A flint-stone with a hole in it hung over the bed's head will prevent nightmare; or place your boots when taken off 'coming and going' – that is, the heel of the one beside the toe of the other.

East Anglia (1885)

A piece of iron nearby was also thought effective. In an early account of 1564, Thomas Blundeville of Norfolk describes the nightmare as resulting from bad digestion rather than supernatural causes, but then relates a 'fonde foolishe charme' in which his contemporaries believed. This involved a holed stone, to be hung over the sufferer, with an accompanying written charm.

red thread protects

A piece of red thread, tied round a farm animal or a person, was widely
believed to be effective as a protective amulet, particularly in Scotland
and Ireland, but also in the northernmost counties of England, and in
Wales. The thread was particularly effective if wound round a piece
of rowan, as summed up in a well-known couplet which existed in
numerous versions on both sides of the Scottish border:

> Rowan tree and red thread
> Mak the witches tine [lose] their speed.

or

> Rowan ash and red thread
> Keep the devils frae their speed.
>
> Scotland/N. England (1937)

The protective thread is most commonly described as effective for
cattle, but it was also useful for vulnerable humans, especially children.
The belief in red thread was already in circulation in medieval Britain,
as it is mentioned in the Saxon manuscripts edited by Cockayne
(*Leechdoms*, 1864), although the Saxon scribes copied most of their
material from classical and continental sources. It was certainly around
a long time before that, as evidenced by its inclusion in the writings
of St John Chrysostom of Antioch (AD 390) where he complains of
its use to protect children as being unchristian.

the magic bone of toads and frogs

A number of traditions relate that there is a particular bone in a toad's
body which, if located and removed in the right way, will confer
important power on its owner. This bone was regularly cited as the
key to the horseman's word, which involved uncanny mastery over
horses. There are several ways of obtaining this bone. The simplest
part was to place the toad on an ant hill and wait for the flesh to be
consumed:

> Then take the bones and go down to a good stream of runnin'
> water an' throw the bones i' the stream. All the bones but one
> will go downstream an' that one as won't go downstream is the
> breast-bone. Now, you must get 'old of this 'ere bone afore the

Devil gets it, an' if you get it and keep it allus by you – in your pocket, or wear it – then you can witch; as well as that you'll be safe from bein' witched yourself.   Lincolnshire (1936)

Other versions add extra details of things happening to test the resolve of the operator.

The belief in the power of this bone has been around in Britain for a long time. Reginald Scot mentions it in his *Discoverie of Witchcraft* (1584), where he describes it as engendering love. The whole idea was probably imported by writers of Scot's generation from the writings of the Roman writer Pliny, who was a great favourite with them. Pliny's account describes letting ants clean the bones of a frog, throwing a special bone into boiling water, and using the bone to gain mastery over dogs and, if it is worn as an amulet, it acts as an aphrodisiac.

touching iron and touching wood

Touching iron and touching wood are often regarded as two aspects of the same superstitious impulse, but whereas the 'touching' part is similar, they are used in very different contexts. Records show that the most common use for touching iron was when someone had uttered a forbidden word, such as 'pig' while at sea, or when confronted by a potentially dangerous or unlucky person, such as a witch:

A custom . . . prevailed till recently among the fishermen of the east coast of Scotland . . . the practice was to touch iron – 'cauld iron' as they called it. It was apparently derived from the belief in witchcraft and always was occasioned by some person or object present, or by an expression used by a person present. I have, for example, been told by a venerable housekeeper that once, when speaking to one of these men in her kitchen, she was interrupted by the entrance of an old woman, reputed to be a witch. The fisherman's consternation was great, and he made it exceedingly emphatic by uttering the words 'Cauld iron!' and affecting at the same time a successful dash towards an iron hook fixed in the ceiling.   Scotland (1906)

Touching iron was also not recorded nearly so often as the ubiquitous touching wood, and only seems to have been widely used in Scottish fishing communities in the nineteenth and twentieth centuries, but as iron was very widely valued as protective in other contexts, it seems that it was only the 'touching' part which was new. The earliest

reference so far found, as quoted by Iona Opie and Moira Tatem, is
from the 1730s:

> In Queen Mary's reign 'tag' was all the play; where a lad saves
> himself by touching cold iron.   *The Craftsman* (4 February 1738)

The earliest references to 'touch wood' are also to a children's game.
'Touching wood' is one of the best-known superstitions in the British
Isles today. We touch wood and/or we say 'touch wood' whenever we
have boasted, or tempted fate in some way:

> We 'tap wood', for instance, after saying I've never had a fall from
> my bicycle (some of us do this instinctively almost before the
> sentence is out of our mouths).   Northumberland (1929)

As indicated here, for many people the action is almost involuntary.
If superstitions were subject to the laws of evolution, the ultimate
evolutionary goal for a belief would be that it becomes so much part
of everyday life and speech that it ceases to be regarded as a belief at
all. This is what has happened to 'touch wood'. Even for those who
do not believe the notion of tempting fate, boasting is still seen as
mildly unacceptable social behaviour, and many say 'touch wood' as a
way of signalling to listeners that we are aware of the social niceties
and to add a touch of humility to balance our transgression.

As usual with well-known superstitions, this one is not nearly as
old as it is often claimed to be, and can only be traced to the early
nineteenth century, and even then not in the form we know it. The
two most popular explanations of origin are that the belief goes back to
pagan times when we believed in tree spirits, or that we are invoking
Christ's protection by referring to the wood of the Cross. The former is
nothing but guesswork, based on the conviction that all superstitions
must be ancient, and it has the usual problem of spanning thousands of
years with no evidence at all of its existence, or, for that matter, any
evidence that 'we' ever believed in tree spirits. The second may have
some truth in it, in that devout Christians often found religious connotations for everyday actions, and although it is unlikely to be the origin of
the custom, it may well have been a significant factor in its continuance.

The real origin appears to be much more prosaic. The two earliest
references, as identified by the indefatigable Iona Opie and Moira
Tatem, are as late as 1805 and 1828, and both refer to a children's game,
Tiggy-touch-wood, or similar. In this chasing game, one is safe when

touching wood, and there were spoken elements, such as 'Tiggy, tiggy, touch wood, I've got no wood', chanted to tease the chaser. Tiggy-touch-wood was an extremely well-known game, and it is most likely that the phrase passed into everyday language. This is not a new origin theory. When the custom was discussed by contributors to *Notes & Queries* in 1906, many of the writers assumed that the phrase and the action were simply extended from the game.

wraiths

A wraith is the spectral double of a person, which appears to others at a distance, while s/he is still alive. Although sometimes used as a synonym for 'ghost', it is useful to preserve the distinction between the ghost as spectre of the *dead* and the wraith as spectre of the still *living*, although, to complicate matters, the latter might be just on the point of dying. Wraiths can appear for various reasons and purposes, and can be summoned by others or appear of their own volition, depending on the context. The four most pertinent to the present study are those summoned by particular love-divination procedures; those summoned in porch watching; those which are seen in second-sight visions, and those which appear to distant family and friends, usually at the point of death of the real person. Accounts of encounters with wraiths of those about to die are common in the folklore literature, and are often characterized by the matter-of-fact and underplayed tone in which they are related:

> Esther Morton, of Black Heddon, was gathering sticks, and made out of the way of the farmer, on whose land she was, and whom she was on the point of meeting; suddenly she remembered that he was very ill, and could not be there. She returned home alarmed, and found that her neighbour had just died. Northumberland (1860/62)

LUCKY AND UNLUCKY NUMBERS

Various superstitions include an element of numbers, but there does not seem to have been any systematic numerology in British traditional lore. The only general rule was that odd numbers were lucky, and sometimes that even numbers were unlucky, but even this did not hold true across the board. Particular numbers can be special in particular instances, but attempts in popular books to brand any number as 'holy' or 'mystical' are grossly misleading.

counting

A deep-seated principle of superstition is that one must not tempt fate, and a visible confidence in the future must therefore be avoided lest it bring retribution in the form of bad luck, or worse. In addition, there are vindictive beings, whether witches, fairies, bad neighbours, or rival tradesmen, who wish us harm at every turn, and it is best if these potential malefactors are prevented from obtaining too close a knowledge of our affairs. With these everyday problems in mind, there has long been an aversion to measuring, weighing, and counting, in many walks of life:

> All fishermen know how unlucky it is to count one's fish until the catch has been landed, as, however freely they may be biting, counting them would invariably stop all sport for the day.   Guernsey (1864)

> A Suffolk shepherd, for instance, will seldom willingly tell even his master the number of lambs born until the lambing-season is over for fear of bad luck.   Suffolk (1943)

> It is not good to count the cakes when done baking. They will not
> in that case last any time. Highland Scotland (1900)

An aversion to numbering too closely can be found in both biblical
(2 Samuel 24: 10) and classical sources, but the earliest British examples
date from only the late seventeenth century. It is quite possible that
the belief entered the British tradition direct from the Bible and
classical literature in medieval times or later, but as the notion seems
so basic to normal superstitious thinking it is equally possible that it
had been here for much longer. Counting also features in other beliefs
– it was unlucky, for example, to count the stars – but the one context
where counting was obligatory was in cures, especially those for warts.

odd numbers good

In general, superstitious people preferred odd numbers to even
numbers:

> A friend and I were visiting an old woman of 82 years, who was
> suffering from rheumatism. The latter asked me to give her seven
> drops of oil of juniper from a bottle standing near. From curiosity
> I asked, 'Supposing it was six or eight drops, would that make much
> difference, Mrs. Lee?' She answered: 'Aw, me dear, that wouldn't
> never du; it must be odd numbers to have any vartue'. Devon (1927)

> [Diary entry of Edith Olivier] I rather dread 1928. Don't like years
> with even numbers. Wiltshire (1989)

This preference for odd numbers was well established even by Shakespeare's time (e.g. *The Merry Wives of Windsor*, 1597) and was also
prevalent in classical times (e.g. Pliny, *Natural History*, AD 77). Individual odd numbers, especially three and seven, and to a lesser extent
five and nine, occur regularly in a positive light in other beliefs and
cures, but again this is not an invariable rule, as the number three, for
example, turns up in several bad luck superstitions. It should also
be remembered that numerous everyday items which have positive
overtones come in even numbers: twelve apostles, ten commandments,
four evangelists, four elements, four points of the compass, and so on.
And in certain contexts, odd numbers of people were carefully avoided,
particularly at wedding feasts and funerals, as death omens.

three

As indicated, in British superstition in general, odd numbers are held
to be preferable to even ones, and three is often included in that
positive light. But in other contexts, the number is definitely unlucky:
a death in a community will always be followed by two others; break
one thing, break three; lighting three cigarettes from one match is
fatal; and it is usually three knocks that are heard to announce a death.
In addition, there is the general 'rule' that bad things come in threes,
which can be interpreted as narrowly or broadly as necessary:

> Bad luck and tragedy had to be tidied up for our Mum by running
> in threes, whether it was another dreaded conception by one of her
> neighbours, the death of a public figure, a whitlow, or a broken tea
> cup, the fates combined to keep her on tenterhooks until she had
> heard of a second and third occurrence.   London (1920s)

'Bad things come in threes' is still heard regularly, but so is 'third time
lucky'.

> This is the third Thursday we have retired to rest hoping that the
> next morning we should welcome home my aunt and cousins –
> may the third bring its reputed good fortune.
>
> New South Wales (Scottish) (1848)

This notion has been proverbial since at least the fourteenth century,
but the wording varies considerably – 'the third is a charm', 'the third
pays for all', 'the third time pays home', or, as in the fourteenth-century
poem of *Gawain and the Green Knight*, 'third time prove best'.

A specialized version of the general idea that bad luck comes in
threes holds that if you break something, it will be the first of three:

> One of my servants having accidentally broken a glass shade, asked
> for two other articles of little value, a wine bottle and a jam crock,
> that she might break them, and so prevent the two other accidents,
> perhaps to valuable articles, which would otherwise follow the
> accident to the glass shade.   (1891)

The idea was reasonably widespread in the late nineteenth century,
but has so far been traced back only to the 1860s.

The worst example of the negative sides of the number three
maintains that once death has visited a community, it will come three

times. 'One funeral makes three', they say (Lincolnshire, 1908). As
with the other unlucky-three superstitions, this one has not been
traced before the 1850s, but it was widely known right into the late
twentieth century – and may be believed still.

seventh son or daughter

A seventh son was widely believed to have certain gifts by virtue of
his birth, both in the direction of healing and in psychic powers. The
usual rule was that he had to be the seventh in an unbroken line of
males, from the same parents, and the seventh son of a seventh son
had even more pronounced powers. There has been some disagreement about whether seventh daughters were also gifted. Many authorities flatly denied it, while others argued that in the case of females it
was the *ninth* child which mattered. A significant number, however,
accepted that seventh daughters were just as good as seventh sons:

> I had an intimate knowledge of a seventh child, a relative, who was
> said to possess the power of healing by touch, and also the gift of
> clairvoyance, because she was born at midnight in All-Hallows –
> so her Derbyshire friends asserted. She certainly had clairvoyance
> to some degree, and had a curious way with young girls, after a
> quiet look at their faces telling them things concerning their future
> lives, some of which came about afterwards. Her touch was singu-
> larly soothing, and gave relief to pain.   Derbyshire (1914)

The most widely known attribute of the seventh child was that s/he
could cure the King's Evil (scrofula) simply by touch, in the same way
as the ruling monarch used to do, but all other diseases and complaints
came under their remit, too. Many simply touched the patient, while
others also used charms, herbs, medicines, and so on, to increase their
efficacy. Some made a living at this, but many reports stressed the
belief that they would lose their gifts if paid for their services, or even
if they were thanked. Seventh sons were often nicknamed 'doctor' in
their communities, and a regular motif in descriptions is that they
would have followed the medical profession if their parents could have
afforded it.

The seventh-son belief was extremely widespread, and was found
in every quarter of Britain and Ireland. It has been documented
regularly since at least the sixteenth century, with Thomas Lupton's *A*

Thousand Notable Things (1579) providing the earliest clear description. But a probable predecessor is found 300 years earlier, in the medieval Welsh manuscript published as the *Physicians of Myddvai* (*c.*1250), which shows that the seventh son was already regarded as special. The origins of the belief remain obscure. The usual assumption that it is simply a manifestation of the presumed 'mystical power' of the number seven is barely more than guesswork, as there is little evidence that seven was prized any more than any other odd number between one and ten in British tradition. Virtually the same belief was found in France and, to a lesser degree, other European countries, and it is probable that an origin should be sought there. It is probably no accident that France also had a strong tradition of kings healing by touch, which developed at roughly the same time as in Britain.

thirteen

One of the most widely distributed superstitions of modern times is that the number thirteen is unlucky. This notion occurs in numerous guises, but in particular in the belief that Friday 13th is an unlucky day, that thirteen people at a gathering or meal is so unlucky that one of them will die within a year, and that houses, flats, ocean liner cabins, hotel rooms, and so on, numbered thirteen are so unpopular that they are invariably changed to 12a or 14.

> To meet the views of superstitious people, the Harrow Council have decided in future to substitute 12a for 13 in the numbering of houses. It is rather astonishing that the present year is not referred to as 1912a.   London (1913)

Despite the modern popular opinion that fear of the number thirteen is an ancient belief, the idea of thirteen as an unlucky number, or Friday 13th as an unlucky day, cannot be traced back further than the mid nineteenth century, and appears to be a Victorian invention. Only in the sense of thirteen at table, or thirteen in a company, can we find any earlier references, and that belief first took shape around the turn of the eighteenth century.

A number of questionable origin-theories have been put forward to explain the dislike of the number. Some, for example, claim that sixteenth- and seventeenth-century witches organized themselves in covens of thirteen, thus giving the number a bad name for the godly.

The evidence for covens is scant, as they mainly existed in the imaginations of the prosecutors, and even where witches' confessions speak of groups and gatherings, thirteen is hardly ever mentioned. The whole notion of covens of thirteen was floated by Margaret Murray in her attempts to prove that witchcraft was the survival of an old pagan religion, which it was not, but her theories have been enthusiastically perpetuated by influential writers such as Robert Graves and Gerald Gardner, and many modern devotees who appreciate the value of a good conspiracy theory to underpin belief. Murray's ideas have been entirely discredited.

The other main theory is that the number is unlucky because there were thirteen people at the Last Supper, and Jesus was killed soon after. This explanation probably has a grain of truth, but not in the way it is generally presented. Put simply, before the Reformation, it was standard Christian practice to replicate the way that Jesus did things whenever possible, and this included the organization of personnel into groups of thirteen. The *Oxford English Dictionary* thus gives one of the early uses of 'convent' as meaning 'a company of twelve (or, including the superior, thirteen) "religious" persons whether constituting a separate community or a section of a larger one'. After the Reformation, however, such activities were re-branded as 'superstitious' by the new Protestant churches, and forbidden. Almost overnight thirteen was officially changed from 'good' to 'bad'. Any generally negative aspects of the number thirteen in Britain can thus date from only the late sixteenth century at the very earliest.

In fact, the earliest reference we can find for thirteen being generally unlucky was published in 1852:

> Odd numbers. They are lucky, except the number thirteen, which
> is the unluckiest of numbers.   Yorkshire (1852)

This notion is repeated occasionally in the literature from then until the end of the century, but after that it rapidly became widely known and, it must be said, fashionable.

thirteen at table or in company

The only one of the superstitions regarding thirteen which can be traced back beyond the Victorian era is that thirteen people at a table, or in a company, is unlucky.

> Dining lately with a friend, our conviviality was suddenly interrupted by the discovery of a maiden lady, who observed that our party consisted of thirteen. Her fears, however, were not without hope, till she found, after a very particular enquiry, that none of her married friends were likely to make any addition to the number. She was then fully assured that one of the party would die within the twelvemonth.   *Gentleman's Magazine* (1796)

The one to die soon is usually specified as the first one to rise from the table. Several of the published accounts detail tricks to avoid the fate once the number of guests has been realized: in addition to everyone standing up at the same time, the hostess quietly leaves the room and eats in the kitchen; one person sits at another table; the house cat joins the company; or they discover that one of the women present is pregnant and therefore counts as two.

The earliest intimation that we have of this danger of thirteen in a company is found at the end of the seventeenth century. In a letter written in 1697 by the antiquarian John Aubrey to Awsham Churchill, the London bookseller, published in the fourth edition of Aubrey's *Miscellanies* (1857), he refers to 'a very pretty remark' in the *Athenian Mercury* of June 1695, which tells the story of two women who were close friends, but one became very ill with small-pox. She sent for her friend, but the latter failed to come as she was worried about catching the disease. The sufferer died, and her ghost later appeared to her friend, warning her 'you have not long to live, therefore prepare to die; and when you are at a feast, and make the thirteenth person in number, then remember my words'. The piece ends with the key words: 'The gentleman that told this story, says that there is hardly any person of quality but what knows it to be true.' In other words, it was a contemporary legend (a ghost story spread like a rumour) of the time. By the second known reference (*Spectator*, 8 March 1711) the superstition has taken on all the details we recognize.

In the absence of other evidence to the contrary, it is almost certain that the point of origin of this particular superstition comes between these dates, 1695 and 1711, and is based on a popular ghost legend of the time, in which the 'thirteen' is a mere detail. However, in common with the other 'thirteen' beliefs, this one has attracted its fair share of invented origins based on guesswork. Most people are satisfied with the simple explanation that there were thirteen at the Last Supper, and this explanation has been widely accepted since the mid nineteenth century at least, but it has never been intellectually satisfying. Certainly, the Last Supper was soon followed by death (of two of the principals, in fact – Judas and Jesus), but there must have been many other gatherings of the Disciples, including meals, at which the thirteen were present which were not at all unlucky. One must also face the sleight of hand of popular writing on superstition. When a writer states that the superstition of thirteen at the table is based on the Last Supper, the implication is that it dates from that time, but as we have seen, this rests on the assumption that it existed, but went unrecorded for some 1,600 years.

A different explanation, which is currently popular in certain circles, claims roots for the belief in Norse mythology. It cites a banquet that Odin held at Valhalla for twelve guests, which Loki gatecrashed and during which he murdered Balder. Unsurprisingly, nothing here is correct. Folklorist Jacqueline Simpson demolishes the whole idea, with reference to the original poem called 'Lokasenna':

> The feast in question was held by Aegir, god of the sea, at his hall; 18 gods and goddesses are named as present (that includes Aegir, the host, Loki, the gatecrasher, and Thor, who arrived late); and the murder of Balder took place on an entirely different occasion.
>
> *FLS News* (November 2001)

Friday 13th *see* lucky and unlucky days.

number 666

On the authority of the Bible, the number 666 is the 'number of the Beast':

> 16 And he causeth all, both small and great, rich and poor, free and bond, to receive a mark in their right hand, or in their foreheads: 17 And that no man might buy or sell, save he that had the mark, or the name of the beast, or the number of his name. 18 Here is wisdom. Let him that hath understanding count the number of the beast: for it is the number of a man: and his number *is* Six hundred threescore *and* six.   Revelation 13:16–18

Ever since the Bible became generally available, these verses have fascinated people and prompted them to attempt to unravel the mysterious language. In London in 1666 – clearly a date which would increase interest in the topic – Samuel Pepys recorded in his diary that he found a book by Francis Potter entitled *An Interpretation of the Number 666*, published in 1642, 'mighty ingenious' (16 February 1665/6; 10 November 1666).

The main manifestation of this concern in the realm of modern superstition is more down to earth, in that the number is believed to be extremely unlucky in all contexts. Fortunately, unlike the number thirteen, which is a common house-number, the Beast's number does not occur often in everyday life. One exception is in car-registration numbers, and the popular press occasionally runs pieces which show that any car thus encumbered brings dreadful luck to its owner. Consider poor Mr Quinn, whose car registration was HFR 666S and whose woes were detailed in 'Devil Plate Has Wrecked My Life', with the sub-title 'Wife died, burgled twice, and garage burnt' (*Sun*, 26 April 1993). It has since been reported that no more 666 number-plates are being issued. In another context, the local council of the London Borough of Croydon was asked by relatives to renumber grave 666 in a local cemetery (*Croydon Advertiser*, 3 December 1993).

Attempts to decode the number 666 have continued, and indeed have greatly increased in recent years, using a variety of alpha-numeric codes and systems, and many have succeeded in proving that the number refers to the Roman Catholic Church, the Pope (individually and Popes collectively), Napoleon, the American government, any recent American president one cares to name, communism, the Soviet Union, Adolf Hitler, and so on. Interested readers are invited to carry out a search on the Internet (try '666 beast') and they will get more information on the subject than anyone could possibly need. For a synopsis of similar concerns in the nineteenth century, see William Jones, *Credulities Past and Present* (1880).

For those who are happy to accept 'the Beast' as Satan, the text of verses 16 and 17 offers ample scope for concern. The text has been ingeniously identified as referring to the invention of bar codes, and there is a widespread conspiracy theory that all bar codes have a secret 666 encoded in them, and that 'the government', under the control of the Devil, is planning to implant everybody with microchips which are similarly encoded. It is not clear what will happen once we all have this 'mark' on us, but it will be very bad. Again, an Internet search provides ample evidence of the wide-ranging international nature of this hypothesis, including the basic assumption that anyone who questions the reality of such theories is by definition part of the conspiracy.

The Natural World

❧

ANIMALS

Lucky Meeting a black cat • Hairs from a donkey's back • Meeting an elephant • Carrying a hare's or rabbit's foot • Seeing the first lamb of spring facing you • Letting a goat run with your cows

Unlucky Kittens born in May • Letting cats near a baby • Hearing a howling dog • Meeting a hare • Rats or mice leaving your house • Handling a toad

❧

BIRDS

Lucky Robins, wrens, swallows, housemartins • Rooks nesting near your house • Money in your pocket when you hear the first cuckoo

Unlucky Birds pecking at your window • Birds in the house • Cock crowing at the wrong time • Seeing a single magpie • Harming a robin or seagull • Taking peacock's feathers indoors

❧

INSECTS

Lucky Telling the bees of a death in the family • Killing the first butterfly or wasp you see • Finding a ladybird

Unlucky Killing a beetle • Handling a caterpillar • Killing a spider or cricket

❧

PLANTS

Lucky Finding a four-leafed clover • Finding white heather • Kissing under mistletoe

Unlucky Picking blackberries after Michaelmas • Handling dandelions • Bringing small numbers of snowdrops or daffodils into the house •

Bringing hawthorn blossom indoors • Picking up flowers in street or churchyard

❧

TREES

Lucky Planting a holly tree near the house • Catching a falling leaf • Carrying a piece of rowan

Unlucky Fruit and blossom on same tree at the same time • Bringing holly indoors before Christmas Eve • Speaking when passing a monkey puzzle tree

❧

NATURAL PHENOMENA AND WEATHER

Lucky Turning money and bowing at the new moon • Seeing the new moon over your right shoulder • Planting crops at the waxing of the moon

Unlucky A rainbow with two ends on the same island • Pointing at the moon • Counting the stars • Seeing the new moon through glass

ANIMALS

animals kneeling

A widespread belief held that at midnight on Christmas Eve all the cattle and other farmyard animals knelt in their stalls or in the fields in honour of the birth of Christ:

> Christmas Eve – The country people have a notion that on this evening oxen kneel in their stalls and moan. In boyhood I was induced more than once to attend on the occasion; but whether for want of faith, or neglect of the instructions given me, I know not – they would not do their duty.   N. England (1829)

Some writers report that their informants claimed to have successfully witnessed these events on a regular basis, but others regarded it as sacrilegious to attempt to do so.

As with other seasonal beliefs, the reform of the calendar in 1752 caused confusion for the faithful, who were forced to choose between the new official calendar and 'old style' dates eleven days later, and many cattle chose to stick with tradition, at least for a while. Variations on the same theme existed in the less common beliefs that at Christmas bees in the hives hum the old One Hundredth Psalm, animals in the field turn to the east and bow, and that donkeys kneel at Easter.

These beliefs are a clear example of the standard motif that nature observes the Christian calendar, which provides both a charming vignette to be told to children, and a proof and legitimization of the religion for the faithful. Belief in the Holy Thorn and the sun dancing at Easter have the same basis. The first clear documentation of the cattle kneeling is by John Brand in 1790, and it was widely reported through the nineteenth and early twentieth centuries, although on present evidence, it seems that Scottish animals were less devout than others in the British Isles. Brand suggests that the belief originated in a popular print of the stable scene, in which the oxen are shown kneeling down, and this certainly seems likely.

cats

According to tradition, cats were viewed with more suspicion than affection in Britain, and there were far more superstitions about cats than any other domestic animal. Many have been forgotten, despite being very widely known in their time, and only one or two survive in anything like the vigour of previous times. Ask a British person nowadays about cat beliefs and they are likely to reply 'black cats are lucky', and perhaps that 'witches have black cats', or 'cats have nine lives' and leave it at that.

black cats

That black cats are lucky is now almost universally accepted in Britain. Good-luck cards bear their pictures, lucky charms are on sale, and brides are happy to meet one:

> A well-known firm of soap manufacturers recently used as an advertisement a charming picture, obviously a photograph, of a family wedding group standing on the church steps and watching, with evident delight, a black cat walking up to the bride.   (1957)

The historical picture, however, is less straightforward, and there are plenty of references which make it quite clear that for some the black cat was a far from good omen:

> it is a very unfortunate thing for a man to meet early in a morning an ill-favoured man or woman, a rough-footed hen, a shag-haired dog, or a black cat.   John Melton, *Astrologaster* (1620)

Cat beliefs are confusing, and often contradictory, and it is not always possible to reach a satisfactory synthesis. This is partly because we have nowadays lost many of the complexities and subtleties of past beliefs, as, for example, in this instance, where the situation of how and when you met the cat dictated much of the meaning:

> A black cat crossing one's path is a lucky omen. A black cat passing by a window foretells the arrival of a visitor.   Guernsey (1975)

The relative luckiness of black cats is not specifically mentioned until Melton's piece in 1620, and references before 1800 are almost non-existent, although there are numerous reports which specify a black cat in cures. Contrasting this paucity of material with the plethora of references from the 1850s onwards at least allows us to say that the belief was nowhere near as popular in the earlier period as it was later to become, and it seems to be a classic example of the growth of a superstition over time.

cats' behaviour

The idea that certain aspects of a cat's behaviour have meaning above and beyond its nature has a long history, and although there is not complete agreement over meanings, the general outline has remained remarkably constant for centuries. The most widespread has been the notion that when the house cat washes itself, if it washes behind or over the ears it presages rain, or a major change in the weather:

> It froze in the afternoon and the barometer still rising, but in the evening it thawed and some rain fell. I was saying before dinner that there would be an alteration of weather soon as I a long time observed one of our cats wash over both her ears – an old observation, and I must now believe it to be a pretty true one.
>
> Norfolk, James Woodforde, *Diary* (30 January 1794)

This meaning has remained relatively constant from at least 1507 to the late twentieth century. Another belief is that the cat sitting with her back to the fire also predicts the weather – snow or frost in some versions or, again, rain. However, the worst weather is predicted by a cat's sudden unexplained activity – chasing its own tail, much scratching of the furniture, for example – which means high winds or storms.

cats have nine lives

The notion that a cat has nine lives was already proverbial in the
sixteenth century:

> No wyfe, a woman hath nyne lyves like a cat,
>> John Heywood, *Proverbs* (1546)

It was quoted by dramatists and poets regularly throughout the seventeenth century and has remained in common parlance to the present
day. It is not clear where the idea originated, although one early
reference links it specifically to witches:

> A cat hath nine lives, that is to say, a witch may take on her a cat's
> body, nine times.   W. Baldwin, *Beware the Cat* (1584)

But again it is not known whether he was quoting a genuine origin or
was repeating an invented legend of origin such as those so often
presented in the present day in similar situations.

May kittens

It was commonly believed that cats born in May were unlucky, sickly,
of little use as mousers, and prone to catching other creatures:

> Kittens born in May will bring snakes into the house – They are
> also unlucky, apparently. Owing to the snake story the servant of a
> friend of mine was about to drown an entire family of kittens born
> in May, but owing to her remonstrance two were spared: one came
> to an untimely end, being murdered by her own pet dog and the
> other was eaten by a rat in its early infancy. On inquiry I find the
> snake legend obtains in my own kitchen.   Devon (1901)

Although May is an unlucky month in other contexts, there is no clue
as to why cats in particular were singled out in this way, although a
few informants claim that other domestic animals, and even human
children, born in the month were also unlucky and unlikely to thrive.
Available references show that the superstition was known in most
parts of England, but evidence from elsewhere in the British Isles is
lacking. It appears also to spring into life, fully formed, all over the
country in the 1850s, so it must have been around for at least a while
before that time.

cats and death

In many areas, when death occurred in a house, the family cats and dogs would immediately be removed:

> The household companions of dog and cat were rigidly excluded from the stricken house; indeed, it was not uncommon for the cat to be imprisoned beneath an inverted tub, for it was believed that if either of these animals should jump or cross over the dead body, the welfare of the spirit of the deceased would certainly be affected.
>
> S.W. Scotland (1911)

The reasons given for this exclusion are not always exactly the same. The rationalist explanation is that animals left with a corpse might maul it in some way, or worse. But this does not explain the very real fear evinced even when the body was already in its coffin, or when the funeral procession was under way. If a cat or dog did succeed in jumping on to or over the corpse, the animal was immediately and unceremoniously killed. The custom was already widespread in the eighteenth century, and is probably much older.

Another belief centres on the ability of cats and dogs to predict a coming death, either by a natural but unexplained sense, or by a supernatural ability:

> When a person lay seriously ill at home and the family cat refused to stay indoors, then it was certain that the sick person would soon die.   Cambridgeshire (1969)

cats dangerous to have around

It is still fairly common to hear people advise against leaving sleeping babies and cats in the same room. The danger is usually expressed that the cat will 'suffocate the baby' by lying across its face, or that cat hairs cause asthma, but this can be seen as just the latest phase in a long tradition of concern about the generally dangerous nature of cats. In previous times, it was said that cats would 'suck the babies' breath away':

> A child of eighteen months old was found dead near Plymouth; and it appeared, on the coroner's inquest, that the child died in consequence of a cat sucking its breath, occasioning a strangulation.
>
> Devon (1791)

The idea that cats are dangerous and unhealthy to have around was easily combined with notions of the supernatural:

> That the breath of these animals is poisonous, that they can play with serpents and remain uninjured, whilst their fur communicates the infection of the venom of those reptiles, that they lend themselves readily to infernal agents and purposes, that certain portions of their bodies possess magical properties and were efficacious in the preparation of charmed potions, and that they are partly supernatural creatures, endowed with a power of bringing good or evil fortune upon their possessors . . . was once devoutly believed by the illiterate, as it is partially at this very day.
>
> *The Mirror* (10 March 1832)

Nevertheless, the assumption that a witch's familiar will necessarily be a black cat is a relatively modern one, but is now irrevocably fixed by countless cartoon films and children's books. Cats became the dominant species for familiars only in the later nineteenth century, and before that time any small animal might be chosen.

dogs

Dogs do not feature so widely in British superstitions as cats do, although they certainly have a traditional 'uncanny' side and are believed to be sensitive to the supernatural. A dog howling was one of the most widespread death omens, but they had other methods of prediction. For example:

> Dogs scratching holes in the earth were looked upon by country folk as digging graves, and it was confidently expected that a death would surely follow in the locality. So great was the belief in this omen, that I have heard of persons who would follow a dog and fill up the holes it had made.   Wiltshire (1893–5)

Furthermore, they must never be allowed to jump over a dead body. They also featured in cures, both as active and passive agents.

dogs howling

The idea that a dog howling is an omen of death is so commonly reported that it has almost reached the status of cliché in folklore writing:

The mournful howling of a dog, termed in Welsh *Udo*, during the night, especially if close to the house of a sick person, was deemed a presage of death. The writer has many times heard it stated by those who knew the dog that an old dame living in *Pen dre* (top of the town) had an aged terrier, which seemed gifted with the faculty of foretelling death, as there was scarcely a person who died without 'old Pal's' dog having his howl in the street.   Montgomeryshire (1877)

Many writers simply include the howling dog in their list of omens without further comment, but where details are included the most common are that the howling must occur at night, and be directly outside a particular house, for it to be taken seriously. The notion that dogs can sense supernatural beings, such as ghosts, which humans cannot has also long been a commonplace of popular belief, and the howling omen is most likely an extension of this belief.

For Shakespeare, and other early writers, a howling dog was not necessarily a symbol of death, but a certain omen of evil – along with owls, crows, and the like:

> The owl shrieked at thy birth – an evil sign;
> The night-crow cried, aboding luckless time;
> Dogs howled, and hideous tempests shook down trees;
> The raven rooked her on the chimney's pot;
> And chattering pies in dismal discords sung.
>
> *Henry VI Part 3* (c.1592)

The earliest reference in English is found in the *Gospelles of Dystaves* (1507), but that describes the tradition of the Low Countries rather than Britain, and it is not till the seventeenth century that a clear example is found in this country: 'That dogs . . . by their howling portend death and calamities is plain by history and experience' (A. Ross, *Arcana Microcosmi*, 1651). The belief was still being quoted in the later twentieth century.

dogs as lucky or unlucky animals

The general behaviour of dogs was watched for signs of good or bad luck, but again these have not been reported as frequently as those concerning cats. To be followed in the street by a strange dog, or for one to come into your house, was generally regarded as lucky:

Good fortune was predicted for one of my sisters, because a strange
dog followed her when she was a babe in arms.

Lincolnshire, Grantham Journal (22 June 1878)

The first clear reference to this belief is in the *Connoisseur* of 1755, but
Iona Opie and Moira Tatem quote a related belief from about 1700
that it was evidence of forthcoming ill-fortune if your own dog
would not follow you. Nevertheless, in certain circumstances, a dog's
appearance was not welcome. A dog crossing the path of a funeral
party, or coming between bride and groom during the wedding ceremony, was occasionally cited as very unlucky indeed.

donkeys

In common parlance, the donkey is characterized as stubborn, stupid,
and totally unglamorous, but it features in a positive light in several
superstitions and cures. At the root of this positive reputation is the
fable which explains that the black markings on the donkey's back and
shoulders form a cross, which first appeared after it bore Jesus Christ
into Jerusalem (or, in some versions, the Holy Family on their way to
the stable):

> [Circus worker] Anna said that the donkey was God's animal. She
> said her nan had taught her that. She said that it had a cross on its
> back.   England (1990s)

One result of this cross is that 'The devil can turn himself into every
animal except a donkey' (Co. Tyrone, 1972). Donkeys are thus said to be
generally lucky to have around, and they have figured in two well-known
cures for various childhood diseases. First described in 1851, one of these
cures involved placing a lock of the donkey's hair in a bag worn round
the sufferer's neck. In the other, the child was passed over and under
the animal's body a requisite number of times. This cure was regularly
reported from the 1820s until the mid twentieth century.

elephants

A few twentieth-century references claim that meeting an elephant
was regarded as lucky:

> [Lucky things for wedding to meet] . . . and so, rather curiously, is
> an elephant. The odds against encountering an elephant on the

way to an English wedding would seem to be fairly high, yet the superstition is well known. I was once at a marriage at Morecambe when the bridegroom did meet such a beast as he drove to church, and afterwards received numerous congratulations on his singular good fortune.   Lancashire (1957)

frogs

Frogs and toads are regarded as interchangeable in many traditions, but where toads were often seen as ugly and poisonous, frogs were viewed in a more positive light. They were widely used in cures for human ailments, but surprisingly few other superstitions about them have survived, and even those which are recorded are often off-shoots of beliefs about other creatures. Frogs were recommended in a wide range of medicinal contexts, but the method of using the animal varied considerably. For ailments affecting the throat and respiratory organs, such as thrush and whooping cough, the frog was held in front of the patient's mouth and then released, to take the disease with it. But a more widespread cure for a range of diseases involved wearing frog's or toad's legs in a bag round the neck:

> A charm for fits was a leg of a frog sewn up in a heart-shaped woollen bag with some incantations. The patient dared not open the bag or the efficacy would be void.   Devon (1934)

Another method was to swallow small live frogs, or make them into a soup, which was recommended for consumption, whooping cough, and other ailments. All these methods were also used in conjunction with other creatures, such as spiders and mice, and were widely known in folk medicine.

see also **toads**

goats

Goats featured surprisingly little in the superstitions of Britain and Ireland, and such beliefs as have been recorded are scattered and contradictory, so that no consistent overall view seems possible. The only belief which was widely reported was that keeping a goat with cattle and horses was beneficial, and farmers across Britain and Ireland followed this practice. Apart from being generally 'lucky', the goats were reputed to have a calming effect on the cattle, and also, more specifically, to prevent abortion in the cows:

> The practice of keeping a goat among a herd of cows to prevent abortion is by no means confined to Leicestershire. It must be a Billy goat, and the more it stinks the better. How the charm works nobody knows. Since I introduced a he-goat among my shorthorns, abortion has ceased. Previously it was very troublesome.
>
> Gloucestershire (1910)

Some farmers believed that goats ate certain 'herbs' which were noxious to cattle, while others claimed that the smell of the goats was somehow protective, or that they actually attracted diseases to themselves and thus prevented infection of the cows. Goats were believed to have a similarly beneficial effect on horses, and were regularly kept in stables. There is no doubt that the practice was widespread and literally believed, and it has the hallmarks of an old custom, but no evidence can be found of its existence before about 1840. Similar claims were made, less commonly, for donkeys, but the earliest reference is still only from 1799.

Considering the centuries-old propensity for portraying the Devil as a goat, which still survives in countless films and book illustrations, there seems to be little in traditional belief to reflect this idea. A handful of reports suggest an affinity, but in a very mild, almost homely fashion:

> A superstition prevails both in England and Scotland that goats are never to be seen for twenty-four hours together, owing to their paying Satan a visit once during that period to have their beards combed.   *The Mirror* (10 March 1832)

hares and rabbits

Hares have a strangely mixed reputation in the traditions of Britain and Ireland. They have been described consistently as unlucky, unfit to eat, uncanny, and as witches in disguise, but newborn children were formerly fed on hares' brains, and numerous people have carried a hare's or rabbit's foot for luck or to cure or prevent disease. The documentary record for hare beliefs is unusually full, and a significant number are mentioned by medieval writers, while some have lasted well into living memory.

hare's foot and rabbit's foot

The carrying of a hare's or rabbit's foot was a well-known cure for a variety of ailments, including rheumatism and cramp:

> The bone also in a hare's foot mitigateth the crampe, as none other bone nor part else of the hare doth.
>
> <div align="right">Reginald Scot, <i>Discoverie of Witchcraft</i> (1584)</div>

And Samuel Pepys carried one for colic:

> So homeward, in my way buying a hare and taking it home – which arose upon my discourse today with Mr. Batten in Westminster-hall – who showed me my mistake, that my hares-foot hath not the joint to it, and assures me that he never had his cholique since he carried it about him, for I no sooner handled his foot but my belly begin to loose and to break wind.   Samuel Pepys, <i>Diary</i> (20 January 1665)

These descriptions of the curative properties of hares' feet pre-date any references to their being carried as lucky amulets, but were probably taken direct from classical sources, such as Pliny's *Natural History* (AD 77), in the sixteenth century.

A rabbit's foot is a well-known lucky amulet in the present day, but its history is strangely difficult to pin down. The earliest reference links a hare's foot with protection:

> [My mother] also carries a hare's foot in her pocket, to guard against attacks in that quarter [by witchcraft] by day.   Westmorland (1827)

But there are no more references until well into the twentieth century, when it is always a rabbit's foot which is valued. Given its current reputation as a 'lucky charm', it is strange that so few historical references have come to light. This is in complete contrast to the United States, where it is probably the most widely known amulet of all. It is likely that the current awareness of the rabbit's foot in Britain today is an introduction from North America, in the post-Second World War era.

meeting hares or rabbits

The good or bad luck which is attached to meeting particular animals or people at the beginning of a journey is a common motif in superstition, and the animal most often singled out is the hare (or occasionally the rabbit):

> If a person on going to his work, or while going on an errand, were to see a hare cross the road in front of him, it was a token that ill luck would shortly befall him. Many under such circumstances would return home and not pursue their quest until the next meal had been eaten, for beyond that the evil influence did not extend.
>
> W. Scotland (1879)

The vast majority of informants claim that meeting a hare is a powerfully bad omen in itself, but a few distinguish between whether the animal approaches from the right (good) or left (bad), while others state that seeing the hare is all right, it is only if it actually crosses your path that it is unfortunate. It is unusual to have more than one confirmation of the existence of a belief in the medieval era, but both John of Salisbury (1159) and Nigel de Longchamps (1180) show that it was already well known in Britain in the twelfth century.

The belief has been found in every quarter of the British Isles, is unusually well documented into the late twentieth century, and has remained remarkably stable in meaning, considering its longevity. The general association between hares and witches in British superstition was formerly widely known, and this may possibly be at the root of the fear of meeting one.

hares as witches

It was common knowledge, for centuries, that witches could turn themselves into hares. Many folklore collections have a version of a tale about hunters trying to shoot or catch a hare which continually eludes them, until it is finally injured and seen to enter a nearby house. When the men get into the house they find an old woman with the same injuries as had been inflicted on the hare. In some versions the hare can be harmed only by a silver bullet. It is a striking characteristic of traditional British witches that they usually turned themselves into small and relatively harmless creatures – hares, cats, mice, and the like

– and the height of their mischief when thus transformed was to milk cows illicitly:

> It has been a frequent complaint, from old times, as well as in the present, that certain hags in Wales, as well as in Ireland and Scotland, changed themselves into the shape of hares, that, sucking teats under this counterfeit form, they might stealthily rob other people's milk.   Gerald of Wales, *Topographica Hibernica* (1184)

This is the earliest known mention of witch-hares, but the notion was recorded regularly right up to the twentieth century.

hedgehogs

It was very widely believed in past centuries that hedgehogs sucked milk from cows' udders as the cattle lay in the fields, and they were thus killed on sight by farmers and their workers. Cows giving bloody milk was taken as particular evidence of a hedgehog's involvement. The earliest documentary records show that the belief was the basis of official policy from Tudor times, and it probably existed before that time. Churchwardens' accounts from Ecclesfield, for example, quoted in *Notes & Queries* (1851), show that regular payments were being made for dead hedgehogs, along with other vermin, from at least 1590 to the 1740s.

While educated Victorian writers tried hard to eradicate this erroneous belief, it proved remarkably durable, and was still being claimed as true in many parts of the country well into the twentieth century.

horses

Horses featured in a wide range of superstitions and traditions, which reflects the vital part they have played in human life in the past. Horses and cows, as the most valuable animals in the farm economy, were particularly prone to witchcraft and ill-wishing. With cows such spite focused largely on their milk yield, but with horses the main evidence of their being bewitched was that they refused to work. Witches could make horses stand stock still, and refuse to budge, until released – a power which was also credited to those who knew the 'horseman's word'. But horses are far more intelligent than cows, and, together with dogs and cats, were thought sensitive to ghosts and other supernatural forces. The fact that horses could easily be 'overlooked' meant that one had to be particularly careful when buying and selling them.

It is very unlucky to refuse a good offer for a horse. If you do, some accident will befall the animal shortly afterwards.   Shropshire (1883)

Horses were believed to have been hag-ridden when they were found wild-eyed and exhausted, their coats matted with sweat as if they had been ridden hard all night, even though the stable door had been locked all the time. Stumbling was long regarded as a bad omen, especially when starting on a journey, but earlier writers show that a horse stumbling was particularly feared. John Melton recorded it in his list of superstitions in 1620, and a few years later John Webster included it with other well-known omens:

> How superstitiously we mind our evils!
> The throwing down salt, or crossing of a hare,
> Bleeding at nose, the stumbling of a horse,
> Or singing of a cricket, are of power
> To daunt whole man in us.

Duchess of Malfi (1623)

white horses

A range of other traditions focused on a horse's colour, particularly piebald and white animals. The most common superstition concerning the piebald horse was the strange belief that a sure cure for whooping cough could be obtained by asking the rider of such a horse to recommend something, and then to follow his instructions to the letter.

The piebald shared with the white horse the attribute that it was lucky to meet one, provided certain precautions were taken:

To meet a piebald horse was lucky. If two such horses were met apart, the one after the other, and if then the person who met them were to spit three times, and express any reasonable wish, it would be granted within three days.   W. Scotland (1879)

Nevertheless, references to white horses in this context outnumber those to piebalds by two to one. Documentary evidence for this belief starts only about 1850, but one informant, writing from Devon in 1852, described the custom in his 'own boyhood', so this may well put it back into the 1830s or beyond. It was collected in most parts of England and Wales, less often in Scotland or Ireland.

Another children's custom was to count the white horses seen, and make a wish when you reached 100. For children's author Alison Uttley, who grew up in Derbyshire in the 1890s, the target was even more complicated:

> White horses brought luck, the village children said. We used to count them and save them up, as children now count cars. A hundred white horses, a blind man, a chimney sweep, and a fiddler together brought the power of making a wish. To make a wish that would really come true was something much desired. Each day we looked out of the train window on the way to the grammar school and counted the white horses we saw in the fields and roads. The same horse must not be counted twice, and it took several weeks to make an original hundred ... When we had made the wish we began again.

lambs: first one seen

One of the simple prognostications of good or bad luck in springtime, and thus one of the important symbolic beginning points in the year, focused on the first new lamb that you saw:

> A friend familiar with rustic affairs told me the other day, that in seeing young lambs for the first time in the fields, they should be looked at in front, as it was most unlucky to take sight of them behind, as something would go wrong in consequence.   (1880)

Exactly the same was said of foals and other animals. The symbolism is reasonably obvious, and is rarely commented on, but informants occasionally said something on the lines of 'if you see the tail first you'll go backwards all year'. The belief was very widely noted across England, Scotland, and Wales, but not, it seems, in Ireland. Nevertheless, it cannot be shown to be very old, as the earliest known reference is only in Chambers' book of Scottish rhymes published in 1826.

lions

Presumed connections between nature and human fertility take several forms, but one of the oddest was the belief that the time when certain animals gave birth to their young was very dangerous for women who were about to do the same. The animals in question were occasionally bears and elephants, but most frequently lions:

> Several women attended by a local midwife having died in child-bed, a neighbour of this woman assured me that she was not to blame for these occurrences, because this was 'the Lion-year'. My informant explained to me that every seven years 'the lioness' had a litter of young, and that if anything went wrong with either mother or cubs on this occasion, many lying-in women died during the year; that 'the lioness' had just cubbed, and that one of her off-spring was dead, this being the sole cause of the deaths in the midwife's practice. She also said that she recollected a similar occurrence seven years previously, with like results. I find on enquiry that this belief is general in the district.   Yorkshire (1884)

Most informants named seven years as the natural cycle involved, but for others it was three years. Some farm animals, particularly pigs it seems, were similarly affected. The earliest reference dates from only the 1870s, but it was still being said in the 1950s, and the belief was sustained by stories which circulated every time a travelling menagerie came to the area, as was a different tradition which held that lions and tigers could not stand to be approached by a pregnant woman. The latter belief was mentioned in Smollett's novel *Humphry Clinker* (1771) and then a handful of times in the late nineteenth century, but those informants made it clear that it was widely known at the time.

The royal menagerie in the Tower of London was formed in 1235 and lasted until 1835, when the surviving animals were moved to the Zoological Gardens. In its time, the collection usually included one or more lions, which were the centre of attraction. At some point the lions in the Tower became associated in the public mind with the ruling sovereign in that the king's death was thought to be preceded by the death of one of the animals:

> The king has been ill. It was generally thought he would have died
> . . . for the oldest lion in the Tower, much about the king's age, died
> a fortnight ago.   Letter from Lord Chesterfield to his son (21 November 1758)

It is not clear when this tradition first started, but the earliest reference found so far is in the *Free-Holder* for 1716, and it is mentioned by other eighteenth-century writers as a common belief of the period.

moles

Many small animals were used extensively in folk medicine, but in classical times, as well as in Britain centuries later, moles seem to have been particularly highly regarded in this sphere. In the same way as the feet of hares or rabbits were kept for luck or as a cure, moles' feet were regularly carried, or worn round the neck, to prevent toothache or to relieve rheumatism. Nearly all informants agreed that the mole must be alive when its feet were taken, and many said that the charm would only work if the mole was then set free to die in its own time. The belief was clearly well known, at least in England, from the early eighteenth century, and it lasted well into the twentieth. In addition, several sources reported a belief that if you caught a live mole and then let it die in your hand, you would henceforth have healing powers. Moles' blood was also considered particularly powerful and was prescribed for a range of ailments, including epilepsy.

The appearance of moles in the garden would seem to be too common an occurrence for comment, but a handful of sources report various beliefs that moles can be seen as unlucky, or even as omens of death, simply by showing their presence:

> If a mole burrows under the washhouse or dairy, the mistress of the home will die within the year. If a molehill be found among the cabbages in the garden, the master of the house will die before the year is out.   Wales (1909)

mice *see* rats and mice

pigs

Pigs featured in a fair number of superstitions in their own right, as well as being prone to witchcraft and ill-wishing, as were all farmyard animals. The killing of the family pig was an immensely important event for the future economy of the household, and it was clearly necessary to get it right and leave little to chance. An extremely widespread belief dictated that the pig be killed at the waxing of the moon, or the meat would be spoilt. There were also strong local traditions covering who should receive parts of the meat, as a courtesy or reward for assistance, and fine distinctions between relatives and neighbours were reflected in who received which particular cuts. Another superstition covered this area:

> It is but neighbourly to send a dish of pig's fry ('pig-fare' as the term is) to a friend; but the dish must on no account be washed when it is returned. It must be left soiled, else the bacon will not cure. So with the 'beestlings' (the milk of the first three milkings after a cow has calved); the pail must never be washed, or the cow will 'go dry'.   Lincolnshire (1886)

There was also the general restriction on the activities of menstruating women: it was believed the meat would spoil if they handled it.

A number of superstitions exist which include the basic motif that it is unlucky to meet certain people or animals first thing in the morning, or when starting a journey. Hares and single magpies were commonly cited in this context, and also commonly reported as unlucky were pigs. The earliest reference we have for this idea is in the 1780s, and although reported occasionally from southern England and Wales, the overwhelming majority of references are from the northern counties of England and Scotland. No sensible reason for this fear of pigs has been put forward, but another strand of belief among fishermen, that the word 'pig' must not be uttered on board a boat, adds to the general impression that pigs were regarded as uncanny in many communities in a rather undefined way. This may simply reflect the animal's appearance in Bible stories. There was the story of the Gadarene swine of Mark 5:11–15 and Luke 8:32–3, and Deuteronomy 14:7–8 declares the animal unclean.

> We don't kill a pig every day, but we did a short time since; and after its hairs were scraped off, our attention was directed to six small rings, about the size of a pea, and in colour as if burnt or branded, on the inside of each fore leg and disposed curvilinearly. Our labourer informed us with great gravity, and evidently believed it, that these marks were caused by the pressure of the devil's fingers, when he entered the herd of swine which immediately ran violently in the sea.   (1853)

However, these biblical stories do not seem sufficient to explain the range of beliefs collected in the last 200 years. It is also noticeable that none of the pig superstitions are documented before the mid eighteenth century, and most are found only from the nineteenth onwards.

It was commonly reported that bad weather could be predicted from watching pigs' behaviour, and the idea that they can 'see the wind' is still commonly stated, although presumably not literally believed. According to a tradition collected from Welsh Gypsies, it would be easy enough to test the notion: 'If you wash your eyes with sow's milk you will see the wind as red as fire.' Another erroneous notion – that they cannot swim, because their trotters cut their throats if they try – is less often heard nowadays, and now sounds somewhat ridiculous.

rabbits *see* hares and rabbits

rats and mice

'Like rats from a sinking ship' is still a widely known proverbial saying, which has a long history. In the earliest versions, it was mice or rats leaving a house which predicted that it would soon fall down:

> It is found by observation, that rats and dormice will forsake old and ruinous houses, three months before they fall, for they perceive by an instinct of nature, that the joints and fastening together of the posts and timber of the houses, by little and little will be loosed and so thereby that all will fall to the ground.
>
> Thomas Lupton, *Thousand Notable Things* (1579)

At this stage, it was clearly taken literally. In later traditional versions, however, it was not simply a prediction about the building, but an omen of death for one of its residents.

Less well known is the idea that a sudden influx of the rats is as bad as their departure:

> The sudden appearance of rats or mice in Cornish houses is said to be a certain forerunner of sickness and death.   Cornwall (1887)

This omen does not appear to be anything like the age of that of the rodent exodus, being first reported only from the mid nineteenth century. Nevertheless, it must have been reasonably well known by that time, as its first known appearance, in the *Illustrated London News*, is in an article parodying current superstitions.

getting rid of rats and mice

Rats and mice, it seems, respond well to civility and/or legal formulae, and a time-honoured method of getting rid of them is to ask them politely to leave – either verbally, or by writing on a piece of paper which is put down their hole, or pinned up nearby:

> When these creatures become superabundant in a house of the humbler class, a writ of ejectment, in the following form, is served upon them, by being stuck up legibly written on the wall:
>
> > Ratton and mouse
> > Lea' the puir woman's house
> > Gang awa' owre by to 'e mill
> > And there ane and a' ye'll get your fill.
> > Scotland (1870)

Although not found in British sources before the early seventeenth century, this notion is of considerable age. Iona Opie and Moira Tatem quote a passage from *Geoponika* from the first century AD, which advises one to 'Take some paper and write these words', 'adjuring' the mice to leave.

rats gnawing

Rats or mice gnawing one's clothes, or the furniture and fittings of one's room, has long been regarded as a sign of bad luck, or even death:

> That it is a great signe of ill lucke, if rats gnaw a man's cloathes.
> John Melton, *Astrologaster* (1620)

This notion was only reported a few times in the later folklore collections, but it has a venerable history. It was presumably behind Chaucer's comment in *The Parson's Tale* about 'hem that bileeven on divynailes, as by . . . gnawynge of rattes', and the idea was certainly prevalent in classical times. Theophrastus' *Superstitious Man* (c.319 BC) was worried by a mouse gnawing his meal-bag, and Pliny wrote of General Carbo's death being predicted by mice chewing his shoelaces (*Natural History*, AD 77). Even St Augustine of Hippo (*De Doctrina Christiana*, AD 396) denounced the superstition, and added the dry comment, attributed to Cato but still very relevant today:

When consulted by a man whose shoes had been gnawed by mice, observed that there was nothing strange about the fact, but that it would have been strange indeed if the shoes had gnawed the mice.

shrews

Shrews enjoyed a baneful reputation, reflected in a widespread belief that they were poisonous, and had the power to lame humans and cattle simply by crawling over them. The agreed way to cure animals of this affliction was to treat them with a branch from a 'shrew-ash', which was a tree in which a live shrew had been imprisoned and allowed to die. The earliest reference to the shrew-ash motif is in Robert Plot's book on Staffordshire natural history (1686), but the notion of the shrew's venomous nature was probably introduced directly to British tradition by educated readers translating classical sources. The idea lived on in many rural areas well into the twentieth century. Another peculiar misconception about shrews, taken directly from Pliny's *Natural History* (AD 77) in the seventeenth century, was that they were unable to cross paths or cart ruts without dying in the attempt.

snails

Snails were used extensively in cures (especially for warts) and they were also commonly eaten for medicinal purposes – snail broth was reputedly good for consumption. They also featured in a regular love-divination procedure which relied on the random movements of a snail to reveal the letters of the future spouse's name:

> To know the name of the person you are destined to marry, put a snail on a plate of flour – cover it over and leave it all night; in the morning the initial letter of the name will be found traced on the flour by the snail.   Ireland (1888)

Variations included throwing the snail over your shoulder, and even baking the poor thing to interpret its writhings. The procedure was reported most often from Ireland, where May Day was a favourite time for its operation, but the earliest reference is from John Gay's evocation of English milkmaids and shepherds, *The Shepherd's Week* (1714), and it was still being reported in the 1950s.

Superstitions regarding meeting or seeing a snail varied considerably in meaning. Some references reported decidedly negative reactions, while others were equally positive. These beliefs were not recorded before the early nineteenth century.

A widespread rhyme was chanted by children all over Britain as they picked up a snail, in the apparent belief that it would do as instructed:

> Snail, snail, put out your horns
> I'll give you bread and barleycorns.
>
> Lancashire (1849)

The wording varies considerably from version to version, and forms of it have been reported almost the world over. In Britain the earliest reference is mid seventeenth century.

snakes

It was very widely believed that snakes, however badly injured, would not die until sunset:

> A snake, 3 ft long, was killed at noon by a schoolboy in a Dorsetshire village and brought to me at once. On my offering to handle it, I was warned by one of the children that it was not dead, and when I pointed out that its battered condition was incompatible with it being alive, I was at once told that 'this was not real death, as neither snakes nor slow-worms can ever really die till after sunset'.
>
> Dorset (1904)

Although not exclusive to the south of England, the majority of reports have come from there, and the earliest dates only from 1850. Thomas Hardy used the motif in his Wessex novel *Return of the Native* (1878). In the absence of any other explanation, it must be assumed that the belief simply arose through mistaken observation of nature.

There has long been a superstition that the adder has no power of hearing:

> 'Deaf as an adder' is a common saying in the fen, and

> If I could hear as well as see
> No man would be the death o' me,
>
> Huntingdonshire (1880s)

And many formerly believed that the markings on the belly of the snake actually said these words. The notion that the adder is deaf has biblical precedent, as Psalm 58:4 states, 'Their poison is like the poison of a serpent; they are like the deaf adder that stoppeth her ear.' The belief probably entered British tradition after the publication of the King James Bible made such literal borrowings possible. In a similar way, the slow-worm was believed to be blind.

A handful of reports indicate a belief that a snake coming to your doorstep, or into your house, foretold a death in the family:

> I was told in Orcop that an adder coming to the door was a sign of death. A doorstep seemed an unlikely place for an adder, but my informant assured me she had known this 'come true'.
>
> Herefordshire (1912)

This does not seem to have been a well-known belief, and was only reported a handful of times between 1885 and 1915.

On seeing the first snake of the year, whether dangerous adder or harmless slow-worm, it was believed one should kill it immediately:

> The mother of a member met an old woman who stopped and beat a 'sleu' (slow) worm to death, breaking her umbrella over it. Asked why she did this she replied, 'Ah! Now I have killed all my enemies.'
>
> Suffolk (1924)

This is reported only from the late nineteenth century, and not very widely. The motif of killing the first of a particular species that you see is also featured in beliefs about other creatures, notably butterflies and wasps, and in the latter case it was said that this action ensured that you would triumph over your enemies.

A range of disparate traditions indicate faith in the curative and magical properties of snake-skins. The most common is the use of a snake-skin to cure or ward off headaches by wearing it in your hat. The second common medical use of a snake-skin is in the extraction of thorns or splinters, although care must be taken to use it the right way because it repels rather than draws the thorn.

toads

Toads have traditionally been regarded as poisonous to both animals and humans. Some species do in fact have sacs of toxins on their skin, but traditional belief goes one better and maintains that they can actually spit their venom. The poisonous nature of toads was already widely believed in the sixteenth century, and is mentioned by Shakespeare in *As You Like it* (1600). It was still being taken for granted by many right into the twentieth century.

It was also firmly believed, at least from the fifteenth century, that certain toads had a jewel-like stone in their heads, which could be extracted and worn as an amulet:

> The editor is possessed of a small relique, termed by tradition a toad-stone, the influence of which was supposed to preserve pregnant women from the power of daemons, and other dangers incidental to their situation. It has been carefully preserved for several generations, was often pledged for considerable sums of money, and uniformly redeemed from a belief in its efficacy.
>
> Walter Scott, *Minstrelsy of the Scottish Border* (1802)

Other useful attributes were that the stone was believed to change colour when poison was near, and it cured bites and stings at a touch. A traditional way of obtaining the stone was to place a dead toad in an anthill; the same method was employed to find the magic bone used to control horses. When surviving toadstones have been examined, they usually turn out to be fossilized teeth of fish or sharks.

BIRDS

Birds feature widely in British superstitions, both in their own right and as adjuncts to other beliefs. One must dispose of any hair very carefully, for example, because if birds get it they will weave it into their nests and you will suffer headaches. The catalogue of bird beliefs is almost endless, and a few examples must stand for all. In particular, any unusual behaviour exhibited by birds was seen as ominous, especially if it appeared to single out a particular person or house:

> When trouble is about to visit you a bird will come sighing or 'tweedling' about you so as to give you warning . . . When a man is in trouble a bird will always haunt him. He will see that bird wherever he goes. Derbyshire (1895)

Some superstitions are relevant to all birds, but many species have their own traditions. Unlike most animal-based superstitions, however, there are numerous good luck as well as bad luck omens. Records show that some birds were protected from harm – robins, wrens (some of the time), swallows, martins – while others, like the unfortunate yellowhammer, were killed on sight. Some were dreaded – owls hooting after dark, single magpies – others, such as cuckoos, were welcomed if the circumstances were right.

People were particularly suspicious of large black or white birds, and the latter often feature in death-omen traditions which adhere to particular families. A bird appearing at a window was widely interpreted as an ill omen, and if there was a sick person in the household it was taken as evidence that they would soon die:

Birds pecking at a window announce a death. The coincidences I
have known in respect of this are certainly so remarkable as almost
to justify the superstition. I was in a house, where at daybreak a
large number of pigeons settled themselves along bedroom window
ledges, making great pecking and noise, and awakening the inmates.
About two hours later it was announced that the master of the
house had died about the time referred to.   Berkshire (1888)

Any bird acting in this way was an omen, but many people particularly
feared robins in this context. A wild bird entering a house was another
death omen to many people:

If a bird flies into your house, a death will follow within three days.
I remember I had got the kitchen door open when I was cooking
the dinner and this bird flew in the back door. I nearly went mad
trying to get it out and in three days my sister died suddenly, that
was in 1953, so that proved it was true.   Lincolnshire (1993)

The fear of birds in the house normally concerned only wild birds, but
some took the idea further and eschewed caged birds, while others
even refused to have representations of birds on china, Christmas
cards, wallpaper, and so on.

When I had a hardware shop I would never stock cups, saucers,
plates, dishes with a picture of a bird on them as I knew I wouldn't
be able to sell them.   Yorkshire (1973)

Two superstitions feature bird droppings. Despite the understandable
annoyance of being hit by bird droppings, it is often regarded as lucky:

I was on my way to an important meeting in London, and my
shoulder was suddenly covered in bird's mess. My colleague, helping
me to clear it off, remarked, 'I think it's meant to be lucky when
that happens'.   London (1992)

This notion has been current since at least the 1870s. On the other
hand, birds dropping on you was formerly quoted as one of the
traditional punishments for not wearing new clothes at Easter or
Whitsun.

Considering the widespread rural practice of 'birds'-nesting' – which
involved boys destroying every nest and egg they could find (with
the exception of a few protected species) – and the equally popular

pastime for both boys and adult naturalists of amassing collections of eggs, it is odd to find a superstition that it was unlucky to bring birds' eggs into the house:

> But, regarding those birds' eggs, we have a very foolish superstition here; the boys may take them unrestrained, but their mothers so dislike their being kept in the house, that they usually break them; their presence may be tolerated for a few days, but by the ensuing Sunday are frequently destroyed, under the idea that they bring bad luck, or prevent the coming of good fortune.   Gloucestershire (1830)

It was particularly dangerous when someone was sick. Although not commonly reported, references are widely enough spread to confirm the general existence of this belief, at least in England from the 1830s onwards, and into the 1950s.

albatrosses

The belief that it is extremely unlucky to kill an albatross is entirely due to its inclusion in Samuel Taylor Coleridge's tremendously popular poem *The Rime of the Ancient Mariner* (written in 1797 and published the following year). The albatross motif was suggested by Coleridge's fellow-poet William Wordsworth, who had come across the idea in Captain George Shelvocke's *A Voyage Round the World by Way of the Great South Sea* [in] *1719–1722* (published 1726). There is no evidence that the albatross superstition existed in Britain before the publication of Coleridge's poem, and, indeed, it was its very air of exotic mystery that suited the poem, in a way that a prosaic local belief would not have done.

cockerels

Traditional views of the cockerel show some ambivalence; they were certainly considered uncanny birds at times, but good or bad by turn. They featured in a number of very widespread beliefs, mostly concerned with their role as messenger and when and where they crow.

> The cock crows: Once for a wedding/Twice for a birth/Three times for sorrow/ Four times for mirth.   Norfolk (c.1895)

The most widespread superstition in the nineteenth century about cocks was that one crowing directly at the door of the farmhouse betokened a visitor, or, occasionally, news from afar:

> I remember lately visiting an old friend in the country, and on making my appearance I was hailed with the salutation, 'Come awa, I knew we would have a visit from strangers today, for the cock crowed thrice over with his head in at the door'.
>
> W. Scotland (1879)

The symbolism is fairly obvious, given the long-standing metaphor of a cock crowing as messenger. The belief is first recorded in Scotland about 1820 and is widely reported throughout the rest of the nineteenth, and the first half of the twentieth century. A cock crowing at the 'wrong' time, or in the wrong way, however, was always regarded as a bad sign – and usually interpreted as predicting illness and death. The wrong time was either at night, or in the afternoon, especially if habitual:

> Almost everyone in Shropshire knows that a cock crowing at midnight is a sign of death. We are told of a farmer's wife who killed her cock because 'he would crow at twelve at night'.
>
> Shropshire (1883)

Broadly similar beliefs were recorded from all parts of the British Isles. The earliest records in British tradition appear in the sixteenth and seventeenth centuries, but there are classical antecedents, such as Petronius Arbiter (c. AD 65), quoted by Iona Opie and Moira Tatem, and St John Chrysostom's *Homilies on Ephesians* (c. AD 390).

crows

In general, crows are not liked in British superstition, and although in certain limited circumstances they can be seen as lucky, in the vast majority of cases they are treated with suspicion. Records show that they were particularly feared if they seemed to be focusing their attention on a particular person or building, and this applied both to single birds and groups:

> I have heard women in the fields remark that such and such a farmer then lying ill would not recover, for a crow had been seen to fly over his house but just above the roof-tree.   Wiltshire (1878)

The belief in the basic unluckiness of crows has a long history in Britain, and was mentioned by many leading literary figures, including Chaucer and Shakespeare, and before that in classical times.

see also **rooks**

cuckoos

The cuckoo features widely in the folklore of Britain and the rest of Europe, in a variety of genres, as well as in poetry, drama, and music. The bird has an essentially pastoral role in songs and poems as the key harbinger or personification of spring, appears in numerous weather predictions, and has traditional tales all of its own, such as the 'numskull' story of the villagers who try to prolong summer by building a wall to keep the cuckoo in. In proverbs and sayings, the cuckoo is synonymous with foolishness (as in the April 'gowk' or April Fool), and has bawdy connotations through the word 'cuckold', and its propensity for leaving offspring in other birds' nests.

It is therefore not surprising that the cuckoo also features in a number of superstitions, but most of those reported are variations on a single basic theme, based on the well-known principle of the importance of beginnings: whatever you are doing or whatever situation you are in when you first hear the cuckoo dictates, or at least indicates, how things will go for you for the rest of the year. If you have money, are in good health, or have a full stomach all well and good, but if you are lying down you will be ill, and if you are hungry or have no money in your pocket, then things will be bad indeed.

> And now take this advice from me,
> Let money in your pockets be,
> When first you do the cuckow hear,
> If you'd have money all the year.
>
> *Poor Robin's Almanack* (1763)

The symbolism can be less direct, as in the idea that to hear the cuckoo's call from your right-hand side is good, but from the left is bad, or to be standing on grass is preferable to a hard surface like a road, because the latter leads to a 'hard life'.

These beliefs regarding the effect of the cuckoo's call on the hearer were extremely widespread, and were reported well into the twentieth century. But they have not yet been traced back earlier than the 1760s, and the similarity between these and superstitions regarding the New Year and, more particularly, the first sight of the new moon, lead one to hazard a guess that they may have been formed as extensions of these much older traditions.

The oldest prognostication from the first cuckoo's call is also the simplest – the number of notes you hear predicts how many more years you have to live. This was first mentioned in the fourteenth century and was still going strong in the twentieth. For young people, the bird could help with other concerns, as it also had an important role in many love-divination procedures.

housemartins *see* swallows and housemartins

magpies

In general, magpies get a mixed press in the superstitions of Britain and Ireland. In many traditions they are very unlucky to meet, and are sometimes regarded as outright death omens. In other beliefs, however, they are neutral – such as forecasting the arrival of a stranger – and in the ubiquitous rhyme ('One for sorrow') they have good connotations when they appear in certain numbers. Nevertheless, overall they are disliked and feared. This bad reputation remains largely unexplained. On the European continent, where numerous negative magpie beliefs have also been recorded, the bad reputation is sometimes explained by the belief that witches regularly turned themselves into magpies, but this explanation hardly ever appears in the British Isles. Some writers, however, refer to it as 'the Devil's bird':

> [The magpie] was sometimes called 'the devil's bird' and was believed to have a drop of the devil's blood in its tongue. It was a common notion that a magpie could receive the gift of speech by scratching its tongue, and inserting into the wound a drop of blood from the human tongue.   N.E. Scotland (1881)

Other traditional legends which seek to explain the magpie's character are less damning:

> A north-country servant thus accounted for the unluckiness of the 'pyet' to her master, the Rev. H. Humble. 'It was', the girl said, 'the

only bird which did not go into the ark with Noah; it liked better
to sit outside, jabbering over the drowned world'.   Co. Durham (1886)

Noah's Ark is a favourite setting for fables which explain the characteristics of specific species. Another story explains that the magpie is
black and white because it was the offspring of the dove and the raven,
the first two birds sent out by Noah as the flood neared its end, and it
was not baptized during the Flood.

The oldest of the magpie superstitions, by some considerable
margin, is that the sound of a chattering magpie denotes the coming
of a stranger:

When a magpie chatters on a tree by the house it declares the
coming of a stranger thither that night.   John Aubrey, *Remaines* (1686)

The earliest known reference dates from 1159, and a number of subsequent authors confirm this meaning as generally known. It is
reported rarely, however, after the sixteenth century. It is interesting
to note that this belief invariably stresses the sound made by the
magpie (i.e. its chattering), while later superstitions are almost always
concerned with seeing or meeting the bird.

There are plenty of references to the fear of meeting a single magpie:

A single magpie crossing your path is esteemed an evil omen, and
I once saw a person actually tremble and dissolve into a copious
perspiration, when one of these birds flitted chattering before him.
                                Lincolnshire, *Gentleman's Magazine* (1832)

Some versions require specific behaviour on the part of the bird – it is
bad if it hops towards you, or flies from your left, or if you see it in
the morning, while others worry if it approaches the house. But similar
things are said of other birds.

The earliest reference in English to the magpie as definitely ominous
is found in the *Gospelles of Dystaves* (1507), but this is a translation of a
Belgian book and is thus not clear evidence of British tradition. Certainly, by Shakespeare's time the magpie shared attributes with other
ill-boding signs. He writes that 'chattering pies in dismal discords sung'
in a passage which includes shrieking owls, ravens, howling dogs, and
hideous tempests (*Henry VI Part 3*). From then on the unluckiness of
magpies is reported only sporadically until the deluge of references to
the number rhyme, detailed below, take over in the late eighteenth

century. Similarly, specific procedures for counteracting the bird's evil
influence – spitting, making the sign of the cross, showing respect by
bowing, raising the hat, speaking politely to the bird, or reciting
defiant words – do not appear in the record until relatively late.

The idea that the significance of meeting or seeing magpies is
dependent on the number of birds seen is without doubt one of the
best-known superstitions in Britain today. This is mainly because of
the catchy rhyme, of which almost everyone can recite at least the first
two lines. The belief is listed in all the major collections of the
nineteenth and early twentieth centuries, although often only in passing, precisely because it was so well known. The rhyme exists in
numerous versions, but there is evidence of standardization in recent
decades, as people now rely more on books of nursery rhymes than on
local or family tradition for their folklore. Two relatively 'standard'
versions:

> One for sorrow
> Two for joy
> Three for a girl
> And four for a boy
> Five for silver
> Six for gold
> Seven for a secret never to be told.
>> South London (author's family)

> One for sorrow
> Two for mirth
> Three for a wedding
> Four for a birth
> Five for heaven
> Six for hell
> Seven you'll see the de'il himsell.
>> Lincolnshire (1891)

Nevertheless, a close examination of a large number of versions shows
that there is far less variation than is apparent at first sight. Similar
symbolism occurs again and again but in a different order. There is
certainly no definable pattern which can be discerned in the attributes
assigned to individual numbers, except for 'one', which is almost
always bad. Indeed, the pattern is clearly dictated by the exigencies of

rhyme and rhythm, and the need for contrasting couplets, rather than any intrinsic belief in the numbers themselves. As indicated, the rhyme was known all over the British Isles, but England and Scotland provide the bulk of the references. On present evidence, the rhyme was not often reported from Wales or Ireland.

The idea that the number of magpies seen is significant cannot be shown to be anywhere near as old as other magpie beliefs, as the first references date only from the 1780s. Similar things were also said of crows.

owls

Owls were generally disliked and feared, and their screech was a proverbial death omen:

> When a screech-owl is heard crying near a house, it is an indication of death on the premises. When a barn-owl alights on a house, hoots, and then flies over it, an inmate will die within the year.
>
> Wales (1909)

This interpretation of the owl has a very long literary history, from Chaucer's *Parliament of Fowls* (c.1380) 'The oule eke, that of deth the bode bringeth', to numerous writers of the sixteenth and seventeenth centuries for whom the owl, raven, and howling dog were stock motifs signalling horror and tragedy – instantly recognized by audiences and readers.

peacocks

From the mid nineteenth century to recent times, many have regarded peacock's feathers as unlucky, and have refused to have them in the house, or even handle anything made with them:

> I recently heard a harrowing story of a certain poor woman, a strong believer in this superstition, who to her horror received a Christmas present of a box of chocolates with a picture of the noxious birds upon the cover. True to her convictions, she mortified her flesh and defied the devil by throwing the whole lot into the dust-bin.
>
> Yorkshire (1932)

General bad luck is usually cited as the result of ignoring this super-stition, but one specific which is sometimes given is that the presence of the feathers has an adverse effect on the matrimonial prospects of the daughters of the house. More than with other superstitions, there seems to have been a distinct division in society between those who believed and those who did not. In Victorian times and after, peacock feathers were fashionable in fans and hats, and were common as household arrangements at all levels of society, so the superstition cannot have been universally known or believed. It suddenly springs, fully fledged, into the documentary record in the mid 1860s, and there is no reason to believe it much older than that in this form.

pigeons

Pigeons have a largely negative reputation in British traditional belief, and in a range of superstitions they were connected with death, in one way or another. The pigeon's reputation as a straightforward death omen has been largely forgotten, but from the early seventeenth to the early twentieth century it was widely regarded with suspicion and horror right across the British Isles:

> It is unlucky for a pigeon to settle on the house. Send it off! If it comes down I'll wring its neck. One settled on the wash-house where I was working, and the woman's old man died. London (1926)

In some reports it was specifically a white or black pigeon that was feared, or it was the particular circumstances of its appearance, such as its perching near the window of a room where someone lay sick. These are all standard motifs found in other bird omens.

The supposed connection between pigeons and death was also indicated in an odd sort of belief which held that the last thing an invalid craved to eat was pigeon, and if they did so it was taken as a sure indication that they were dying. This has only been recorded irregularly since the 1850s, but enough times, and on a wide enough geographical spread, to confirm its independent existence. The pigeon also made a regular appearance in other death-bed scenes. A recurrent theme in folk medicine is the use of live animals, skinned, dismembered, or simply cloven in two, which are applied to the sick or wounded person in one way or another. In many of these cases, the implication is that the animal provides both natural healing heat and acts beneficially by *drawing* the sickness out of the patient's body. Live pigeons were the most often cited creatures to suffer and serve in this way, and there are numerous reports of their use from the seventeenth to the late nineteenth centuries. What seems strange to modern eyes is that for much of this period the pigeon was actually applied to the sufferer's feet, even in cases of general fever or problems with the head. This was because it was believed that the feet and head were physiologically closely linked. Samuel Pepys twice mentioned the treatment, in a matter of fact way:

> (21 January 1668) News from Kate Joyce that if I would see her husband alive, I must come presently . . . and find him in his sick bed . . . but his breath rattled in his throat and they did lay pigeons to his feet while I was in the house; and all despair of him.

And, writing of the Queen's current illness:

> (19 October 1663) It seems she was so ill as to be shaved and pigeons put to her feet.

The implication is usually that the pigeons were the last resort, and administered when the patient was *in extremis*. The treatment was sufficiently well known to become a literary cliché in seventeenth-century writing – 'I would sooner eat a dead pigeon taken from the soles of the feet of one sick of the plague than kiss one of you fasting' (John Webster, *Duchess of Malfi*, 1623), and both William Congreve (1695) and Thomas Otway (1681) use a similar image in their plays.

It was also widely believed that pigeon feathers in a mattress prevented anyone 'dying easy' in that bed, and condemned the sufferer to a prolonged and difficult passing. Last, but not least, in the annals of pigeon-lore, their hearts were sometimes roasted and/or stuck with pins, as an integral part of witchcraft spells, either as counter-magic or in a love charm.

ravens

The ominous nature of the raven is a standard motif in beliefs across the British Isles:

> Another sign of death is a black raven appearing a few nights before a person dies . . . Nearly every time a person dies down near Bannow, the raven will be seen and heard on one of the old walls of the church and he will go along the top of the wall and make some of the most awful noises that ever you heard.   Co. Wexford (1938)

The bird's cry is evidence enough of its meaning, and all it needed to do was fly over or settle near someone's house, especially if accompanied by another, and if someone was already ill. Similarly, the raven as death omen is almost a cliché in literature, from the sixteenth century onwards, where its dark side was expressed in synonyms such as 'night-crow' or 'night-raven'. Shakespeare uses the image at least four times, as do other playwrights of his generation, and later writers repeat the same themes. There is no need for any other explanation than common sense to discover why the raven had such a bad reputation. Its size, colour, carrion-eating habits, and raucous cry are sufficient. Its reputation was also well known in the classical era, and both Virgil and Pliny comment on its ominous nature.

robins

Perhaps the oddest mixture of superstitions pertaining to one bird is that which surrounds the robin. On the one hand the bird has been generally welcomed and protected from harm, while in certain contexts it has been feared as an omen of death and is still sometimes considered unlucky when depicted on the apparently innocuous Christmas card.

A handful of birds were traditionally protected from molestation – swallows, martins, and wrens, for example – but by far the most widespread was the robin redbreast. All over Britain and Ireland it was strongly believed that the robin should be left alone, and versions of a traditional rhyme are reported in most folklore collections:

> The robin red-breast and the wren
> Are God Almighty's cock and hen.
> East Anglia (1830)

This was taken very seriously – even by birds'-nesting boys – and the robin and its nest were unmolested:

Should any boy [take its eggs], his companions hoot and hiss at him, singing all the while: 'Robin takker, robbin takker, Sin, sin, sin!' until he is driven from their midst. Yorkshire (1890)

In addition to the direct action of disapproving juveniles, there were many other penalties for ignoring this interdiction. They varied from the general 'you'll have bad luck for ever', to the specific 'your cows will give bloody milk', 'your hand will shake thereafter', 'you will break an arm or leg', 'you or a loved one will die', and, more strangely, 'all the crockery in your house will break'.

A number of reasons were given for the robin's status. There were several versions of an international legend connecting the bird with the crucifixion of Christ, which explained its red breast:

> it was the robin that plucked out the sharpest thorn that was piercing Christ's brow on the cross; and in so doing the breast of the bird was dyed red with the Saviour's blood, and so has remained ever since a sacred and blessed sign to preserve the robin from harm and make it beloved of all men.   Ireland (1888)

The earliest clear reference to the robin being a protected species appears in the *British Apollo* (1709), in which a correspondent points out the 'malicious and envious' nature of the bird in real life, and asks 'why many people should have so much esteem for this bird, as to account it a crime to do it any injury'. Only four years later, a writer in the *Guardian* (1713) suggests that robins 'owe their security to the old ballad of the *Children in the Wood*'. The latter story started life as a play (1595), became a broadside ballad, a children's song around 1800, and later (as *The Babes in the Wood*) a popular pantomime. Most of these popular manifestations included the motif of robins covering the bodies of the two lost children with leaves out of pity.

Despite the general popularity of robins, and these strong traditions protecting them from harm, the bird has also been regarded in some contexts as an omen of death. Any bird tapping or 'crying' at a window, for example, was taken as a death sign, particularly if someone in the house was ill, but the prediction was believed to be especially potent if the bird was a robin.

> The people in our neighbourhood believe that if a robin attaches himself to a house and afterwards pecks upon the window, there will certainly be a death in the house. It happened in our house; a robin pecked upon the window and a death did follow.
>
> Cardiganshire (1928)

Tapping at the window may be the most overt sign, but robins simply hanging around a house was also enough to unnerve some people. It is just possible to square the protected status with the fear of the robin, if one regards the tapping and crying as a beneficent 'call' to a new life, but there is no hint that any informants believed this, and this death omen was feared in the same way as all others were. It does not, however, seem to be very old, as the earliest reference so far found dates from only 1829. It is much more widely reported in the twentieth century.

Similarly, any bird flying into a house was widely regarded as a sign of forthcoming misfortune or death, but again for many people the omen was particularly bad if that bird was a robin. There is no evidence that this particular concern with robins is any older than late Victorian times, although it certainly existed with regard to other birds since at least the seventeenth century.

In what is probably an extension of the idea that birds in the house are extremely unlucky, some people go so far as to eschew Christmas cards which depict robins:

> Doreen Fleet says that whenever she buys a box of assorted Christmas cards, 'any with a bird on get thrown out' – the poor robins end up in the bin.   Yorkshire (1993)

Although only noticed occasionally in the literature, this belief was certainly quite widespread in the second half of the twentieth century, and is still in existence.

rooks

Large black birds, such as crows and ravens, have an almost invariably negative reputation in British superstition, but the traditional view of rooks is more mixed, and in some people's belief it was actually lucky to have them around:

> Rooks building near a house are a sign of prosperity.
>
> East Anglia (1830)

> Rooks are very much liked in our neighbourhood; they are supposed to keep the crows away, and, as the crow steals chickens, the rook is thus regarded as a protector.   Cardiganshire (1928)

In the most widespread tradition about them, rooks were closely linked with death, but this belief was couched in a less direct way than most death omens. The superstition in question maintained that if the head of the family on whose land they nested died, the rooks would immediately vacate their nests. In some cases, the sequence was reversed, and rooks vacating their rookery was taken as a sign that a family bereavement was imminent. On the other hand, there were some people who thought rooks were definitely unlucky. Many people did not make any distinction between crows and rooks, and it is likely that some of the negative beliefs about the former contaminated those of the latter.

> We believed that a crow or rook carried a plague or brought a disease that could kill you, and that's why they are unlucky.
>
> Lincolnshire (c.1930s)

seagulls

In coastal areas, seagulls were viewed with suspicion, or at least caution. They were usually left unmolested, but the reason varied. The strongest tradition was that they were the souls of seamen who died at sea, but their behaviour could also be interpreted as a death omen:

> When they mew incessantly around a seafarer's home it is said to presage a death. When a very well-known *Haut pas* boat-owner died immediately before the 1939–45 war it was noticed by all the neighbours how restless and noisy flocks of gulls were around the house all day as he lay dying. They were said to have been agitated in the same fashion around the places inland where members of his family were working.
>
> Guernsey (1975)

Given the nature, look, and cry of the seagull, one would expect there to have been beliefs about them in the distant past, but at present none have been found before late Victorian times.

swallows and housemartins

The swallow and the housemartin mostly shared the same positive characteristics in British tradition, although the former featured much more often. In general, they were both lucky to see and to have around the house, as long as they stayed, and they were thus protected from harm. Their specially protected status, which they shared with robins and wrens, is summed up in the widespread quatrain:

> The robin and the wren
> Are God Almighty's cock and hen
> The martin and the swallow
> Are God Almighty's bow and arrow.
>
> Warwickshire (1842)

The first two lines of this verse were remarkably stable throughout the British Isles, but the second two varied considerably, presumably because it was difficult to find a decent rhyme for 'swallow'. This wide variance in meaning also suggests that, in contrast to robins and wrens, there was no widespread belief or legend to support that part of the rhyme. Penalties for harming the birds ranged from the common 'bad luck' to specific misfortunes such as death, broken limbs, and the cows giving bloody milk, which were also said of those who hurt robins.

The protected nature of the swallow was already established in the early seventeenth century, when Martin Parker mentioned it in his poem on the *Nightingale* (1632), and over a century earlier it was included in the Low Countries text translated into English as the *Gospelles of Dystaves* (1507). Nevertheless, despite the almost universal positive reputation of the swallow across most of the British Isles, for some communities in Scotland and Ireland it was 'the devil's bird', and its protection based more on fear than admiration.

wrens

A handful of birds were believed to be lucky to have around and generally protected from molestation, even by birds'-nesting village boys. Swallows and housemartins were often afforded this honour, but the most widespread in this category was the robin, and second was the wren. The latter was traditionally regarded as female, and wife of the robin, and it seems that most of the protection it received was because of the close association of the two. An extremely widespread couplet summed it up: 'The robin and the wren/Are God Almighty's cock and hen', while other rhymes threatened retribution if they were harmed:

> He that hurts a robin or a wren
> Will never prosper sea or land.
>
> Cornwall (1871)

But all was not sweetness and light for the wren. It also featured in a St Stephen's Day calendar custom called 'Hunting the Wren', in which it was mercilessly hunted, killed, decorated, and paraded round the village accompanied by music and song. The custom was most widespread in Ireland, but also took place in Wales, the Isle of Man, and some parts of England:

The wren is mortally hated by the Irish; for on one occasion when the Irish troops were approaching to attack a portion of Cromwell's army, the wrens came and perched on the Irish drums, and by their tapping and noise aroused the English soldiers, who fell on the Irish troops and killed them all. So ever since the Irish hunt the wren on St. Stephen's Day, and teach their children to run it through with thorns and kill it whenever it can be caught.

Ireland (1888)

INSECTS

bees

The key characteristic of bees in the superstitions of Britain and Ireland is that they are very sensitive and censorious creatures. They are quick to take offence if not treated with respect, they know what is going on in the world of humans, and their behaviour is also useful as an indicator of future events. By far the most common manifestation of this sensitivity to the doings of their human masters is the belief that they should be informed of any major change of circumstance in the owner's family, and in particular must be told of any death:

> About thirty years ago, an old woman in my parish told my wife that her bees had died: a circumstance which she attributed to her having forgotten to tell her bees of the master's death . . . I mentioned it [recently] to my nurse, and asked her if she had ever heard of a similar custom. She said, 'Yes', and that she herself having lost her bees on the death of her first husband, was told by her neighbours that this had happened because she had neglected to tell the bees of her husband's death. She further said that in her village it was the custom, on the death of the master of a family, not only to inform the bees, but also to give them a piece of the funeral cake, together with beer sweetened with sugar. Nottinghamshire (1869)

Records show that this 'telling the bees' often followed a set routine – tapping gently on each hive, often with the house key, for example – and reciting a set phrase, while others prescribed a more elaborate process of inviting them to the funeral, placing black cloth on the hives, and giving them a share of the food and drink served to mourners. Another part of the custom, reported in many areas, was 'lifting' or 'turning' the hives, apparently symbolizing the bees accompanying the funeral procession. Many keepers also told their bees of other major family events, such as weddings. In one form or other, 'telling the bees' is reported from all over England, plus a few places in Wales and Ireland, but not, on current evidence, in Scotland. Considering its ubiquity in England in the nineteenth and twentieth centuries, it might be presumed that the custom of telling the bees has a long history, but at present this cannot be proved. Iona Opie and Moira Tatem located the earliest reference, in P. Camerarius' *Historical Meditations* (1621), which comments on the belief that on the death of the master or mistress of the house, beehives should be moved elsewhere, and John Brand (1813) quotes a newspaper from 1790 describing 'turning' the hives in a similar situation. But 'telling the bees', or dressing their hives for a funeral or wedding, does not appear until the first decades of the nineteenth century, and at present we have no grounds for believing it much older than that.

Several other superstitions attested that bees were sensitive to human behaviour. They would not thrive in a quarrelsome family, they objected to bad language, and there were traditional restrictions, from at least the eighteenth century, on how they changed hands:

> There is not one peasant, I believe, in the village, who would sell you a swarm of bees. To be guilty of selling bees is a grievous omen indeed, than which nothing can be more dreadful. To barter bees is quite a different matter. If you want a hive, you may easily obtain it in lieu of a small pig, or some other equivalent.   Hampshire (1854)

Away from their hives, bees' behaviour could also be meaningful. Rural dwellers took careful note of where swarming bees settled, and judged it lucky, or more usually unlucky, according to the place chosen. The most common belief was that it was a sure sign of death if they settled on a dead branch or hedge stake, especially if near the house, as was widely reported across England and Wales since its earliest appearance in John Gay's pastoral poem *The Shepherd's Week* (1714).

From the 1850s onwards, a bee entering the house could mean different things to different people, although the most common was that it predicted a visitor in the near future. As such, this could be regarded as neutral, or even positively lucky, but a few regarded it as a death omen, and this seems to be the older tradition, as an early reference (*c.*1050) states that dreaming of bees entering a house portends its destruction.

beetles

> Rain-beetles were never killed by the village boys, for that would make rain pour down, they said.   Derbyshire (*c.*1890s)

This was very well known across most parts of England, with occasional references from Wales and Scotland, but no explanation for the belief is given in any of the available sources. The earliest is 1852, and it was still being said in the 1980s, but was presumably much rarer by then. Records show that in some parts of Ireland and Scotland, however, beetles were regarded as unlucky and deliberately killed on sight. This destruction was excused by reference to a traditional story about the insect's betrayal of the Holy Family:

> The boys of Sutherland will never allow a beetle to escape them; they stamp on the insect and cry, 'Beetle, beetle, you won't see tomorrow'. The practice is without doubt connected with a legend which may be heard in the counties, a legend of special interest as a type of those curious Scottish stories wherein New Testament history and modern realism are interblent. Here it is: As they fled into Egypt, Joseph and Mary and the child Christ passed through a field where men scattered corn seeds. The Virgin said to the men, 'Should any ask of you if we have journeyed this way, make answer, "A man, a woman, and a child crossed the field as we sowed the corn".' The men promised to do her bidding. That night the grain sprouted, grew rapidly, and ripened, so that next day the labourers brought their sickles and began to reap it. Now a band of soldiers came and questioned them: 'Have you seen a mother and child on an ass with a man leading it, go this way?' The men replied: 'As we sowed the corn which we now reap, they passed'. When they heard these words, the messengers of the king were about to turn back, but a black beetle cried aloud: 'Yesterday, yesterday, the corn was sown, and the son of God passed through the field'.   Sutherland (1895)

This is typical of a range of stories which relate how creatures helped or hindered Jesus' flight.

butterflies

To modern minds it will come as a surprise that something as harmless and attractive as a butterfly could have sufficient negative reputation that several traditions dictated that it should be killed on sight. At the very least people were advised to kill the first one they encountered in the year, for luck:

> they always chase and try to kill the first butterfly of the season; and, should they succeed, they will overcome their enemies.
>
> Cornwall (1887)

The motif of the first sight of a particular species being significant is a commonplace of superstition, and it was also said of snakes and wasps. A range of other butterfly superstitions have been noted, almost all of them negative, but none of them have been recorded often enough for us to judge how widespread they were. Some are simply contradictory in all essentials:

> To see three white butterflies together is lucky, so my old Grannie used to tell me.   Cambridgeshire (1969)

> Death omen – the sight of a trio of butterflies.   Northamptonshire (1851)

caterpillars

Caterpillars were widely distrusted, and children, in particular, even thought them poisonous:

> When visiting at a farmhouse in the neighbourhood of Box, during the last summer, whilst walking in a field I picked up a very pretty hairy caterpillar (woolly bear). A little boy, who was with me at the time, cried out to me at once, 'Drop it, drop it, or it will kill you' and ran off in considerable fear.   (1876)

Some species of caterpillar can apparently cause painful irritation to human skin if handled, but this hardly explains the particular fear that if the creature curled round your finger to make a ring, you would certainly die. Other sources also report negative attitudes to the caterpillar, which seem to have a long history:

> How now, fool! How now, caterpillar? It's a sign of death when such vermin creep hedges so early in the morning.   Anon, *Wily Beguiled* (1606)

But occasional reports say quite the opposite: 'If you throw a black hairy caterpillar over your shoulder you have good luck' (Dumfries, 1957). Caterpillars, spiders, woodlice, and other small insects were also used extensively in cures of ailments such as whooping cough and the ague, by being imprisoned alive in a bag and worn around the sufferer's neck until they wasted away.

crickets

Crickets featured widely in superstition across Britain and Ireland, but there was no consensus as to their meaning, and even in the same geographical area there could be a wide divergence of opinion. The majority of references claimed that the presence of crickets in the house was decidedly lucky (see, for example, Charles Dickens's *The Cricket on the Hearth*, 1846), and by extension, it was considered unwise to kill one:

> [From a schoolboy's composition on 'Insects'] Crickets are those insects that sing behind the firegrate. Never kill crickets, for I tell yer I once killed a cricket while my mother was a mangling and I was rocking the baby by the side of the mangle, lookin in the fire, and then my mother began crying, saying baby would never have no luck. Then I cried, and then the baby started crying and wouldn't go to sleep. I'm sure I shant kill no more crickets, for I loves our baby more than yer think.   London (1889)

The penalty for this crime varied from general ill luck to certain death, but it was often reported that the crickets would eat the clothes of the party responsible for the cruel deed. In many instances, however, the cricket's very presence was seen as generally unlucky or even as an omen of death. All the seventeenth-century examples fall into this latter category, including the earliest known, in which the playwright John Webster (*White Devil*, 1612) brackets the cricket's chirp with the dreaded screech of an owl and yellow spots on the fingernails. Another strand of belief maintained that it was the departure of the crickets 'where they have bin many yeeres', or their sudden proliferation, which was the sign of death.

In general, the historical trend has been from bad to good, with the earlier writers stressing the evil portent and the later ones the good fortune, but there is no simple chronological or geographical pattern. At least one writer has claimed biblical precedent for the death omen:

'And the grasshopper shall be a burden, because man goeth to his long home' (Ecclesiastes 12:5). The occasional Irish reference indicates that there crickets were regarded almost as household sprites, old, wise, able to understand what was said about them, and liable to take offence if not well-treated.

ladybirds

The ladybird is the one insect which has received a consistently positive press in British belief and custom. It was generally thought to be lucky, and was protected from harm – in the same way as robins were in the bird realm – and also featured in a love-divination procedure designed to predict the direction of the future lover's home. The latter was first reported by John Gay (*The Shepherd's Week*, 1714) and lasted well into the twentieth century.

From at least the 1850s onwards, it was considered very unlucky to harm a ladybird, and unspecified, but dire, consequences would follow if anyone was foolish enough to ignore this warning. The insect had numerous local names, including lady-bug, bishop barnabee, lady-cow, and God Almighty's cow, and all the different strands of belief could be accompanied by a rhyme which was recited as the ladybird settled on the hand, or when it was seen. The rhyme is still widely known, but it varies considerably across the country. A consistent theme is the house on fire and children:

> Lady-cow, lady-cow, fly thy ways home
> Thy house is on fire, thy children are gone
> All but one, and he is Tum [Tom]
> And he lies under the grindelstun [grindstone].
>
> Shropshire (1883)

See Iona and Peter Opie (1951) for British and foreign versions.

spiders

Spiders enjoy a surprisingly positive reputation in British superstition, as elsewhere in Europe. Apart from their former use in cures, which invariably ended in their death, they have been widely protected from harm by closely linked beliefs which hold that they are lucky to have around, and that it is very unlucky to harm them.

> My grannie was a Calbourne woman, and when I was setting up
> house she warned me thus: 'Now my child, you are young, but
> whatever you do in your life never kill a spider. If you are sweeping,
> and come on a web, don't destroy it till the spider is safe, then you
> may sweep away the web; but if you kill the spider it will surely
> bring poverty to your house.'   Isle of Wight (1917)

A reason for this prohibition is rarely given, but where it is, it is
invariably a reference to one of the legends which claim that the spider
acted to help or protect Jesus in some way:

> A minister visiting an old Border woman in her last illness, observed
> a spider near her bed, and attempted to remove it, when the invalid
> desired him to let it be, and reminded him that when our Blessed
> Lord lay in the manger at Bethlehem, a spider came and spun a
> beautiful web which protected the Babe from all the dangers which
> surrounded Him – cold and frost and the searchers and soldiers of
> King Herod.   England/Scotland Borders (1935)

A more developed story has Mary and her baby taking refuge in a
cave, and a spider quickly weaving a complicated web across the
entrance to fool the pursuers into believing that no one had recently
entered. This is a widespread international folk-tale motif, reported
across Europe and also in Asia and Africa, and told of various heroes
and religious figures.

Despite its widespread nature, this general belief in the luckiness,
and resultant protection, of spiders can be traced only to the eighteenth
century, except in the specialized case of the 'money-spider':

> There is a small black spider that often gets on our clothes or hats;
> this is called a 'money spider', and if you kill it you will be sure to
> suffer for it by lack of the needful.   Yorkshire (1852)

These tiny spiders are thus generally called 'money spiders' or 'money
spinners'. In many cases it was simply enough that the spider land on
you, but others advised particular rituals to ensure the good fortune,
including putting the spider in your pocket, eating it, or throwing it
over your shoulder. The superstition can confidently be traced to at
least the late sixteenth century – in Nashe's *Terrors of the Night* (1594),
the creature is already termed a 'spinner' ('If a spinner creep upon him
he shall have gold rain down from heaven') – and it has been reported

regularly ever since, although the vast majority of published references are from England. Many people still call tiny spiders 'money spiders'.

spiders' webs and kisses

A curious connection between cobwebs and kissing has been reported, in the form of a popular saying:

> In Hampshire, if a cobweb is seen, 'it is a sign that the housemaid wants kissing'. On inquiring the meaning of this expression, I was told that when the housemaid is saluted she naturally holds up her head and thus becomes aware of the neglect.   Hampshire (1863)

Spiders were also very widely used in cures for various ailments, particularly ague and whooping cough. The most common method was to imprison a live spider in a bag which the sufferer wore round their neck. As the spider died and wasted away, the disease was believed to disappear. This procedure, which derives from the writings of classical authors, was extremely widespread until the latter half of the nineteenth century, and even later. Other cures involved swallowing spiders whole (often sweetened with jam or honey), and cobwebs were regularly put on wounds to stop bleeding.

wasps

In common with butterflies and snakes, it used to be said that the first wasp you see in the year should be killed at once:

> The first wasp seen in the season should always be killed. By so doing you secure to yourself good luck and freedom from enemies throughout the year.   Northamptonshire (1850)

The 'freedom from enemies' motif was often claimed, although not explained. Only a handful of examples of this belief have been noted, dating from 1850 to the 1920s, and it is therefore difficult to gauge its relative popularity from such a small sample.

PLANTS

blackberries

An extremely widespread tradition concerning blackberries is that after a certain date each year they are at best no longer palatable and at worst poisonous. The date varies from place to place, but is often Michaelmas (29 September) or in early October. Blackberries do indeed deteriorate rapidly late in the season, but the traditional explanation is that on that day the Devil goes round and spits on them, or wags his tail over them, or puts his foot on them, and so on. This tradition has been noted from most parts of the British Isles and is still heard, but it does not seem to have been common before the early nineteenth century. A few other miscellaneous beliefs about blackberries have been noted, including several medicinal uses, but the only one that seems to have been at all widely known is that horses, cats, and babies are often not well when the blackberries are ripe: 'Baby's not well – it's blackberry time' (Devon, 1959).

clover

The four-leafed clover is one of the best-known symbols of good luck in modern Britain, and has been so for nearly 500 years or more. The modern belief is that to find and keep one bestows luck and prosperity, and this has been one of the main benefits right from the earliest references:

That if a man walking in the fields, finde any foure-leaved grasse, he shall in a small while after finde some good thing.

John Melton, Astrologaster (1620)

In addition to the general good-luck meaning, a four-leafed clover (or sometimes, paradoxically, a two-leafed one, called a 'clover of two') is part of a widespread love divination when linked with an ash-leaf with an even number of leaflets:

> Even ash and four-leaved clover
> You are sure your love to see
> Before the day is over.

New Forest (1867)

The other useful attribute of a four-leafed clover in earlier times was to protect against evil eye and witchcraft, and, more than that, to enable the possessor to see through any tricks and deceptions wrought by ill-wishers, fairies, or charlatans.

The general good luck and love connections are reported from at least the sixteenth century, with Reginald Scot's *Discoverie of Witchcraft* (1584) being the first. The notion of conferring the ability to see through tricks is regularly reported from only the early nineteenth century onwards, but it was clearly well known across large parts of the British Isles.

daffodils

Robert Herrick's poem *Divination by a Daffodil* (1648) belies the cheerful image of the flower as a welcome sign of spring:

> When a daffodil I see,
> Hanging down his head t'wards me,
> Guess I may, what I must be:
> First I shall decline my head;
> Secondly I shall be dead;
> Lastly, safely buried.

It appears to be the drooping head of the flower which triggered the gloomy prognostication. This belief was not widely recorded, but was still found in the twentieth century. The most common superstition about daffodils, which they shared with primroses, was the idea that they were closely linked with goslings and chicks:

My friend had been out for a walk in the meadows, near the river; along its banks the daffodils are very abundant. He picked one and put it in the button-hole of his coat. When he got back to the farm-house he pulled out the flower and laid it on the table. Soon after a servant came into the room and saw the flower, and at once exclaimed, 'Who brought in this daffodil? Did you, Mr. G.? We shall have no ducks this year!' My friend enquired the reason for such a superstition, but he could get no satisfactory answer; only that it was so . . . I am informed that a single flower is unlucky for the ducklings; but if a handful is brought in, it is in their favour, and the season will be fortunate.   Devon (1877)

This idea was only reported from the nineteenth century onwards, and was probably based on nothing more than the coincidences of colour and time of year between the plant and the young birds.

dandelions

Dandelions have long been recommended as a cure for numerous ailments, including warts, eczema, indigestion, jaundice, and liver disease. They were also used to treat diseases of the urinary tract and to clean the kidneys and the bladder, which presumably gave rise to the extremely widespread children's belief that picking dandelions caused bed-wetting:

Buttercups and daisies were our first favourites [for flower chains], dandelions being shunned somewhat, because . . . the handling of them was supposed to induce 'undesirable consequences at night'. In fact, we called dandelions in Derbyshire 'pisabeds'.

Derbyshire (1901)

The plant had similar local names all over the country.

Children all over the British Isles have also blown the seeds off the dandelion to tell the time – or to answer simple questions such as how many years till marriage, or 'she loves me, she loves me not'. The earliest reference so far found is from 1830.

picking up flowers

It was considered very unwise to pick up a flower found in the street, even by children who were not overly squeamish about what else they picked up:

> It was not a rare occurrence, particularly near the stall at the top of our street or in the Fulham market, to see a cut flower lying on the ground, and if one of the younger children went to touch it, the rest of us dragged him back gasping 'pick up a flower, pick up a fever'.   London (1920s)

Or, more graphically:

> Pick up flowers, pick up sickness
> Pick up sickness, fall down dead.
> Buckinghamshire (1913)

As with most flower superstitions, this one has not been found before the turn of the twentieth century, and it has been suggested, albeit with no evidence, that it was based on a fear of handling flowers used in funerals.

flowers from churchyards

Flowers are connected with death in popular tradition in many different ways. Not only have they formed an integral part of funerals for centuries, but various varieties formerly had the reputation of predicting or even causing death if brought indoors. Another tradition was that flowers in churchyards should not be removed. This was true for flowers growing, and also those bought for placing on the grave:

> At one cemetery in South London plants are sold at the lodge for placing on the graves. I bought one as I went out on my way home, and I noticed that the seller seemed surprised. I was afterwards told that it was very unlucky to bring a plant or a flower home from a cemetery.   London (1926)

red and white flowers

Although a handful of beliefs centre on red flowers, such as roses, it does not seem to be their colour which causes concern, but other situational factors, such as the petals falling:

> To scatter the leaves of a red rose on the ground is unlucky, and
> betokens an early death.   (1880)

The mixing of red and white flowers in the same vase, however, is widely considered to be unlucky, or even an omen of death. The addition of just one flower of any other colour breaks the spell, and the placing of red and white blooms in separate vases in the same room is usually acceptable. It appears to be the mixing that causes the unease and which people try to avoid. This avoidance is particularly common in hospitals, and is still well known to nursing staff, but many people also avoid the combination in their own homes. In all cases the combination of the flowers is seen as 'unlucky' in some way, but while to some it is a sign of a death to come, others regard it as an invitation to, or even a cause of, that death. One family at least believed that the hospital staff would use the flowers as a sign:

> The family of a friend of mine went to visit their mother in hospital
> in Galashiels. When they got there they were very upset to see a
> vase of red and white flowers placed on the locker beside her bed.
> They complained to the sister, and told her that they would rather
> be told that the hospital thought that their mother was going to
> die, instead of having them dropping hints. They thought that the
> red and white flowers indicated that the hospital had given up hope
> with their mother.   Selkirkshire (1985)

The most often quoted reason for the ban is that red and white flowers represent 'blood and bandages'. Given this association, the avoidance is understandable outside the hospital environment, as people do not, after all, wish to be reminded of sickness and death in their homes, but why thinking of 'blood and bandages' should be avoided in their proper context of a hospital ward is not at all clear. It is likely that this supposed connection is a back-formed or post-facto explanation, probably based on the earlier red and white stripes on the pole used to advertise barbers' shops, for which the same explanation used to be given, with a similar lack of real evidence.

The earliest reference so far located is in the *Sunlight Almanac* for 1896, where it is claimed that to dream of red and white flowers is a prediction of death. The belief is not listed in the main regional folklore collections, nor in the nineteenth-century books on plant-lore, and a search of a number of Victorian and Edwardian dream books also failed to locate relevant examples. There are, however, numerous beliefs about the unluckiness of white flowers, both individual species and in general, from earlier periods. Some of these are otherwise identical with the *Sunlight Almanac*, as, for example, 'to dream of white flowers has been supposed to prognosticate death' (T. F. Thiselton-Dyer, *Folk-Lore of Plants*, 1889), and it is conceivable that the ban on red and white flowers has grown from the avoidance of the white.

Various individual species of white flowers are considered unlucky, particularly if brought into the house, but some people have clearly decided that all white flowers should be shunned:

> I have heard from a social worker in London that it is most unlucky
> – almost offensively unlucky, in fact – to give any white flowers,
> even those not native to England, like white chrysanthemums, to
> sick people. Apparently some implication that, being white, they
> would be suitable for the funeral, is involved. The people to whom
> these particular white chrysanthemums were given were quite
> young, moderately well educated, typical Londoners, and yet super-
> stitious on this point – which they said was well known to everyone.
>
> London (1931)

This general aversion to white flowers is relatively well reported through most of the twentieth century, but there is little evidence of such a belief before that time.

flower petals

One of the simplest and most widely known forms of love divination is to pluck the petals from a flower while reciting 'She loves me, she loves me not'. However widely known these words are today, this is not the only form of words which can be found in this context:

> Gathering a daisy, she commences plucking the petals off, saying
> with each one, 'Does he love me – much – a little – devotedly – not
> at all', and the last petal settles the question.   Wales (1909)

and other rhymes can also be used in the same context, such as the ubiquitous 'tinker, tailor'. None of these rhymes can be traced before the nineteenth century, but the connection between love and daisies was current much earlier. Evidence comes, for example, from Thomas Killigrew's play *Thomaso* (1663), where 'plucked daisies' is included in a list of love-related items such as bent coins, valentines, and yarrow.

hawthorn blossoms smell like death

The most widely reported of the many beliefs about unlucky flowers held that it was very unwise to bring hawthorn or 'may' blossom into the house. At best it was unlucky, but in many minds it was an omen, or even a cause, of a coming death in the family:

> Hawthorn was never brought into the house during the month of May. Indeed it was never taken into our rooms. There was a strong feeling against it in every cottage and farmhouse, for it was a portent of death in that year.   Derbyshire (1890s)

Some informants claimed more specific deaths would result from hawthorn blossoms indoors – children were told that their mother would die if they ignored the prohibition, while others thought a child would die. Many of the people who acted on this superstition claimed that the blossom 'smelled like death' or, more specifically, like the plague. This assessment of the flower goes back to at least the early seventeenth century, long before the Great Plague of the 1660s. In the earliest reference known to us, Francis Bacon wrote that the plague had a scent 'of the smell of a mellow apple and (as some say) of May flowers' (*Sylva Sylvarum*, 1627).

Certainly, the flowers of some species of hawthorn do decay rapidly when picked, and emit a pungent smell. The popular assessment that this 'smells like death' is more than simply a superstitious fancy, as pointed out by plant-lore expert Roy Vickery (*Dictionary of Plant-Lore*, 1995):

> More recently it has been shown that trimethylamine, one of the first products formed when animal tissues start to decay, is present in hawthorn flowers.

Other popular explanations also existed. One is that the superstition arose at the Reformation because may blossom was popular in Catholic churches for decorating statues of the Virgin Mary. It was therefore forbidden and branded as evil by the new Anglican Church. This explanation is probably still being quoted, but is not supported by history. The strong connection between Mary and the month of May only started in the eighteenth century, in Italy, and it came to Britain and Ireland considerably later. May devotions were not introduced until the nineteenth century. Another explanation is that Christ's 'crown of thorns' was made from the hawthorn.

heather

Along with four-leafed clover and shamrock, white heather is one of the best-known 'lucky' plants, most closely associated with Scotland, where it can often be seen in lapels on special occasions, in bride's bouquets, and so on. Elsewhere in the British Isles, bunches of 'lucky white heather' are still regularly hawked by street sellers. The earliest references so far found to white heather are all in writings concerning Queen Victoria and her family, from 1855 to 1893, and it is likely that this was one of the pieces of folklore which she made popular by her example. We have no record of the belief before her time, but it is unlikely she or Prince Albert actually invented it. It has been reported sporadically ever since, but it is strangely absent from most turn-of-the-century Scottish folklore books.

lilac

Like many other sweet-smelling flowers, lilac is widely regarded as an unlucky plant to bring indoors, especially white-flowered varieties:

> 'Doan't yew dare bring that in, 'cos I 'on't hev it. Tha's unlucky tew hev in housen, laylock allus wor!' Chris's aunt gave vehement emphasis to the belief she shared with most village folk, that white lilac was unlucky if taken into the house.   Essex (c.1920)

No references to this belief have yet come to light from before the early twentieth century, but it is still widely believed.

mistletoe

In AD 77, Pliny the Elder famously wrote that Druids revered mistletoe growing on an oak as their most sacred plant, and harvested it with a golden sickle: this short piece is responsible for more disinformation in British folklore than almost any other. Whatever its merits in itself, it has been repeated, ad nauseam, by countless British writers, and has been used as the basis for innumerable flights of fancy about Druids and the ancient origins of our customs and beliefs. This situation led plant-lore expert Roy Vickery (*Dictionary of Plant-Lore*, 1995) to write, in some exasperation it seems, 'More nonsense has been written about mistletoe than about any other British plant.'

This Druid preoccupation with the plant is assumed to be the basis of our modern custom of kissing under the mistletoe at Christmas, and also as the reason for the erroneous idea that mistletoe has always been banned from Christian churches because it is a 'pagan' plant. Stating a succinct case against such popular notions which have become entrenched by constant repetition and elaboration is very difficult, because the whole premise and chain of thought is in question as well as the individual facts. To put it simply: Pliny was writing about the Gauls, not the British. We do not know where or from whom he got his information. Classical authors, however reliable they may be in other respects, are at their shakiest, and most gullible, when describing foreign peoples and their lands (see, for example, Caesar's delightful description of the elk in his *Conquest of Gaul*, Bk 6, Ch. 4). There is no hint anywhere else to support Pliny's report, and there is no other mention of the sacred nature of mistletoe in Britain until antiquarians start reading and believing Pliny, some 1,500 years later. Even if Pliny's description was accurate, there is no evidence that the practice continued into historical times, or had any influence on later lore. Modern mistletoe beliefs are reported almost exclusively from England – not the Celtic areas where, we are told (but we do not believe), the Druid traditions continue to have resonance. And so on.

There is no discernible connection between this description and the dominant British mistletoe tradition of kissing at Christmas, first reported in 1813, and how the supposed sacred mistletoe of the Druids got transformed into this excuse for boys and girls to indulge in Christmas horseplay is rarely considered. Keeping our feet planted on more solid ground, the mistletoe does not make much of an appearance in British traditions apart from the Christmas kissing. It had something of an international reputation in cures, much of which was again copied from Pliny by literate herbalists. Otherwise, its lore is almost entirely concerned with its role in Christmas decoration.

nettles

The application of a dock leaf has been recommended for a nettle sting for at least 650 years, and remains almost universally known. Many people are still convinced that docks and nettles always grow in close proximity simply for human convenience. In the past, however, the dock leaf itself was only one half of the cure, because it was also thought necessary to recite a certain charm to make it effective. Many people still know versions of the charm, although it is now usually regarded simply as a rhyme for children rather than an essential part of the cure. The words vary considerably, but nearly always follow a similar simple pattern.

> Nettle in, dock out
> Dock in, nettle out
> Nettle in, dock out
> Dock rub nettle out.
>
> Northumberland (1876)

This rhyme was already proverbial in Chaucer's time, as when Troilus protests that he cannot simply switch his love to another: 'But kanstow playen raket, to and fro, Nettle in, dok out, now this, now that?' (*Troilus and Criseyde*, c.1374), and similarly, in the sixteenth century it still meant an unsettled state of mind: 'For in one state they twain could not yet settle, but wavering as the wind, in dock out nettle' (Heywood, *Proverbs*, 1546).

parsley

A surprising number of different superstitions have been recorded about parsley, of such a disparate nature that it is difficult to see how they are connected. Despite being valued in numerous cures, and being the subject of semi-humorous notions about who is master in the household, it was widely believed that parsley promised serious bad luck if transplanted:

> Someone gave me a root of parsley and a neighbour said it was unlucky. Anyway, I tossed my head and thought 'so what'. Not long after my husband died. So that's the last I will grow.
>
> Dorset (1995)

This may be linked to a tradition that the plant is in league with the Devil somehow:

> When parsley is sown it goes nine times to the Devil before it comes up. Only the wicked can make parsley grow. Derbyshire (1895)

The Devil motif is usually simply a metaphor for the slowness with which the plant grows in some areas, but the story varies from place to place. Like the other parsley beliefs, this one is not found before the later nineteenth century, but seems quite widespread in the twentieth, at least in England. Some informants simply say that it is unlucky to receive parsley plants as a present, although even this has variants: 'Parsley should never be taken as a gift, but it is very lucky to steal some' (Guernsey, 1904).

There are various traditions reported from southern England about how and when parsley should be sown. Records show that it was one of the plants which were traditionally sown on Good Friday, to ensure good growth and good luck. Parsley also shared with rosemary and sage the tradition that it only grows well where the woman is master in the house, and a few references indicate a connection between parsley and pregnancy, but there are diametrically opposed opinions about the plant's effect.

> If a young woman sows parsley-seed she will have a child.
>
> Lincolnshire (1936)

> When a woman wants a baby, she should go out and pick some parsley.   Oxfordshire (1951)

> Parsley is believed to prevent a pregnancy . . . it is sometimes eaten as a salad by young married women who do not desire to have a family.   Cambridgeshire (1939)

primroses

Primroses are one of several early-blooming flowers which should not be brought indoors for fear of bad luck. As with daffodils, when a reason for this ban was stated, it was often connected to the fate of any chicks or goslings belonging to the household:

> A Suffolk farmer's wife was rather annoyed with her young daughter because on a fine day in early spring the child had brought a bunch

of primroses into the house. 'If you are going to bring primroses indoors', the mother said tartly, 'you'll have to bring in more than that. Take them out and pick a bigger bunch!' ... [A local explained] 'Of course you had to bring in at least thirteen primroses into the house. Do you bring less, it were no use; it didn't serve. Thirteen was the number – or more. It didn't matter if you had more; but you dursn't have less.'   Suffolk (1966)

The belief in the unluckiness of primroses was widespread across England, but rarely reported elsewhere. The earliest references are from the 1850s, but it was already described as old by then and, although the connection with poultry has faded, many people still avoid bringing the flower indoors.

rosemary

It was popularly believed that rosemary grows best in the gardens of families where the woman is the master. Our first knowledge of this tradition is in a query published in the early eighteenth century:

Pray tell me the reason, that where the rosemary grows, there it is said the woman reigns.   *British Apollo* (8 December 1708)

The same idea was reported in later years, and was quite widely known. Similar things were said of sage and parsley.

shamrocks

The shamrock is one of the most widely recognized symbols in the English-speaking world, effectively connoting 'Irishness' as well as 'good luck'. The word 'shamrock' cannot be found earlier than the sixteenth century, when several writers refer to the Irish being fond of eating it, but the spelling varies considerably and is often given as 'sham-root', and it is not always clear what plant is being referred to. The connection with food is the only context in which the shamrock appears until about the 1680s, but from that time it also begins to be described as a national symbol worn on St Patrick's Day, as, for example, 'The vulgar superstitiously wear shamroges, 3-leav'd grass' (1681), and from then on the intimate connection between the plant and Ireland becomes widely accepted. A story which first appeared in the eighteenth century seeks to explain the connection by reference to

St Patrick's teaching, when he reputedly used the three-leafed plant to successfully explain the concept of the Trinity to the pagan Irish.

snowdrops

One of several white flowers which it was thought unlucky to bring into the house, as it brought sickness and death, even well into living memory:

> Last year we picked one from the woods when there were thousands out. When George [neighbour and gardener] came to tie up the raspberry canes he must have seen it on the window-sill for he was full of gloom. He said it foretold a death . . . It is entirely our fault that one of his chickens died and that their egg yield went down . . . So this year we must be more careful. George has told us all the unpleasant things he knows about snowdrops. 'We called them "corpses in shrouds" when we were little, and we never took them indoors at all. All white flowers is unlucky.' *The Times* (15 February 1966)

The phrase 'corpses in shrouds' was used by several informants. It is surprising how seriously these fears could be taken:

> [In the 1870s] When a schoolfellow of mine died of typhoid fever, the lady Principal of the boarding-school wrote to my parents, charging them with being the authors of the calamity, in that they had a short time before sent me a box of snowdrops.

There is some crossover with primroses and daffodils in their traditional connection with chickens. In this context, the number of flowers brought into the house in spring determined the number of chicks that would hatch.

TREES

apples

For some reason, apples seem to have been connected in the popular mind with love and sex, reflected perhaps in the tradition that Eve gave one to Adam, and the main area of superstition in which they feature is therefore love divination. Nevertheless, in another very widespread belief, apple trees had less happy associations, as when a simultaneous appearance of blossom and fruit on a tree was held to predict an imminent death in the owner's family:

> Last year I was walking in the garden of a neighbouring farmer, aged seventy-one. We came up to an apple tree, heavily laden with nearly ripe fruit; and perceived a sprig of very late bloom, a kind of second edition. He told me, rather gravely, that in his boyhood this occurrence was invariably held to herald a death in the family within two or three months. On my joking him about Welsh credulity, he pretended not to believe the idle lore, but evidently was glad to pass from the subject. His brother, aged sixty-eight, in perfect health then, who resided in the same house, was dead within six weeks.

Wales (1854)

There seems to be no rational explanation for such belief, beyond the fact that the superstitious mind abhors anomalies in nature such as albino animals, crowing hens, and birds trying to come indoors. Late blossom on fruit trees is not that rare an occurrence, but it was widely feared. The earliest reference dates from only the mid nineteenth century, and it was still being quoted well into the late twentieth.

elder

The elder is without doubt the hardest plant to classify in terms of its superstitions and traditions. On the one hand it was widely regarded as extremely useful in the prevention and cure of ailments as diverse as epilepsy and saddle sores, and was sometimes reported as generally protective, while on the other it was widely feared and treated with suspicion. Compare, for example, the following:

> The elder tree is a sacred tree and should be planted as near as possible to the back door, the most used entrance in the home. It is credited with being a very good protection against witchcraft.
>
> Guernsey (1975)

> The elder was regarded with considerable awe. In South Wales it was deemed very dangerous to build any premises in or near the spot where an elder-tree stood.   Wales (1909)

This is not simply a geographically based difference, as positive and negative attributes have been reported from nearly all quarters:

> In Cambridgeshire the elder was associated with witchcraft. Elderly residents of Crishall recalled in 1958 that because witches were supposed to have a particular liking for the tree it should never be touched, cut, sawn, or in any way tampered with after dark. Paradoxically, however, some inhabitants of the same village said that the elder tree afforded protection against lightning and that it was particularly lucky to have a tree growing in or near a farmyard because it kept away evil spirits and promoted fertility among the stock.   Cambridgeshire (1969)

Elders were everywhere connected with fairies and witches, although it was not always clear in what way. It was also believed to be the tree on which Judas hanged himself, or that provided the wood for the Crucifixion. Furthermore, it must never be cut down, or the wood burned; it must never be used to make cradles, a wound inflicted with an elder spike was bound to prove fatal, and the tree would 'bleed' if cut. It has proved impossible to reach an adequate synthesis of elder beliefs, because the evidence is patchy and contradictory, and all that can be said is that it was generally agreed to be 'uncanny'. Many of these traditions are some of the oldest we have on record, dating from before the fifteenth century. There is a curious overall sense that the negative and positive feelings stemmed from the same basic notions, and may have depended largely on the general disposition of the informant.

holly

Holly was far and away the most popular plant for Christmas decorations, and is mentioned in that context in early records, such as the Churchwarden's Accounts of St Laurence, Reading (1505): 'Payed to Mackrell for the holy bush agayne Christmas'. Similarly, John Stow (1598) reported an occurrence at Christmas 1444 when a 'tempest of thunder and lightning', created by a malignant spirit, brought down a street decoration of holly and ivy.

As such, it came under various prohibitions covering decorations – in particular not being brought into the house before Christmas Eve; there were also disagreements about whether or not it should be burnt afterwards, and whether male or female varieties should be used. Outside the Christmas season, holly was held in a generally positive light, although unlucky to bring into the house. It was thought unlucky to cut it down or otherwise harm it:

> about fifteen years ago two holly trees were cut down in the parish. Locals protested violently, saying this would produce poltergeist havoc.   Devon (1971)

It was also thought to be immune from lightning strikes, and to protect against the harmful activities of witches:

> Pieces of holly along with rowan were placed inside over the door of the stable to prevent the entrance of the nightmare.
>
>   Aberdeenshire (1889)

The earliest reference to holly being protective seems to be by John Aubrey (1686).

leaves falling

A predominately children's belief holds that it is lucky to catch a leaf which is falling from a tree:

> I could never restrain the impulse to dart among the shower [of autumnal leaves] and catch a falling leaf. As a small boy I had whimsically been taught that there was magic in a falling leaf, if you caught it before it touched the ground.   Sussex (1930s)

Most authorities state that you will have a happy month for each one caught, and they agree that the leaf must not touch ground. It was widely known and is still passed on from parents to small children on autumnal walks, but is not recorded before the late nineteenth century.

monkey puzzle tree

A modest set of beliefs surround the peculiar tree nicknamed the monkey puzzle. Since at least the 1930s, children have believed that one must not say a word in its vicinity:

> The writer was told in Caterham, Surrey, in 1953, where a handsome monkey puzzle stood in front of the then council offices, that one should never speak while passing the tree, or otherwise attract its attention, lest some misfortune follow.   Surrey (2001)

Versions of this superstition have been noted in various parts of England, and it was clearly quite widely known. A different belief links the devil with the tree:

> It was an old Fenland belief that if a monkey puzzle tree was planted on the edge of a graveyard it would prove an obstacle to the Devil when he tried to hide in the branches to watch a burial. Many elderly Cambridgeshire people believe the tree is an unlucky one.
>   Cambridgeshire (1969)

These associations with the Devil may well explain the children's fear of speaking near the tree, or 'attracting its attention', although if the tree generally 'puzzled' the Devil it would logically be a lucky one. This story is also a statutory lesson to those who assume that stories of devils and churchyards are necessarily ancient. The monkey puzzle was only introduced to Britain, from Chile, in the 1790s.

rowan (mountain ash)

Of all the various recorded traditional ways of protecting people, animals, and property from witches, fairies, or any other form of ill-wishing, a piece of the rowan tree was one of the most widespread. It was valued across the British Isles, and particularly in Scotland and Ireland.

> A horse-shoe nailed over the threshold was supposed to afford perfect immunity, neither witch nor warlock being able to enter a dwelling where this mode of protection had been adopted. By some a branch of rowan tree was looked upon with equal favour, and bundles of small rowan tree twigs were constantly kept suspended over the doorway, or attached to the top of the box-bed or corner cupboard.   Dumfriesshire (1890/91)

Pieces of rowan, often wound round with red thread, could also be sewn into a garment to provide personal protection. The protective qualities of the rowan were known at least as far back as 1597, when James I included it in his book of *Daemonologie*.

yew

The yew appears in a number of minor superstitions, but the overwhelming question about the tree is how to explain its regular, and noticeable, presence in older churchyards. Yews appear so often in this context that accident can be ruled out, and a deliberate policy presumed, and there are numerous stories which are told to explain this. The most common in the present-day is that the wood of yew trees was used to make bows, and as the security of the realm depended on a ready supply of bows and bowmen, it was ordered that yews be planted in every churchyard in the land. Another is that because yews are poisonous to cattle, they were planted in churchyards to ensure that neighbouring farmers kept their fences in order, to keep their stock out of danger. A third combines the two. There is no evidence to support any of these explanations, and they do not hold together internally – why, for example, if bows were so important, did they plant only one or two yews in each churchyard? Who made the rule, and why cannot we find any record of it? These explanations are no more likely to be true than any other guesses, but they are still widely known and believed. It is most likely that there was a traditional connection between yews and death or mourning in medieval times in Britain, but its exact nature has yet to be satisfactorily explained.

NATURAL PHENOMENA
AND WEATHER

Many natural phenomena such as comets, shooting stars, and major storms have had traditions and beliefs attached to them, usually of an ominous kind, and some still linger even in this scientific age.

Aurora Borealis

Spectacular celestial phenomena such as eclipses, comets, and major storms were regularly taken as portents or the result of great things afoot. The grander the show the more elevated the people or events that were involved. The Aurora Borealis have excited awe and interest in all cultures that can see them, and Britain is no exception.

> The Northern Lights were seen with great foreboding – some thought a national disaster was imminent, others that the end of the world was nigh.
>
> Essex (*c.*1920)

comets

The idea that comets mark or predict great happenings has been common in many countries since at least the classical era, and was already known in eighth-century Britain:

> Comets are long-haired stars with flames, appearing suddenly, and presaging a change in sovereignty, or plague, or war, or floods.
>
> Bede, *De Natura Rerum* (*c.* AD 725)

Despite sceptical voices from the seventeenth century onwards, this idea was taken seriously until quite recent times, and coincidences such as the appearance of Halley's Comet and the death of Edward VII served to keep traditional belief alive into our own era. If comets could presage major national events, great storms too could be interpreted as marking the death of important persons:

> Waked with a very high wind, and said to my wife, 'I pray God I hear not of the death of any great person, this wind is so high'; fearing that the Queen might be dead.
>
> Samuel Pepys, *Diary* (19 October 1663)

rainbows

Rainbow superstitions in Britain and Ireland reveal an ambivalence that is difficult to synthesize or explain. Modern beliefs appear to be mostly positive, including the idea that one should make a wish when you see one, and the now ubiquitous connection between the rainbow and the pot of gold:

> Sometimes it is said one may wish upon a rainbow; and a master at Ballingry, Fife, found his class believed that the first to see a rainbow was lucky, provided the person called out to his friends, 'First to see a rainbow'. He recollected that this had also been the practice when he was a boy (at Cowdenbeath c. 1944).   Fifeshire (1959)

Other superstitions, however, reveal a much darker side to the rainbow, at least in certain circumstances: 'A rainbow with both ends on one island is a sign of death' (Orkney, 1909); 'A rainbow over a house is a sign of death' (Co. Longford, 1936). This unequivocally gloomy view of the rainbow seems restricted to Scotland and Ireland.

A further strand of tradition lies in the reactions of children on seeing a rainbow, as, for example, in rhymes recited which are similar to those with which they have long greeted ladybirds, crows, and other natural phenomena. It was also held by some to be unlucky to point at a rainbow, just as it was to point at the moon or stars. None of these superstitions is reported before about the 1820s.

A widespread children's belief maintained that it was possible to make a rainbow disappear by 'crossing it out':

When a schoolboy [before 1850s] I recollect that we were wont, on the appearance of a rainbow, to place a couple of straws or twigs on the ground in the form of a cross, in order to dispel the sign in the heavens, or, as we termed it, to 'cross out the rainbow'.

N. England (1895)

Twentieth-century children also had a similar custom of 'stepping on' a rainbow, but by this they meant the coloured patches of petrol on the road which were held to be the place where the rainbow had stood.

'rain, rain, go away'

Rain has featured in superstition only in certain situations, for example when it fell on a funeral it was considered 'lucky' for the deceased, or on certain days (e.g. Ascension Day) it had marked curative properties. A very widespread children's rhyme, still well known today, invites the rain to 'go away'.

Little children have a custome, when it raines to sing, or charme away the raine; thus they all join in a chorus and sing thus, viz.

> Raine, raine, goe away,
> Come again a Saterday.
> John Aubrey, *Remaines* (1686)

In some of the earlier reports, the implication is that the rhyme was expected to work as a charm which really could influence the weather. The earliest version so far found dates from 1659, but as it was then included in a book of proverbs, it was presumably already in wide circulation.

stars

From Victorian times a belief, or more likely just a cute story told to children, maintains that a shooting star is a sign that a new baby (often specifically a boy) has been born. But this is in direct contrast to how things were seen in earlier times, when a shooting star meant a general calamity or even a specific death:

A Huntingdonshire woman was telling me of the death of her baby, on June 5, after five days' illness. She said: 'I had a warning that it was to go. The night before it was took I was passing your gate,

Sir, and a great star fell down from the sky plump before me. It did not go into the ground, but burst about a foot above the road. As soon as I got home I told mother about it, and said it was a warning for someone. She said, "Perhaps it's for grandfather." I said, "May be, mother; but I fear it's for someone nigher." The next day my poor babe was took.'

Huntingdonshire (1866)

A widespread superstition held that it was unlucky to point at, or try to count the stars, in the same way as it was unwise to point at the moon or a rainbow. In many cases the prohibition was couched in terms of 'sin' and 'irreverence' rather than 'luck':

I remember being rebuked more than once for pointing at the stars when a child . . . I do not think any definite reason was given, but I was made to feel that I had been guilty of shocking irreverence.

Nottinghamshire (1902)

storms

Traditions about thunder and lightning include some superstitious elements, but are mostly concerned with practical advice on how to stay safe. A widespread strategy for dealing with the perceived danger of a storm was to open all doors and windows to ensure that if it hit the house, it could escape without causing damage. The second important way to protect the household was to cover all mirrors and other reflective surfaces. This included items made of metal, such as knives and forks, scissors and needles, and even jugs of water. Neither of these protective strategies have been found before the mid nineteenth century, but they were still current in the 1970s.

A few references deal with apparently linked beliefs warning against drawing attention to thunder and lightning, by pointing, counting, or even speaking of it:

It is wicked to point towards the part of the heavens from which lightning is expected. I have seen a little boy, for this offence, made to kneel blindfold on the floor, to teach him how he would feel if the lightning came and blinded him.

(1862)

These can be compared with the more common notions about the impropriety of pointing at the moon, stars, and rainbows. It was also reported, from Essex about 1917, that it was unlucky to count the interval between the lightning flash and the thunder clap. This is surprising, as many people do this in modern times to work out how far away the storm is.

tides

Considering the ubiquity of notions that the moon's phases affect many aspects of human life and health, it is not surprising that the tide was believed to have somewhat similar effect, especially in coastal areas:

> A very widely-spread belief exists all along the sea-coast of Wales as to the effect the tide has on human life. It is believed that children are born as the tide comes in, and people die as the tide goes out. The late Mr. Noott, of Cardigan, a doctor with a large practice, was firmly persuaded that this was the case, and he ushered hundreds of children into the world in his time and stood beside very many death-beds.   Wales (1898)

The state of the tide was anxiously watched when anyone lay ill in the house, as they would be in particular danger every time the tide turned. This idea was expressed by the East Anglian agricultural writer Thomas Tusser in 1557, and it was clearly known to Shakespeare when he described Falstaff dying at the turn of the tide (*Henry V*, 1600). Dickens also used the idea in *David Copperfield* (1850). Surprisingly, the notion was still current at the end of the twentieth century:

> Question: Does anyone have evidence suggesting that sheep tend to give birth when the tide is high in coastal regions?
>   *Guardian* (1 December 1989)

The basic belief was well known all over Europe, and was also well documented in classical times, as evidenced, for example, by Pliny's *Natural History* (AD 77). In some Scottish fishing communities, the state of the tide, like the phase of the moon, was taken even more seriously, regulating when people got married, when important tasks were commenced, when eggs were set under hens, and even when to pull up weeds in the garden.

the moon

The moon features so strongly in past British superstitions that it is hardly an exaggeration to say that superstitious people were obsessed by it. But despite the wide range of beliefs that have been recorded, they are all concerned with just two principles. The first is that the waxing and waning of the moon has direct effect on natural life on earth, and the second is that the new moon is one of the beginning points at which practices aimed at divination or for luck should be carried out.

> When living, a few years ago, in Ayrshire, our housekeep used to make obeisance several times to the new moon when she observed it, looking very solemn the while. And when I asked her why she did so, she replied that by so doing she would be sure to get a present before the next moon appeared. She wished me (then a very young girl) to do so too, and when I told her it was all nonsense, she 'fired up' and said her mother had done so, and she would continue to do so. I rather think this is no uncommon practice, for our previous servant did the same thing, and neither of them was older than about forty or fifty.   Ayrshire, *Scotsman* (27 December 1889)

The form of the obeisance varies considerably. Bowing or curtseying are by far the most common, but nodding, raising the hat, kissing the hand, and so on, are also reported. The number of stipulated times can be any odd number from one to nine. This bowing motif is very often combined with other elements of 'new moon' belief, such as making a wish or reciting a rhyme to divine future partners, but the most common direct result of paying one's respect is that you will get a present, or find something nice, before the next new moon.

The earliest references show that the custom was already widespread by the seventeenth century, across Ireland, Scotland, and England. As with other new-moon beliefs this was also extremely widespread in the nineteenth, lasted well into the late twentieth century, and is probably still done by some people. Reading the mass of examples, the overall impression is of 'paying respect' rather than 'worshipping', and few of the direct reports use language to suggest the latter interpretation, except where collectors have introduced their own slant. There is indeed no evidence that these actions are a remnant of moon worship as cultural survivalists would like to believe. Neverthe-

less, without suggesting a direct line of descent, it must be acknowledged that earlier peoples had apparently similar procedures for
greeting the moon – the biblical Job (31:26–7), for example, speaks of
kissing one's hand when beholding the moon, and Psalm 81 (verse 3)
exhorts 'Blow up the trumpet in the new moon'. Similarly, in classical
times, Horace (*Odes* 3:23) wrote 'if thou lift thy hands to heaven when
the moon is new'. It is more than possible that the British superstitions
in this respect were based on the Bible.

how to look at the new moon

> A new moon seen over the right shoulder is lucky, over the left
> shoulder unlucky, and straight before prognosticates good luck to
> the end of the moon.   Devon (1851)

This belief is reported from most parts of the British Isles, and
although regularly reported in the Victorian period it is recorded from
only the 1830s onwards. Another widespread superstition regarding
how the new moon is first seen, dictates that it is very bad luck to see
it through glass:

> An elderly Cambridge man recalled in 1958 that when he used to
> stay with his grandmother in Ely when he was a boy, he remembers
> being told by her to stand by an open kitchen window to warn her of
> an appearance of a new moon so that she could join him and see it
> from the doorstep and not through a window.   Cambridgeshire (1969)

The penalty for ignoring this interdiction is usually cited as generally
'very bad luck', but some informants specified that the result would be
that you would 'break glass' during that moon. It is not entirely clear
why viewing through glass is counted as so significant, although
similar prohibitions were reported, much less commonly, in other
contexts. It was formerly believed, for example, that it was bad luck
to see a funeral through a window. The only clue which emerges from
the mass of references to the new-moon belief is an impression, and
it is no more than that, that it is somehow *disrespectful* to the moon
not to see it face to face. The superstition was extremely widespread
in the nineteenth and twentieth centuries, and most regional folklore
collections include versions. It has not, however, been found before
1830.

it's rude to point at the moon

Another relatively widespread nineteenth-century superstition prohibited any pointing at the moon, again on the basic grounds of being
disrespectful:

> A lady, upwards of seventy years of age, informs me that when a
> child on a visit to her uncle at Ashburton, she was severely scolded
> by one of the servants, for pointing her finger at the moon. The act
> was considered very wicked, being an insult; and no one knew what
> evil instances it might call down. Devon (1879)

This reference must refer to a time before the 1820s, and no earlier
one has been found. Similar beliefs about pointing at stars and rainbows also date from around the same period. All references are from
England, and the belief does not seem to have lasted well in the
twentieth century.

turn your money at the new moon

One of the most popular moon beliefs presumes a connection between
the new moon and money in the pocket. As with other superstitions
concerning beginnings, the basic belief is that if you have money at
the start of the cycle you will continue to have it for the rest of the period
in question. This is routinely reported as relevant for each new moon
of the year, but is especially potent for the first moon of the New Year:

> You must look at the first new moon of the New Year, bow to it
> three times, and turn your money and you'll have money all the
> year round. Norfolk (c.1895)

In addition to the basic motif of important beginnings, there is
also the idea that as the waxing moon is intimately connected with
'growing', your money will also grow. The obvious conclusion, that it
will shrink when the moon has passed its full, is never mentioned in
this context. The money-turning is very often combined with the
bowing/curtseying and wishing motifs. These notions are remarkably
constant across the British Isles, and were extremely well known
throughout the nineteenth century and into the late twentieth. The
chronological sequence in earlier times is, however, puzzling. The first
known reference in English is quite consistent with later meanings:

> He that hath no money in his purse ought to abstain him from
> looking on the new moon, or else he shall have but little all along
> that moon.   *Gospelles of Dystaves* (1507)

but it is well over 250 years before the next clear sighting. It is distinctly
strange that the belief does not seem to have been mentioned by the
sixteenth- and seventeenth-century dramatists who supply evidence
for so many other superstitions extant at the time, including plenty of
other traditions about the moon. As the *Gospelles* was originally com-
piled in the Low Countries, a tentative interpretation has to be that
although the belief was known abroad as early as 1507, it was not
known in Britain until much later. If it was known here, it clearly
cannot have been as widespread as it became from the turn of the
nineteenth century.

'new moon tell unto me'

The first sight of a new moon is one of those points around which
love-divination customs have traditionally clustered. In some cases it
was the first new moon of the year, but quite commonly any new
moon would do. There were two main categories of divination. In the
first, the supplicant addressed her/himself directly to the new moon,
either making a wish or reciting a traditional rhyme, which varied
only in the details, hoping that she/he would later dream of the future
spouse. The custom could be quite simple:

> The young women of the Lowlands, on first observing the new
> moon, exclaim as follows:
>
> > New mune, true mune, tell unto me
> > If [naming favourite lover] my true love
> > He will marry me
> > If he marry me in haste, let me see his bonnie face
> > If he marry me betide, let me see his bonnie side
> > Gin he marry na me ava, turn his back and gae awa.
> >   Scotland (1826)

It could also be elaborated in both the action and placing of the
participant. Many elements have been borrowed from other key love-
divinatory times, such as when hearing the first cuckoo.

The second main method was to view the moon indirectly, either through some piece of material or reflected in a pail of water or a mirror:

> You should look through a new silk handkerchief at the first new moon in the year, and as many moons as you saw would be years before you'd be married, or turn your back and look at it in the looking-glass, and count the same as with the silk handkerchief.
>
> Northumberland (1929)

The refraction method was reported only from the early nineteenth century onwards, but remained popular throughout the twentieth. Addressing the moon in rhyme, however, was already well known in the mid seventeenth century, as recorded by John Aubrey (1686) and by the compiler of the chapbook *Mother Bunch's Closet Newly Broke Open* (1685).

moon rules all

The regular waxing and waning of the moon was deemed to be of vital importance to life on earth. A wide range of natural processes were widely believed to be directly affected, if not ruled, by the moon's cycle.

In the human sphere it covered things such as hair, fingernails, and corns.

> My mother-in-law in her youth always had her hair cut every month as the moon was growing, never when on the wane. She is now 77, with a wealth of dark hair reaching below her waist, and she attributes it to the care and attention given in early days and cut at the time mentioned.   Kent (1922)

Conversely, nails and corns, whose growth should be retarded, had to be cut when the moon was on the wane. The idea has a long history. Iona Opie and Moira Tatem identify the earliest known British example in a letter from Arabella Stewart, an eleven-year-old girl, to her grandmother, enclosing the 'endes of my heare, which was cut the sixt day of the moone'. The belief was also well known abroad, and was already in vogue in classical times. Opie and Tatem also quote a Hampshire hairdresser in 1987 who believed it to be scientific fact.

In the plant world, farmers and gardeners were advised to pay heed to the moon for planning their planting and harvesting:

> Rule for planting – Everything below ground (i.e. tubers, etc.) on a waning moon; everything above ground (green vegetables) on a waxing moon.
>
> Devon (1961)

More specialist tasks, such as grafting fruit trees, were also ruled by the same principle. Again, the same ideas were held in classical times, and, as horticulture is still largely in the hands of ordinary people rather than professionals, the strictures on planting lasted well into living memory, and are probably still followed in some quarters.

Similar notions held sway for the animal kingdom. It was a matter of common knowledge for centuries that animals must be slaughtered during the waxing of the moon, or the meat would be at best inferior and at worst downright bad. As pigs were the animals most commonly killed at home rather than in professional butchers' premises, the majority of recorded beliefs focus on them:

> [Attempting to book local pig-killer] On my questioning him as to his impending engagements, he made various references to the moon that, to me, were unintelligible. At last he spoke plainly: 'I tell you what it is, guv'nor. If you don't want to lose your pig, you won't let me kill him when the moon's a-going off. Better wait till she's getting near the full' . . . 'Does this only apply to pigs?' – 'No, guv'nor, it holds good with all beasts.'
>
> (1875)

This belief is well documented from the sixteenth century across the British Isles, but it does not seem to have survived the era of home pig-killing which ended in the twentieth century. Those who buy their pork at the supermarket know little of when and how it was killed.

Bibliography

Addy, S. O., *Folk Tales & Superstitions* (Wakefield: EP, 1973; first published as *Household Tales with Other Traditional Remains*, 1895)

Aubrey, John, *Remaines of Gentilisme and Judaisme* (1686; London: Folklore Society, 1880)

Aubrey, John, *Miscellanies upon Various Subjects* (1696; 4th edn, London: Russell Smith, 1857)

Brand, John, *Observations on Popular Antiquities* (London: Bohn, 1849; prev. edns, 1810 and 1813)

Chambers, Robert, *The Book of Days* (London: Chambers, 1864)

Davies, Owen, *A People Bewitched: Witchcraft and Magic in Nineteenth-Century Somerset* (Bruton, 1999)

Davies, Owen, *Witchcraft, Magic and Culture 1736–1951* (Manchester: Manchester University Press, 1999)

Folk-Lore Record, Folk-Lore Journal, Folk-Lore, Folklore (journals of the Folklore Society, 1878 to date)

Gomme, G. L., *The Gentleman's Magazine Library: Popular Superstitions* (London: Eliot Stock, 1884)

Grose, Francis, *A Provincial Glossary, with a Collection of Local Proverbs and Popular Superstitions* (London: S. Hooper, 1787; 2nd edn, 1790)

Hutton, Ronald, *Stations of the Sun: A History of the Ritual Year in Britain* (Oxford: Oxford University Press, 1996)

Kittredge, George Lyman, *Witchcraft in Old and New England* (Cambridge, Mass.: Harvard University Press, 1929)

Mackay, Charles, *Extraordinary Popular Delusions and the Madness of Crowds* (London: Bentley, 1841; 2nd edn, National Illustrated Library, 1852)

Melton, John, *Astrologaster, or the Figurecaster* (1620; reprinted, Los Angeles: Augustan Reprint Society, 1975)

Notes & Queries (1849 to date)

Opie, Iona and Moira Tatem, *A Dictionary of Superstitions* (Oxford: Oxford University Press, 1989)

Opie, Iona and Peter, *Oxford Dictionary of Nursery Rhymes* (Oxford: Oxford University Press, 1951; 2nd edn, 1997)

Opie, Iona and Peter, *The Lore & Language of Schoolchildren* (Oxford: Oxford University Press, 1959)

Scot, Reginald, *The Discoverie of Witchcraft* (1584; reprinted, New York: Dover, 1972)

Shermer, Michael, *Why People Believe Weird Things: Pseudoscience, Superstition, and Other Confusions of Our Time* (New York: W. H. Freeman, 1997)

Simpson, Jacqueline and Steve Roud, *A Dictionary of English Folklore* (Oxford: Oxford University Press, 2000)

Swainson, Charles, *The Folklore and Traditional Names of British Birds* (London: Folklore Society, 1866)

Thomas, Keith, *Religion and the Decline of Magic* (London: Weidenfeld & Nicolson, 1971)

Uttley, Alison, *Country Things* (London: Faber, 1946)

Vickery, Roy, *A Dictionary of Plant-Lore* (Oxford: Oxford University Press, 1995)

Index

Page numbers in **bold** denote a main entry.

abracadabra, **167**
albatrosses, **221**
almanacs, **151–2**
apples, **257–8**
ash-riddling, 152
astrology, 21, 34, 152,
    156, 167
Aurora Borealis, **263**

babies, 26, **31–46**, 173,
    265
beds, 31, **98–101**
bees, 69, **236–8**
beetles, 60, **238**
Bible dipping, **152–3**
birds, 32, 76, **219–35**
birthmarks, **32–3**
blackberries, **244**
blade-bone divination,
    154–5
bouquets, 50–51
bread and cakes, 6, 10,
    11, 17–18, 48, **139–41**
brooms, **101–2**
burials, **65–7**, 68
burning, 76, 145
butterflies, **239**

cakes, 6, 17–18, 48
calendars, **102**
Candlemas, 16

candles, 8, 57, **103–4**
caterpillars, **239–40**
cats, 26, **196–200**
cauls, **34–5**
chairs, 31, 68, **104–5**
charms, **163–4**
cheeks, **78–9**
christening, 36, **38–40**
Christmas, 15–18
churching, 37, **40–42**
churchyards, **65–7**, 247,
    261
cleft palate, 33
clocks, 69, **105–6**
clothes, 8, 37, 51,
    120–21, 124, **131–8**,
    214, 220, 240
clover, **244–5**
coal, 8, **107**
cockerels, **221–3**
coffins, 68, 119, 139
coins, 36, 38, 83, 117,
    129–30
colours, 51–2 *see also*
    green; red
comets, **263–4**
confetti, **52–3**
corpses, **63–5**, **70–71**,
    106, 113, 146, 169
counting, **182–3**, 266
cradles, **42–3**

crickets, **240–41**
Cross days, 20
crows, 23, 201, **222–3**
cuckoos, **223–4**
curses, 53, **166**, 168–9

daffodils, **245–6**
dandelions, **246**
days, 18, **20–27**, 34, 75,
    89
death, 54, **57–72**, 199
decorations, 15–17
dogs, 60, **200–202**
donkeys, **202**
doors, 6, 49–50, 54,
    69–70, 266
dreams, **155–6**

ears, **78–80**, 88
Easter, 9
effigies, **170–71**
eggs, 11, 37, **141–2**
elder, **258–9**
elephants, **202–3**, 210
elf-shot, **171–2**
evil eye, **172–3**
executions, **61–3**
eyes, 64, **80–1**

feathers, 99–100,
    227–8

feet, 66, **87**, 88, 205
fingernails, 22, 44, **85–6**
fingers, **84–5**, 90–91
fires, 8, **107–8**
first footing, **4–7**
flowers, 248–50 *see also*
  specific flower names
Fridays, **22–5**
Friday 13th, **23–5**
frogs, **178–9**, 203
funerals, 54–5, **68–70**

goats, **203–4**
Good Friday, **10–13**
graves, 66, 139
green, 51, 52, **134**

Hallowe'en, **13–14**
hair, 4, 5, 22, 44, **75–8**
handkerchiefs, **135–6**
hands, 36, **84**, 88, 92–3,
  169, 174
hares *see* rabbits
hawthorn, **250–51**
heather, **251**
hedgehogs, **207**
holly, 15, 17, **259**
Holy Innocents' Day,
  18–19
horseman's word, **176–7**
horses **207–9**
horseshoes, 98, **122–3**
housemartins, **233–4**

insects, **237–43**
iron, 124, **179–81**
itching, **88**
ivy, 15, 17

keys, **153–4**
knives, 5, **109–11**
knocking, 59

ladders, **125–7**
ladybirds, **241**
lambs, **209**
leaves, **260**
lilac, **251**
lions, **209–10**

magpies, **224–7**
May, **26–6**, 102, 121,
  198, 251
mending, **132**
mice *see* rats
mirrors, 69, **111–14**,
  266
mistletoe, 15–17, **251–2**
moles, **211**
money, 7, 36, 37, 83,
  108, **127–30**
monkey puzzle tree,
  260
moon, 75, **268–73**
mountain ash *see*
  rowan
mourning, 132

nettles, **253**
New Year, **3–9**
nightmares, **177**
numbers, **183–91**

ornaments, **114–15**
owls, 201, **227**

parsley, 54, **253–4**
peacocks, **227–8**
petals, **249–50**
photographs, **113–14**
pictures, 69, **113–14**
pigeons, 99–100,
  228–9
pigs, 210, **211–13**, 273
pillows, 61

pinching, 133
pins, **115–19**
plants, 15, **244–56**
pointing, 264, 266, 270
porch watching, **156–7**
prams, **42–3**
pregnancy, **31–3**, 66,
  210, 254
primroses, **254–5**

rabbits, 26–7, 33, 135,
  204–7
rain, 70–71, 197, 238,
  265
rainbows, **264–5**
rats, **213–15**
ravens, **229–30**
red, 52, 77, 178, 248–9
rings, 32, 48
robins, 220, **230–32**
rooks, **232–3**
rosemary, 15, 17, 54, **255**
rowan, **261**

sage, 54
salt, **143–7**
scissors, 5, 117
seagulls, **233**
second sight, **157–60**
seven, **185–6**
shamrocks, **255–6**
sheets, **119**
shoes, 119, **136–7**
shrews, **215**
shuddering, **88–9**
sieve and shears, **160**
sin-eater, **71–2**
666, **189–91**
snails, **215–16**
snakes, **216–17**
sneezing, **89–90**
snowdrops, **256**

spades, **117**

spiders, **241–3**

spitting, **90**, 126, 127

spoons, **117–18**

stairs, **118–19**

stars, **265–6**

stones, 98, **168–9**, **175**

storms, **266–7**

swallows, **233–4**

suicides, **61–3**

tables, **119**

tea, **147–8**, 161

teeth, 44–5, **82–3**

tempering, 36

thirteen, 23–5, 106, 142, **186–9**

three, **184–5**

threshold, 49–50

tides, **267**

'tinker, tailor', **161–2**

toads, 178–9, **218**

tongues, **83**

touching, **179–81**

trees, 257–62

Twelfth Night, 16

umbrellas, 119, **137–8**

washing, 8, 12, 18, **92–3**, **120–21**

wasps, **243**

weddings, 23, **45–56**

weighing, 44, **45–6**

wells, 8, 54

windows, 69, 266

wishbones, **162**

wood, **179–81**

wraiths, **181**

wrens, **234–5**

yew, **261–2**